ISBN 0-8373-1287-6
C-1287   CAREER EXAMINATION SERIES

## This is your PASSBOOK® for...

# Fire Fighter

*Test Preparation Study Guide*

*Questions & Answers*

**NLC**

**NATIONAL LEARNING CORPORATION**

Copyright © 2009 by

## National Learning Corporation

**212 Michael Drive, Syosset, New York 11791**

All rights reserved, including the right of reproduction in whole or in part, in any form or by any means, electronic or mechanical, including photocopying, recording, or by any information storage and retrieval system, without permission in writing from the Publisher.

(516) 921-8888
(800) 645-6337
FAX: (516) 921-8743
www.passbooks.com
sales @ passbooks.com
info @ passbooks.com

PRINTED IN THE UNITED STATES OF AMERICA

# PASSBOOK®

## NOTICE

This book is *SOLELY* intended for, is sold *ONLY* to, and its use is *RESTRICTED* to *individual*, bona fide applicants or candidates who qualify by virtue of having seriously filed applications for appropriate license, certificate, professional and/or promotional advancement, higher school matriculation, scholarship, or other legitimate requirements of educational and/or governmental authorities.

This book is *NOT* intended for use, class instruction, tutoring, training, duplication, copying, reprinting, excerption, or adaptation, etc., by:

(1) Other publishers

(2) Proprietors and/or Instructors of "Coaching" and/or Preparatory Courses

(3) Personnel and/or Training Divisions of commercial, industrial, and governmental organizations

(4) Schools, colleges, or universities and/or their departments and staffs, including teachers and other personnel

(5) Testing Agencies or Bureaus

(6) Study groups which seek by the purchase of a single volume to copy and/or duplicate and/or adapt this material for use by the group as a whole without having purchased individual volumes for each of the members of the group

(7) Et al.

Such persons would be in violation of appropriate Federal and State statutes.

*PROVISION OF LICENSING AGREEMENTS.* — Recognized educational commercial, industrial, and governmental institutions and organizations, and others legitimately engaged in educational pursuits, including training, testing, and measurement activities, may address a request for a licensing agreement to the copyright owners, who will determine whether, and under what conditions, including fees and charges, the materials in this book may be used by them. In other words, a licensing facility exists for the legitimate use of the material in this book on other than an individual basis. However, it is asseverated and affirmed here that the material in this book *CANNOT* be used without the receipt of the express permission of such a licensing agreement from the Publishers.

NATIONAL LEARNING CORPORATION
212 Michael Drive
Syosset, New York 11791

Inquiries re licensing agreements should be addressed to:
The President
National Learning Corporation
212 Michael Drive
Syosset, New York 11791

# PASSBOOK SERIES®

THE *PASSBOOK SERIES®* has been created to prepare applicants and candidates for the ultimate academic battlefield – the examination room.

At some time in our lives, each and every one of us may be required to take an examination – for validation, matriculation, admission, qualification, registration, certification, or licensure.

Based on the assumption that every applicant or candidate has met the basic formal educational standards, has taken the required number of courses, and read the necessary texts, the *PASSBOOK SERIES®* furnishes the one special preparation which may assure passing with confidence, instead of failing with insecurity. Examination questions – together with answers – are furnished as the basic vehicle for study so that the mysteries of the examination and its compounding difficulties may be eliminated or diminished by a sure method.

This book is meant to help you pass your examination provided that you qualify and are serious in your objective.

The entire field is reviewed through the huge store of content information which is succinctly presented through a provocative and challenging approach – the question-and-answer method.

A climate of success is established by furnishing the correct answers at the end of each test.

You soon learn to recognize types of questions, forms of questions, and patterns of questioning. You may even begin to anticipate expected outcomes.

You perceive that many questions are repeated or adapted so that you can gain acute insights, which may enable you to score many sure points.

You learn how to confront new questions, or types of questions, and to attack them confidently and work out the correct answers.

You note objectives and emphases, and recognize pitfalls and dangers, so that you may make positive educational adjustments.

Moreover, you are kept fully informed in relation to new concepts, methods, practices, and directions in the field.

You discover that you are actually taking the examination all the time: you are preparing for the examination by "taking" an examination, not by reading extraneous and/or supererogatory textbooks.

In short, this PASSBOOK®, used directedly, should be an important factor in helping you to pass your test.

# FIRE FIGHTER

## DUTIES
Performs firefighting assignments in a specialized line, support or inspectional activity area; and performs other related duties as required.

Under supervision, Firefighters assist in the control and extinguishment of fires, in providing pre-hospital emergency medical care and in the enforcement of laws, ordinances, rules and regulations regarding the prevention, control and extinguishment of fires, as well as perform Fire Safety Education activities; and perform related work.

Some of the physical activities performed by Firefighters and environmental conditions experienced are: wearing protective clothing, such as bunker suit, helmet, boots and breathing apparatus; crawling, crouching and standing, often for prolonged periods, while extinguishing fires; driving fire apparatus; climbing stairs, ladders and fire escapes; raising portable ladders; using forcible entry tools, such as axes, sledge hammers, power saws and hydraulic tools; searching for victims in smoke-filled hostile environments; carrying or dragging victims from dangerous locations; connecting, stretching and operating hose lines; locating hidden fire by feel and smell; providing medical assistance to injured or ill citizens; and providing control and mitigation of hazardous materials incidents while wearing chemical protective clothing.

## SCOPE OF THE EXAMINATION
The written test is designed to test the candidate's ability to learn and to perform the work of a Firefighter. It may include questions involving the understanding of written language and information, using language to communicate information or ideas to other people, memorizing information, recognizing or identifying the existence of problems, applying general rules to specific situations, applying prioritized rules to specific situations, determining position or spatial information within a larger area, visualizing how objects or structures might appear from different perspectives or after changes, finding a rule or concept which fits or describes a situation, and other related areas.

Candidates may be examined for their knowledge of firefighting practices, methods and operations; the purposes, uses, operation and care of assigned equipment; first aid and life-saving principles, practices and techniques; breathing apparatus and resuscitation equipment; fire safety prevention and inspection practices, principles, methods, procedures, codes, rules and laws; traffic laws and ordinances; departmental rules, regulations, policies and operating procedures; principles and practices of human and public relations; reading and understanding technical materials; understanding and following oral and written instructions; establishing and maintaining good working relationships; and dealing tactfully and effectively with others.

# HOW TO TAKE A TEST

I. YOU MUST PASS AN EXAMINATION

A. *WHAT EVERY CANDIDATE SHOULD KNOW*

Examination applicants often ask us for help in preparing for the written test. What can I study in advance? What kinds of questions will be asked? How will the test be given? How will the papers be graded?

As an applicant for a civil service examination, you may be wondering about some of these things. Our purpose here is to suggest effective methods of advance study and to describe civil service examinations.

Your chances for success on this examination can be increased if you know how to prepare. Those "pre-examination jitters" can be reduced if you know what to expect. You can even experience an adventure in good citizenship if you know why civil service exams are given.

B. *WHY ARE CIVIL SERVICE EXAMINATIONS GIVEN?*

Civil service examinations are important to you in two ways. As a citizen, you want public jobs filled by employees who know how to do their work. As a job seeker, you want a fair chance to compete for that job on an equal footing with other candidates. The best-known means of accomplishing this two-fold goal is the competitive examination.

Exams are widely publicized throughout the nation. They may be administered for jobs in federal, state, city, municipal, town or village governments or agencies.

Any citizen may apply, with some limitations, such as the age or residence of applicants. Your experience and education may be reviewed to see whether you meet the requirements for the particular examination. When these requirements exist, they are reasonable and applied consistently to all applicants. Thus, a competitive examination may cause you some uneasiness now, but it is your privilege and safeguard.

C. *HOW ARE CIVIL SERVICE EXAMS DEVELOPED?*

Examinations are carefully written by trained technicians who are specialists in the field known as "psychological measurement," in consultation with recognized authorities in the field of work that the test will cover. These experts recommend the subject matter areas or skills to be tested; only those knowledges or skills important to your success on the job are included. The most reliable books and source materials available are used as references. Together, the experts and technicians judge the difficulty level of the questions.

Test technicians know how to phrase questions so that the problem is clearly stated. Their ethics do not permit "trick" or "catch" questions. Questions may have been tried out on sample groups, or subjected to statistical analysis, to determine their usefulness.

Written tests are often used in combination with performance tests, ratings of training and experience, and oral interviews. All of these measures combine to form the best-known means of finding the right person for the right job.

## II. HOW TO PASS THE WRITTEN TEST

### A. NATURE OF THE EXAMINATION

To prepare intelligently for civil service examinations, you should know how they differ from school examinations you have taken. In school you were assigned certain definite pages to read or subjects to cover. The examination questions were quite detailed and usually emphasized memory. Civil service exams, on the other hand, try to discover your present ability to perform the duties of a position, plus your potentiality to learn these duties. In other words, a civil service exam attempts to predict how successful you will be. Questions cover such a broad area that they cannot be as minute and detailed as school exam questions.

In the public service similar kinds of work, or positions, are grouped together in one "class." This process is known as *position-classification*. All the positions in a class are paid according to the salary range for that class. One class title covers all of these positions, and they are all tested by the same examination.

### B. FOUR BASIC STEPS

#### 1) Study the announcement

How, then, can you know what subjects to study? Our best answer is: "Learn as much as possible about the class of positions for which you've applied." The exam will test the knowledge, skills and abilities needed to do the work.

Your most valuable source of information about the position you want is the official exam announcement. This announcement lists the training and experience qualifications. Check these standards and apply only if you come reasonably close to meeting them.

The brief description of the position in the examination announcement offers some clues to the subjects which will be tested. Think about the job itself. Review the duties in your mind. Can you perform them, or are there some in which you are rusty? Fill in the blank spots in your preparation.

Many jurisdictions preview the written test in the exam announcement by including a section called "Knowledge and Abilities Required," "Scope of the Examination," or some similar heading. Here you will find out specifically what fields will be tested.

#### 2) Review your own background

Once you learn in general what the position is all about, and what you need to know to do the work, ask yourself which subjects you already know fairly well and which need improvement. You may wonder whether to concentrate on improving your strong areas or on building some background in your fields of weakness. When the announcement has specified "some knowledge" or "considerable knowledge," or has used adjectives like "beginning principles of..." or "advanced ... methods," you can get a clue as to the number and difficulty of questions to be asked in any given field. More questions, and hence broader coverage, would be included for those subjects which are more important in the work. Now weigh your strengths and weaknesses against the job requirements and prepare accordingly.

#### 3) Determine the level of the position

Another way to tell how intensively you should prepare is to understand the level of the job for which you are applying. Is it the entering level? In other words, is this the position in which beginners in a field of work are hired? Or is it an intermediate or advanced level? Sometimes this is indicated by such words as "Junior" or "Senior" in the class title. Other jurisdictions use Roman numerals to designate the level – Clerk I, Clerk II, for example. The word "Supervisor" sometimes appears in the title. If the level is not indicated by the title, check the description of duties. Will you be working under very close supervision, or will you have responsibility for independent decisions in this work?

### 4) Choose appropriate study materials

Now that you know the subjects to be examined and the relative amount of each subject to be covered, you can choose suitable study materials. For beginning level jobs, or even advanced ones, if you have a pronounced weakness in some aspect of your training, read a modern, standard textbook in that field. Be sure it is up to date and has general coverage. Such books are normally available at your library, and the librarian will be glad to help you locate one. For entry-level positions, questions of appropriate difficulty are chosen – neither highly advanced questions, nor those too simple. Such questions require careful thought but not advanced training.

If the position for which you are applying is technical or advanced, you will read more advanced, specialized material. If you are already familiar with the basic principles of your field, elementary textbooks would waste your time. Concentrate on advanced textbooks and technical periodicals. Think through the concepts and review difficult problems in your field.

These are all general sources. You can get more ideas on your own initiative, following these leads. For example, training manuals and publications of the government agency which employs workers in your field can be useful, particularly for technical and professional positions. A letter or visit to the government department involved may result in more specific study suggestions, and certainly will provide you with a more definite idea of the exact nature of the position you are seeking.

## III. KINDS OF TESTS

Tests are used for purposes other than measuring knowledge and ability to perform specified duties. For some positions, it is equally important to test ability to make adjustments to new situations or to profit from training. In others, basic mental abilities not dependent on information are essential. Questions which test these things may not appear as pertinent to the duties of the position as those which test for knowledge and information. Yet they are often highly important parts of a fair examination. For very general questions, it is almost impossible to help you direct your study efforts. What we can do is to point out some of the more common of these general abilities needed in public service positions and describe some typical questions.

1) General information

Broad, general information has been found useful for predicting job success in some kinds of work. This is tested in a variety of ways, from vocabulary lists to questions about current events. Basic background in some field of work, such as sociology or economics, may be sampled in a group of questions. Often these are principles which have become familiar to most persons through exposure rather than through formal training. It is difficult to advise you how to study for these questions; being alert to the world around you is our best suggestion.

2) Verbal ability

An example of an ability needed in many positions is verbal or language ability. Verbal ability is, in brief, the ability to use and understand words. Vocabulary and grammar tests are typical measures of this ability. Reading comprehension or paragraph interpretation questions are common in many kinds of civil service tests. You are given a paragraph of written material and asked to find its central meaning.

3) Numerical ability

Number skills can be tested by the familiar arithmetic problem, by checking paired lists of numbers to see which are alike and which are different, or by interpreting charts and graphs. In the latter test, a graph may be printed in the test booklet which you are asked to use as the basis for answering questions.

4) Observation

A popular test for law-enforcement positions is the observation test. A picture is shown to you for several minutes, then taken away. Questions about the picture test your ability to observe both details and larger elements.

5) Following directions

In many positions in the public service, the employee must be able to carry out written instructions dependably and accurately. You may be given a chart with several columns, each column listing a variety of information. The questions require you to carry out directions involving the information given in the chart.

6) Skills and aptitudes

Performance tests effectively measure some manual skills and aptitudes. When the skill is one in which you are trained, such as typing or shorthand, you can practice. These tests are often very much like those given in business school or high school courses. For many of the other skills and aptitudes, however, no short-time preparation can be made. Skills and abilities natural to you or that you have developed throughout your lifetime are being tested.

Many of the general questions just described provide all the data needed to answer the questions and ask you to use your reasoning ability to find the answers. Your best preparation for these tests, as well as for tests of facts and ideas, is to be at your physical and mental best. You, no doubt, have your own methods of getting into an exam-taking mood and keeping "in shape." The next section lists some ideas on this subject.


IV. KINDS OF QUESTIONS

Only rarely is the "essay" question, which you answer in narrative form, used in civil service tests. Civil service tests are usually of the short-answer type. Full instructions for answering these questions will be given to you at the examination. But in case this is your first experience with short-answer questions and separate answer sheets, here is what you need to know:

## 1) Multiple-choice Questions

Most popular of the short-answer questions is the "multiple choice" or "best answer" question. It can be used, for example, to test for factual knowledge, ability to solve problems or judgment in meeting situations found at work.

A multiple-choice question is normally one of three types—
- It can begin with an incomplete statement followed by several possible endings. You are to find the one ending which *best* completes the statement, although some of the others may not be entirely wrong.
- It can also be a complete statement in the form of a question which is answered by choosing one of the statements listed.
- It can be in the form of a problem – again you select the best answer.

Here is an example of a multiple-choice question with a discussion which should give you some clues as to the method for choosing the right answer:

When an employee has a complaint about his assignment, the action which will *best* help him overcome his difficulty is to
- A. discuss his difficulty with his coworkers
- B. take the problem to the head of the organization
- C. take the problem to the person who gave him the assignment
- D. say nothing to anyone about his complaint

In answering this question, you should study each of the choices to find which is best. Consider choice "A" – Certainly an employee may discuss his complaint with fellow employees, but no change or improvement can result, and the complaint remains unresolved. Choice "B" is a poor choice since the head of the organization probably does not know what assignment you have been given, and taking your problem to him is known as "going over the head" of the supervisor. The supervisor, or person who made the assignment, is the person who can clarify it or correct any injustice. Choice "C" is, therefore, correct. To say nothing, as in choice "D," is unwise. Supervisors have and interest in knowing the problems employees are facing, and the employee is seeking a solution to his problem.

## 2) True/False Questions

The "true/false" or "right/wrong" form of question is sometimes used. Here a complete statement is given. Your job is to decide whether the statement is right or wrong.

SAMPLE: A person-to-person long-distance telephone call costs less than a station-to-station call to the same city.

This statement is wrong, or false, since person-to-person calls are more expensive.

This is not a complete list of all possible question forms, although most of the others are variations of these common types. You will always get complete directions for answering questions. Be sure you understand *how* to mark your answers – ask questions until you do.

## V. RECORDING YOUR ANSWERS

For an examination with very few applicants, you may be told to record your answers in the test booklet itself. Separate answer sheets are much more common. If this separate answer sheet is to be scored by machine – and this is often the case – it is highly important that you mark your answers correctly in order to get credit.

An electric scoring machine is often used in civil service offices because of the speed with which papers can be scored. Machine-scored answer sheets must be marked with a pencil, which will be given to you. This pencil has a high graphite content which responds to the electric scoring machine. As a matter of fact, stray dots may register as answers, so do not let your pencil rest on the answer sheet while you are pondering the correct answer. Also, if your pencil lead breaks or is otherwise defective, ask for another.

Since the answer sheet will be dropped in a slot in the scoring machine, be careful not to bend the corners or get the paper crumpled.

The answer sheet normally has five vertical columns of numbers, with 30 numbers to a column. These numbers correspond to the question numbers in your test booklet. After each number, going across the page are four or five pairs of dotted lines. These short dotted lines have small letters or numbers above them. The first two pairs may also have a "T" or "F" above the letters. This indicates that the first two pairs only are to be used if the questions are of the true-false type. If the questions are multiple choice, disregard the "T" and "F" and pay attention only to the small letters or numbers.

Answer your questions in the manner of the sample that follows:

32. The largest city in the United States is
   A. Washington, D.C.
   B. New York City
   C. Chicago
   D. Detroit
   E. San Francisco

1) Choose the answer you think is best. (New York City is the largest, so "B" is correct.)
2) Find the row of dotted lines numbered the same as the question you are answering. (Find row number 32)
3) Find the pair of dotted lines corresponding to the answer. (Find the pair of lines under the mark "B.")
4) Make a solid black mark between the dotted lines.

## VI. BEFORE THE TEST

Common sense will help you find procedures to follow to get ready for an examination. Too many of us, however, overlook these sensible measures. Indeed, nervousness and fatigue have been found to be the most serious reasons why applicants fail to do their best on civil service tests. Here is a list of reminders:

- Begin your preparation early – Don't wait until the last minute to go scurrying around for books and materials or to find out what the position is all about.
- Prepare continuously – An hour a night for a week is better than an all-night cram session. This has been definitely established. What is more, a night a

week for a month will return better dividends than crowding your study into a shorter period of time.
- Locate the place of the exam – You have been sent a notice telling you when and where to report for the examination. If the location is in a different town or otherwise unfamiliar to you, it would be well to inquire the best route and learn something about the building.
- Relax the night before the test – Allow your mind to rest. Do not study at all that night. Plan some mild recreation or diversion; then go to bed early and get a good night's sleep.
- Get up early enough to make a leisurely trip to the place for the test – This way unforeseen events, traffic snarls, unfamiliar buildings, etc. will not upset you.
- Dress comfortably – A written test is not a fashion show. You will be known by number and not by name, so wear something comfortable.
- Leave excess paraphernalia at home – Shopping bags and odd bundles will get in your way. You need bring only the items mentioned in the official notice you received; usually everything you need is provided. Do not bring reference books to the exam. They will only confuse those last minutes and be taken away from you when in the test room.
- Arrive somewhat ahead of time – If because of transportation schedules you must get there very early, bring a newspaper or magazine to take your mind off yourself while waiting.
- Locate the examination room – When you have found the proper room, you will be directed to the seat or part of the room where you will sit. Sometimes you are given a sheet of instructions to read while you are waiting. Do not fill out any forms until you are told to do so; just read them and be prepared.
- Relax and prepare to listen to the instructions
- If you have any physical problem that may keep you from doing your best, be sure to tell the test administrator. If you are sick or in poor health, you really cannot do your best on the exam. You can come back and take the test some other time.

## VII. AT THE TEST

The day of the test is here and you have the test booklet in your hand. The temptation to get going is very strong. Caution! There is more to success than knowing the right answers. You must know how to identify your papers and understand variations in the type of short-answer question used in this particular examination. Follow these suggestions for maximum results from your efforts:

### 1) Cooperate with the monitor

The test administrator has a duty to create a situation in which you can be as much at ease as possible. He will give instructions, tell you when to begin, check to see that you are marking your answer sheet correctly, and so on. He is not there to guard you, although he will see that your competitors do not take unfair advantage. He wants to help you do your best.

### 2) Listen to all instructions

Don't jump the gun! Wait until you understand all directions. In most civil service tests you get more time than you need to answer the questions. So don't be in a hurry.

Read each word of instructions until you clearly understand the meaning. Study the examples, listen to all announcements and follow directions. Ask questions if you do not understand what to do.

### 3) Identify your papers
Civil service exams are usually identified by number only. You will be assigned a number; you must not put your name on your test papers. Be sure to copy your number correctly. Since more than one exam may be given, copy your exact examination title.

### 4) Plan your time
Unless you are told that a test is a "speed" or "rate of work" test, speed itself is usually not important. Time enough to answer all the questions will be provided, but this does not mean that you have all day. An overall time limit has been set. Divide the total time (in minutes) by the number of questions to determine the approximate time you have for each question.

### 5) Do not linger over difficult questions
If you come across a difficult question, mark it with a paper clip (useful to have along) and come back to it when you have been through the booklet. One caution if you do this – be sure to skip a number on your answer sheet as well. Check often to be sure that you have not lost your place and that you are marking in the row numbered the same as the question you are answering.

### 6) Read the questions
Be sure you know what the question asks! Many capable people are unsuccessful because they failed to *read* the questions correctly.

### 7) Answer all questions
Unless you have been instructed that a penalty will be deducted for incorrect answers, it is better to guess than to omit a question.

### 8) Speed tests
It is often better NOT to guess on speed tests. It has been found that on timed tests people are tempted to spend the last few seconds before time is called in marking answers at random – without even reading them – in the hope of picking up a few extra points. To discourage this practice, the instructions may warn you that your score will be "corrected" for guessing. That is, a penalty will be applied. The incorrect answers will be deducted from the correct ones, or some other penalty formula will be used.

### 9) Review your answers
If you finish before time is called, go back to the questions you guessed or omitted to give them further thought. Review other answers if you have time.

### 10) Return your test materials
If you are ready to leave before others have finished or time is called, take ALL your materials to the monitor and leave quietly. Never take any test material with you. The monitor can discover whose papers are not complete, and taking a test booklet may be grounds for disqualification.

## VIII. EXAMINATION TECHNIQUES

1) Read the general instructions carefully. These are usually printed on the first page of the exam booklet. As a rule, these instructions refer to the timing of the examination; the fact that you should not start work until the signal and must stop work at a signal, etc. If there are any *special* instructions, such as a choice of questions to be answered, make sure that you note this instruction carefully.

2) When you are ready to start work on the examination, that is as soon as the signal has been given, read the instructions to each question booklet, underline any key words or phrases, such as *least, best, outline, describe* and the like. In this way you will tend to answer as requested rather than discover on reviewing your paper that you *listed without describing*, that you selected the *worst* choice rather than the *best* choice, etc.

3) If the examination is of the objective or multiple-choice type – that is, each question will also give a series of possible answers: A, B, C or D, and you are called upon to select the best answer and write the letter next to that answer on your answer paper – it is advisable to start answering each question in turn. There may be anywhere from 50 to 100 such questions in the three or four hours allotted and you can see how much time would be taken if you read through all the questions before beginning to answer any. Furthermore, if you come across a question or group of questions which you know would be difficult to answer, it would undoubtedly affect your handling of all the other questions.

4) If the examination is of the essay type and contains but a few questions, it is a moot point as to whether you should read all the questions before starting to answer any one. Of course, if you are given a choice – say five out of seven and the like – then it is essential to read all the questions so you can eliminate the two that are most difficult. If, however, you are asked to answer all the questions, there may be danger in trying to answer the easiest one first because you may find that you will spend too much time on it. The best technique is to answer the first question, then proceed to the second, etc.

5) Time your answers. Before the exam begins, write down the time it started, then add the time allowed for the examination and write down the time it must be completed, then divide the time available somewhat as follows:
   - If 3-1/2 hours are allowed, that would be 210 minutes. If you have 80 objective-type questions, that would be an average of 2-1/2 minutes per question. Allow yourself no more than 2 minutes per question, or a total of 160 minutes, which will permit about 50 minutes to review.
   - If for the time allotment of 210 minutes there are 7 essay questions to answer, that would average about 30 minutes a question. Give yourself only 25 minutes per question so that you have about 35 minutes to review.

6) The most important instruction is to *read each question* and make sure you know what is wanted. The second most important instruction is to *time yourself properly* so that you answer every question. The third most

important instruction is to *answer every question*. Guess if you have to but include something for each question. Remember that you will receive no credit for a blank and will probably receive some credit if you write something in answer to an essay question. If you guess a letter – say "B" for a multiple-choice question – you may have guessed right. If you leave a blank as an answer to a multiple-choice question, the examiners may respect your feelings but it will not add a point to your score. Some exams may penalize you for wrong answers, so in such cases *only*, you may not want to guess unless you have some basis for your answer.

7) Suggestions
   a. Objective-type questions
      1. Examine the question booklet for proper sequence of pages and questions
      2. Read all instructions carefully
      3. Skip any question which seems too difficult; return to it after all other questions have been answered
      4. Apportion your time properly; do not spend too much time on any single question or group of questions
      5. Note and underline key words – *all, most, fewest, least, best, worst, same, opposite,* etc.
      6. Pay particular attention to negatives
      7. Note unusual option, e.g., unduly long, short, complex, different or similar in content to the body of the question
      8. Observe the use of "hedging" words – *probably, may, most likely,* etc.
      9. Make sure that your answer is put next to the same number as the question
      10. Do not second-guess unless you have good reason to believe the second answer is definitely more correct
      11. Cross out original answer if you decide another answer is more accurate; do not erase until you are ready to hand your paper in
      12. Answer all questions; guess unless instructed otherwise
      13. Leave time for review

   b. Essay questions
      1. Read each question carefully
      2. Determine exactly what is wanted. Underline key words or phrases.
      3. Decide on outline or paragraph answer
      4. Include many different points and elements unless asked to develop any one or two points or elements
      5. Show impartiality by giving pros and cons unless directed to select one side only
      6. Make and write down any assumptions you find necessary to answer the questions
      7. Watch your English, grammar, punctuation and choice of words
      8. Time your answers; don't crowd material

8) Answering the essay question

Most essay questions can be answered by framing the specific response around several key words or ideas. Here are a few such key words or ideas:

M's: manpower, materials, methods, money, management
P's: purpose, program, policy, plan, procedure, practice, problems, pitfalls, personnel, public relations

  a. Six basic steps in handling problems:
    1. Preliminary plan and background development
    2. Collect information, data and facts
    3. Analyze and interpret information, data and facts
    4. Analyze and develop solutions as well as make recommendations
    5. Prepare report and sell recommendations
    6. Install recommendations and follow up effectiveness

  b. Pitfalls to avoid
    1. *Taking things for granted* – A statement of the situation does not necessarily imply that each of the elements is necessarily true; for example, a complaint may be invalid and biased so that all that can be taken for granted is that a complaint has been registered
    2. *Considering only one side of a situation* – Wherever possible, indicate several alternatives and then point out the reasons you selected the best one
    3. *Failing to indicate follow up* – Whenever your answer indicates action on your part, make certain that you will take proper follow-up action to see how successful your recommendations, procedures or actions turn out to be
    4. *Taking too long in answering any single question* – Remember to time your answers properly

## IX. AFTER THE TEST

Scoring procedures differ in detail among civil service jurisdictions although the general principles are the same. Whether the papers are hand-scored or graded by machine we have described, they are nearly always graded by number. That is, the person who marks the paper knows only the number – never the name – of the applicant. Not until all the papers have been graded will they be matched with names. If other tests, such as training and experience or oral interview ratings have been given, scores will be combined. Different parts of the examination usually have different weights. For example, the written test might count 60 percent of the final grade, and a rating of training and experience 40 percent. In many jurisdictions, veterans will have a certain number of points added to their grades.

After the final grade has been determined, the names are placed in grade order and an eligible list is established. There are various methods for resolving ties between those who get the same final grade – probably the most common is to place first the name of the person whose application was received first. Job offers are made from the eligible list in the order the names appear on it. You will be notified of your grade and your rank as soon as all these computations have been made. This will be done as rapidly as possible.

People who are found to meet the requirements in the announcement are called "eligibles." Their names are put on a list of eligible candidates. An eligible's chances of getting a job depend on how high he stands on this list and how fast agencies are filling jobs from the list.

When a job is to be filled from a list of eligibles, the agency asks for the names of people on the list of eligibles for that job. When the civil service commission receives this request, it sends to the agency the names of the three people highest on this list. Or, if the job to be filled has specialized requirements, the office sends the agency the names of the top three persons who meet these requirements from the general list.

The appointing officer makes a choice from among the three people whose names were sent to him. If the selected person accepts the appointment, the names of the others are put back on the list to be considered for future openings.

That is the rule in hiring from all kinds of eligible lists, whether they are for typist, carpenter, chemist, or something else. For every vacancy, the appointing officer has his choice of any one of the top three eligibles on the list. This explains why the person whose name is on top of the list sometimes does not get an appointment when some of the persons lower on the list do. If the appointing officer chooses the second or third eligible, the No. 1 eligible does not get a job at once, but stays on the list until he is appointed or the list is terminated.


X. HOW TO PASS THE INTERVIEW TEST

The examination for which you applied requires an oral interview test. You have already taken the written test and you are now being called for the interview test – the final part of the formal examination.

You may think that it is not possible to prepare for an interview test and that there are no procedures to follow during an interview. Our purpose is to point out some things you can do in advance that will help you and some good rules to follow and pitfalls to avoid while you are being interviewed.

*What is an interview supposed to test?*

The written examination is designed to test the technical knowledge and competence of the candidate; the oral is designed to evaluate intangible qualities, not readily measured otherwise, and to establish a list showing the relative fitness of each candidate – as measured against his competitors – for the position sought. Scoring is not on the basis of "right" and "wrong," but on a sliding scale of values ranging from "not passable" to "outstanding." As a matter of fact, it is possible to achieve a relatively low score without a single "incorrect" answer because of evident weakness in the qualities being measured.

Occasionally, an examination may consist entirely of an oral test – either an individual or a group oral. In such cases, information is sought concerning the technical knowledges and abilities of the candidate, since there has been no written examination for this purpose. More commonly, however, an oral test is used to supplement a written examination.

*Who conducts interviews?*

The composition of oral boards varies among different jurisdictions. In nearly all, a representative of the personnel department serves as chairman. One of the members of the board may be a representative of the department in which the candidate would work. In some cases, "outside experts" are used, and, frequently, a businessman or some other representative of the general public is asked to serve. Labor and management or other special groups may be represented. The aim is to secure the services of experts in the appropriate field.

However the board is composed, it is a good idea (and not at all improper or unethical) to ascertain in advance of the interview who the members are and what groups they represent. When you are introduced to them, you will have some idea of their backgrounds and interests, and at least you will not stutter and stammer over their names.

*What should be done before the interview?*

While knowledge about the board members is useful and takes some of the surprise element out of the interview, there is other preparation which is more substantive. It *is* possible to prepare for an oral interview – in several ways:

**1) Keep a copy of your application and review it carefully before the interview**

This may be the only document before the oral board, and the starting point of the interview. Know what education and experience you have listed there, and the sequence and dates of all of it. Sometimes the board will ask you to review the highlights of your experience for them; you should not have to hem and haw doing it.

**2) Study the class specification and the examination announcement**

Usually, the oral board has one or both of these to guide them. The qualities, characteristics or knowledges required by the position sought are stated in these documents. They offer valuable clues as to the nature of the oral interview. For example, if the job involves supervisory responsibilities, the announcement will usually indicate that knowledge of modern supervisory methods and the qualifications of the candidate as a supervisor will be tested. If so, you can expect such questions, frequently in the form of a hypothetical situation which you are expected to solve. NEVER go into an oral without knowledge of the duties and responsibilities of the job you seek.

**3) Think through each qualification required**

Try to visualize the kind of questions you would ask if you were a board member. How well could you answer them? Try especially to appraise your own knowledge and background in each area, *measured against the job sought*, and identify any areas in which you are weak. Be critical and realistic – do not flatter yourself.

**4) Do some general reading in areas in which you feel you may be weak**

For example, if the job involves supervision and your past experience has NOT, some general reading in supervisory methods and practices, particularly in the field of human relations, might be useful. Do NOT study agency procedures or detailed manuals. The oral board will be testing your understanding and capacity, not your memory.

**5) Get a good night's sleep and watch your general health and mental attitude**

You will want a clear head at the interview. Take care of a cold or any other minor ailment, and of course, no hangovers.

*What should be done on the day of the interview?*

Now comes the day of the interview itself. Give yourself plenty of time to get there. Plan to arrive somewhat ahead of the scheduled time, particularly if your appointment is in the fore part of the day. If a previous candidate fails to appear, the board might be ready for you a bit early. By early afternoon an oral board is almost invariably behind schedule if there are many candidates, and you may have to wait.

Take along a book or magazine to read, or your application to review, but leave any extraneous material in the waiting room when you go in for your interview. In any event, relax and compose yourself.

The matter of dress is important. The board is forming impressions about you – from your experience, your manners, your attitude, and your appearance. Give your personal appearance careful attention. Dress your best, but not your flashiest. Choose conservative, appropriate clothing, and be sure it is immaculate. This is a business interview, and your appearance should indicate that you regard it as such. Besides, being well groomed and properly dressed will help boost your confidence.

Sooner or later, someone will call your name and escort you into the interview room. *This is it.* From here on you are on your own. It is too late for any more preparation. But remember, you asked for this opportunity to prove your fitness, and you are here because your request was granted.

*What happens when you go in?*

The usual sequence of events will be as follows: The clerk (who is often the board stenographer) will introduce you to the chairman of the oral board, who will introduce you to the other members of the board. Acknowledge the introductions before you sit down. Do not be surprised if you find a microphone facing you or a stenotypist sitting by. Oral interviews are usually recorded in the event of an appeal or other review.

Usually the chairman of the board will open the interview by reviewing the highlights of your education and work experience from your application – primarily for the benefit of the other members of the board, as well as to get the material into the record. Do not interrupt or comment unless there is an error or significant misinterpretation; if that is the case, do not hesitate. But do not quibble about insignificant matters. Also, he will usually ask you some question about your education, experience or your present job – partly to get you to start talking and to establish the interviewing "rapport." He may start the actual questioning, or turn it over to one of the other members. Frequently, each member undertakes the questioning on a particular area, one in which he is perhaps most competent, so you can expect each member to participate in the examination. Because time is limited, you may also expect some rather abrupt switches in the direction the questioning takes, so do not be upset by it. Normally, a board member will not pursue a single line of questioning unless he discovers a particular strength or weakness.

After each member has participated, the chairman will usually ask whether any member has any further questions, then will ask you if you have anything you wish to add. Unless you are expecting this question, it may floor you. Worse, it may start you off on an extended, extemporaneous speech. The board is not usually seeking more information. The question is principally to offer you a last opportunity to present further qualifications or to indicate that you have nothing to add. So, if you feel that a significant qualification or characteristic has been overlooked, it is proper to point it out in a sentence or so. Do not compliment the board on the thoroughness of their examination – they have been sketchy, and you know it. If you wish, merely say, "No thank you, I have nothing further to add." This is a point where you can "talk yourself out" of a good impression or fail to present an important bit of information. Remember, *you close the interview yourself*.

The chairman will then say, "That is all, Mr. _____, thank you." Do not be startled; the interview is over, and quicker than you think. Thank him, gather your belongings and take your leave. Save your sigh of relief for the other side of the door.

*How to put your best foot forward*

Throughout this entire process, you may feel that the board individually and collectively is trying to pierce your defenses, seek out your hidden weaknesses and embarrass and confuse you. Actually, this is not true. They are obliged to make an appraisal of your qualifications for the job you are seeking, and they want to see you in your best light. Remember, they must interview all candidates and a non-cooperative candidate may become a failure in spite of their best efforts to bring out his qualifications. Here are 15 suggestions that will help you:

**1) Be natural – Keep your attitude confident, not cocky**

If you are not confident that you can do the job, do not expect the board to be. Do not apologize for your weaknesses, try to bring out your strong points. The board is interested in a positive, not negative, presentation. Cockiness will antagonize any board member and make him wonder if you are covering up a weakness by a false show of strength.

**2) Get comfortable, but don't lounge or sprawl**

Sit erectly but not stiffly. A careless posture may lead the board to conclude that you are careless in other things, or at least that you are not impressed by the importance of the occasion. Either conclusion is natural, even if incorrect. Do not fuss with your clothing, a pencil or an ashtray. Your hands may occasionally be useful to emphasize a point; do not let them become a point of distraction.

**3) Do not wisecrack or make small talk**

This is a serious situation, and your attitude should show that you consider it as such. Further, the time of the board is limited – they do not want to waste it, and neither should you.

**4) Do not exaggerate your experience or abilities**

In the first place, from information in the application or other interviews and sources, the board may know more about you than you think. Secondly, you probably will not get away with it. An experienced board is rather adept at spotting such a situation, so do not take the chance.

**5) If you know a board member, do not make a point of it, yet do not hide it**

Certainly you are not fooling him, and probably not the other members of the board. Do not try to take advantage of your acquaintanceship – it will probably do you little good.

**6) Do not dominate the interview**

Let the board do that. They will give you the clues – do not assume that you have to do all the talking. Realize that the board has a number of questions to ask you, and do not try to take up all the interview time by showing off your extensive knowledge of the answer to the first one.

**7) Be attentive**

You only have 20 minutes or so, and you should keep your attention at its sharpest throughout. When a member is addressing a problem or question to you, give him your undivided attention. Address your reply principally to him, but do not exclude the other board members.

### 8) Do not interrupt
A board member may be stating a problem for you to analyze. He will ask you a question when the time comes. Let him state the problem, and wait for the question.

### 9) Make sure you understand the question
Do not try to answer until you are sure what the question is. If it is not clear, restate it in your own words or ask the board member to clarify it for you. However, do not haggle about minor elements.

### 10) Reply promptly but not hastily
A common entry on oral board rating sheets is "candidate responded readily," or "candidate hesitated in replies." Respond as promptly and quickly as you can, but do not jump to a hasty, ill-considered answer.

### 11) Do not be peremptory in your answers
A brief answer is proper – but do not fire your answer back. That is a losing game from your point of view. The board member can probably ask questions much faster than you can answer them.

### 12) Do not try to create the answer you think the board member wants
He is interested in what kind of mind you have and how it works – not in playing games. Furthermore, he can usually spot this practice and will actually grade you down on it.

### 13) Do not switch sides in your reply merely to agree with a board member
Frequently, a member will take a contrary position merely to draw you out and to see if you are willing and able to defend your point of view. Do not start a debate, yet do not surrender a good position. If a position is worth taking, it is worth defending.

### 14) Do not be afraid to admit an error in judgment if you are shown to be wrong
The board knows that you are forced to reply without any opportunity for careful consideration. Your answer may be demonstrably wrong. If so, admit it and get on with the interview.

### 15) Do not dwell at length on your present job
The opening question may relate to your present assignment. Answer the question but do not go into an extended discussion. You are being examined for a *new* job, not your present one. As a matter of fact, try to phrase ALL your answers in terms of the job for which you are being examined.

*Basis of Rating*

Probably you will forget most of these "do's" and "don'ts" when you walk into the oral interview room. Even remembering them all will not ensure you a passing grade. Perhaps you did not have the qualifications in the first place. But remembering them will help you to put your best foot forward, without treading on the toes of the board members.

Rumor and popular opinion to the contrary notwithstanding, an oral board wants you to make the best appearance possible. They know you are under pressure – but they also want to see how you respond to it as a guide to what your reaction would be under the pressures of the job you seek. They will be influenced by the degree of poise you display, the personal traits you show and the manner in which you respond.

# EXAMINATION SECTION

# EXAMINATION SECTION

## TEST 1

DIRECTIONS: Each question or incomplete statement is followed by several suggested answers or completions. Select the one that BEST answers the question or completes the statement. *PRINT THE LETTER OF THE CORRECT ANSWER IN THE SPACE AT THE RIGHT.*

Questions 1-10.

DIRECTIONS: Questions 1 through 10 are to be answered on the basis of the floor plan below. Study it for five minutes. Do not look at it again when answering the questions.

Firefighters must be able to find their way in and out of buildings that are filled with smoke. They must learn the floor plan quickly for their own safety and to help fight the fire and remove victims. Look at this floor plan of an apartment. There is an apartment on each side of this one. It is on the fifth floor of the building.

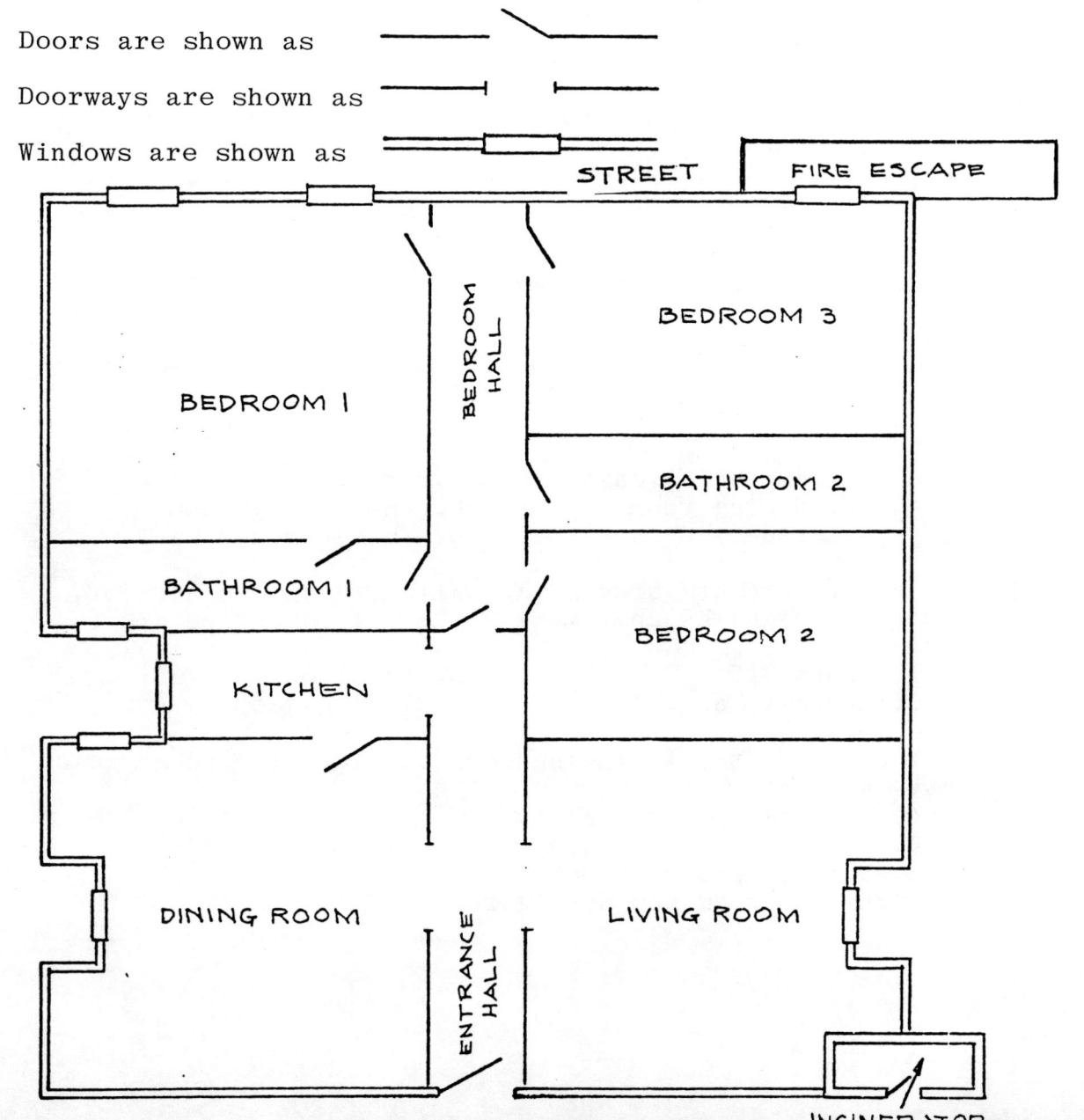

Doors are shown as

Doorways are shown as

Windows are shown as

1.  A person escaping a fire in the apartment can get on the fire escape by going through the window of
    A. Bedroom 1
    B. Bedroom 2
    C. Bedroom 3
    D. Living Room

2.  If there is a fire in bedroom 3 and a firefighter is rescuing a child in bedroom 2, the SAFEST way of escape would be through the
    A. window of bedroom 2
    B. entrance hall and apartment door
    C. bedroom hall and bedroom 1
    D. bedroom hall and window of bathroom 2

3.  Firefighters coming in the apartment's entrance door would have to go the LONGEST distance to get to the
    A. fire escape
    B. dining room
    C. door of bathroom 2
    D. kitchen window

4.  Which one of the following rooms in the apartment CANNOT be closed off by a door?
    A. Living room
    B. Bedroom 1
    C. Bathroom 1
    D. Bedroom 2

5.  A firefighter is in a room from which there is only one way of escape.
    Which one of the following rooms is the firefighter in?
    A. Living room
    B. Dining room
    C. Kitchen
    D. Bedroom 2

6.  There is a fire in the apartment and the ladder of the fire truck in the street cannot be placed against the fire escape.
    The ladder should be raised from the street to reach a window in bedroom
    A. 1
    B. 2
    C. 3
    D. hall

7.  A door from the kitchen leads directly into
    A. the dining room
    B. the living room
    C. bathroom 1
    D. the entrance hall

8.  If a fire breaks through the walls of the incinerator, the people in the apartment NEAREST to the fire are those in
    A. bedroom 2
    B. bathroom 1
    C. the kitchen
    D. living room

9.  Which one of the following choices lists two rooms which have NO windows?
    A. Bedroom 1 and bathroom 1
    B. Bedroom 2 and bathroom 2
    C. Kitchen and bathroom 2
    D. Living room and dining room

10. The door that can be closed to separate the bedrooms from    10.___
    the rest of the apartment is the door between the
       A. entrance hall and the bedroom hall
       B. living room and the entrance hall
       C. kitchen and the living room
       D. dining room and the living room

Questions 11-25.

DIRECTIONS:   Questions 11 through 25 are to be answered SOLELY on
              the basis of the following facts and Building Inspection
              Form. Each box on the form is numbered. Read the facts
              and review the form before answering the questions.

   Firefighters are required to inspect all buildings within their
assigned area of the city. They check conditions within the building
for violations of fire safety laws. While inspecting a building,
they must fill out a Building Inspection Form as a record of the
conditions they observed.

   On June 12, 1992, Firefighter Edward Gold, assigned to Engine
Company 82, is ordered by Captain John Bailey to inspect the building
at 1400 Compton Place as part of the engine company's monthly
building inspection duty. The building is a one-story brick warehouse where books of the S & G Publishing Company are stored before
shipment to stores.

   Firefighter Gold enters the warehouse through the main entrance
door in the front of the building. Though an exit sign is present
above the door, the sign is unlit because of a burned-out bulb.
There is a small office to one side of the main entrance area where
Firefighter Gold goes to meet the warehouse manager, Mr. Stevens.
The firefighter explains the purpose of the inspection.

   Firefighter Gold tells the manager that he will check the
automatic sprinkler system first because if a fire got started in
a warehouse full of stored books, the fire could spread rapidly.
He asks Mr. Stevens for the Certificate of Fitness issued to the
company employee certified to maintain the sprinkler system in
working order. The certificate is dated June 1, 1989, and Gold
observes that it has expired. The manager promises to have the
certificate renewed as soon as possible.

   The firefighter wants to locate the main control valve of the
sprinkler system. He asks Mr. Stevens to go with him and show him
its location. Gold and the manager leave through an office door
which leads into the main working area of the warehouse. They locate
the main sprinkler control valve on the wall in a corner of the work
area behind high shelves stocked with books. The firefighter
observes that the main control valve is sealed in the open position.
Gold next climbs a ladder lying against the storage shelves and
measures the distance between the top of the stack of books on the
highest shelf and the sprinkler heads suspended on pipes below the
ceiling. The distance is three feet.

Firefighter Gold next inspects the remaining exits from the building. A large fire door leads out to the loading dock in the rear of the warehouse. A small door on the side of the warehouse that is used by employees when they leave for the day is partially obstructed by cartons. Lighted exit signs can be clearly seen above both doors. During working hours, only the main entrance door and the fire door to the loading dock are unlocked. Mr. Stevens says he keeps the side door locked to keep employees from leaving early and only unlocks it at closing time.

Firefighter Gold and the manager then walk through the main work area. Gold observes that fireproof rubbish receptacles are placed at frequent intervals. However, they are not covered and the contents are overflowing, resulting in several piles of litter on the floor. *No Smoking* signs are on the walls of the work area, but are difficult to see behind the rows of high storage shelves.

The two fire extinguishers in the work area are found lying on the floor rather than hung on wall racks. The two other fire extinguishers in the warehouse, one in the office and one in the employee lounge, are both correctly hung on wall racks. All four fire extinguishers are fully charged. According to their tags, they were last inspected on March 11, 1992.

Firefighter Gold continues the inspection by checking on the electrical wiring, which appears to be generally in good condition. However, four switch boxes lack covers. The main junction box has a cover, but it cannot be closed because the cover is corroded.

The inspection is now complete, so Firefighter Gold thanks Mr. Stevens for his cooperation and leaves the building. Gold checks that all required information is entered on the Building Inspection Form, including information concerning building violations Firefighter Gold signs and dates the Building Inspection Form and then submits it to Captain Bailey for his review. After reviewing Firefighter Gold's report, Captain Bailey signs the Building Inspection Form.

## BUILDING INSPECTION FORM

| DIVISION (1) | BATTALION (2) | COMPANY (3) |
|---|---|---|

| BUILDING INFORMATION | Name of Business (4) | Address (5) |
|---|---|---|
|  | Type of Business (6) | Occupancy Code Number (7) |

| CONDITION OF EXITS | Number of Exits (8) | Exits Obstructed (9) | Exits unlocked (10) |
|---|---|---|---|
|  | Exit Signs (11) | Exit Sign Lights (12) | Fire Doors (13) |

| HOUSEKEEPING CONDITIONS | Rubbish Receptacles (14) | | No Smoking Signs (15) |
|---|---|---|---|
|  | Clearance of Stock in Feet from Sprinkler Heads (16) | | |
|  | Electrical Wiring (17) | Switches (18) | Junction Box (19) |

| CONDITION OF FIRE EXTINGUISHERS | Charged (20) | Placement (21) | Date of Last Inspection (22) |
|---|---|---|---|

| CONDITION OF AUTOMATIC SPRINKLER SYSTEM | Color of Siamese (23) | Main Control Valve (24) | Shut-off sign (25) |
|---|---|---|---|
|  | Certificate of Fitness (26) | Date of Last Inspection (27) | |

| SPECIAL CONDITIONS | Rubbish/Obstructions (28) | Certificate of Occupancy (29) |
|---|---|---|
|  |  | Heavy Load Signs (30) |

| FIRE DEPARTMENT INFORMATION | Inspector Name _____ Signature _____ (31) | Rank (32) | Date (33) |
|---|---|---|---|
|  | Officer Name _____ Signature _____ (34) | Rank (35) | Date (36) |

11. Which one of the following should be entered in Box 3?
    A. Ladder Company 79      B. Engine Company 12
    C. Ladder Company 140     D. Engine Company 82

12. Which one of the following should be entered in Box 4?
    _____ Company.
    A. G & R Printing         B. S & G Printing
    C. R & G Publishing       D. S & G Publishing

13. Which one of the following should be entered in Box 8?
    A. 2        B. 3        C. 4        D. 5

14. Which one of the following should be entered in Box 9?
    A. Office door            B. Side door
    C. Main door              D. Fire door

15. Which one of the following should be entered in Box 10?
    _____ door and _____ door.
    A. Fire; main             B. Side; office
    C. Fire; side             D. Main; cellar

16. The entry in Box 12 should show that replacement bulbs are needed for _____ light(s).
    A. one      B. two      C. three     D. all

17. The entry in Box 14 should show that covers are missing from _____ of the rubbish receptacles.
    A. two      B. three    C. four      D. all

18. Which one of the following should be entered in Box 16?
    _____ feet.
    A. One and one-half       B. Two
    C. Two and one-half       D. Three

19. Which one of the following should be entered in Box 19?
    A. Faulty circuits        B. Exposed wiring
    C. Corroded cover         D. Good condition

20. Which one of the following entries about the placement of fire extinguishers should appear in Box 21?
    A. One on the floor, three hung on wall racks
    B. Two on the floor, two hung on wall racks
    C. Three on the floor, one hung on wall rack
    D. Four hung on wall racks

21. Which one of the following should be entered in Box 22?
    A. June 1, 1989           B. May 21, 1991
    C. March 11, 1992         D. May 1, 1992

22. The entry in Box 24 should show that the position of the main control valve is
    A. open                   B. half open
    C. one-third closed       D. closed

23. Which one of the following should be entered in Box 26?      23.___
    A. Expired              B. Missing from file
    C. Never issued         D. Current

24. Which one of the following should be entered in Box 28?      24.___
    A. Ceiling plaster cracked
    B. Rubbish piles litter work floor
    C. Second floor stairway blocked
    D. Open paint cans on loading dock

25. Which one of the following should be entered in Box 34?      25.___
    A. John Bailey          B. Edward Gold
    C. John Gold            D. Edward Bailey

---

# KEY (CORRECT ANSWERS)

1. C  
2. B  
3. A  
4. A  
5. D  

6. A  
7. A  
8. D  
9. B  
10. A  

11. D  
12. D  
13. B  
14. B  
15. A  

16. A  
17. D  
18. D  
19. C  
20. B  

21. C  
22. A  
23. A  
24. B  
25. A  

---

# TEST 2

DIRECTIONS: Each question or incomplete statement is followed by several suggested answers or completions. Select the one that BEST answers the question or completes the statement. *PRINT THE LETTER OF THE CORRECT ANSWER IN THE SPACE AT THE RIGHT.*

Questions 1-8.

DIRECTIONS: Questions 1 through 8 are to be answered on the basis of the following items. The sizes of the items shown are NOT their actual sizes. Each item is identified by a number. For each question, select the answer which gives the identifying number of the item that BEST answers the question.

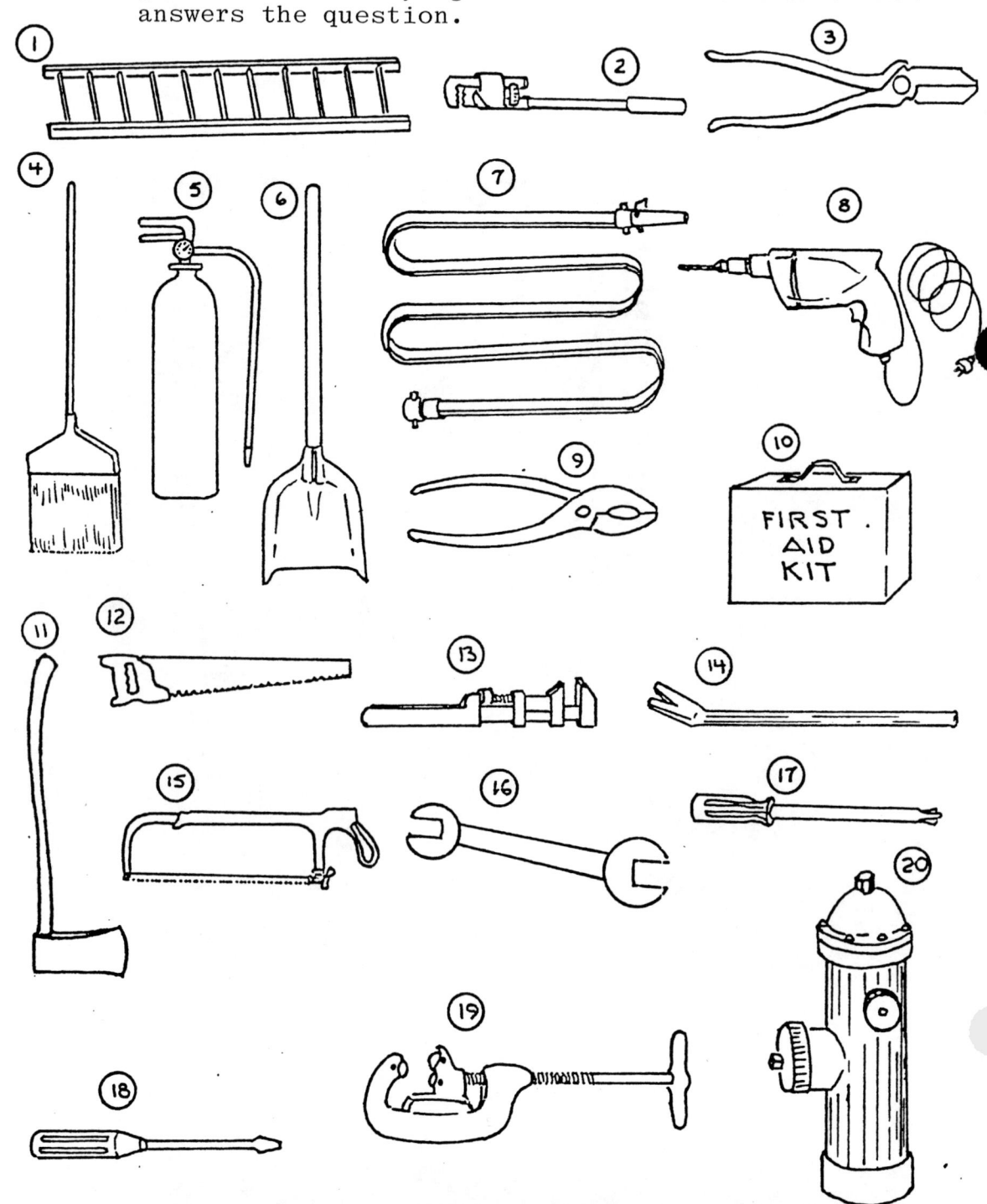

1. Which one of the following items should be connected to a hydrant and used to put out a fire?
   A. 5   B. 7   C. 8   D. 17

2. Which one of the following pairs of items should be used after a fire to clean a floor covered with small pieces of burned material?
   A. 1 and 14   B. 4 and 6   C. 10 and 12   D. 11 and 13

3. Which one of the following pairs of items should be used for cutting a branch from a tree?
   A. 2 and 3   B. 8 and 9   C. 11 and 12   D. 14 and 15

4. Which one of the following items should be used to rescue a victim from a second floor window?
   A. 1   B. 10   C. 15   D. 20

5. Which one of the following pairs of items should be used to tighten a nut on a screw?
   A. 2 and 3   B. 8 and 19   C. 9 and 14   D. 16 and 18

6. Which one of the following items should be used to repair a leaky faucet?
   A. 4   B. 5   C. 12   D. 13

7. Which one of the following items should be used as a source of water at a fire?
   A. 2   B. 6   C. 9   D. 20

8. Which item should be used for cutting metal?
   A. 6   B. 13   C. 15   D. 18

9. An elderly man staggers into the firehouse and tells the firefighters on duty that he is having trouble breathing. Of the following, it would be BEST for the firefighters to
   A. send the elderly man away as his staggering shows that he has been drinking too much
   B. place the elderly man in a chair and quickly call for assistance
   C. tell the elderly man to go to the hospital and see a doctor
   D. help the elderly man leave the firehouse as this is not a problem that firefighters should handle

10. As firefighters travel to and from their firehouse, they usually look around the neighborhood in order to spot dangerous conditions. If they spot a dangerous condition, firefighters will take action to correct it. They do this because they want to prevent fires. While on his way to work overtime at a nearby firehouse, a firefighter passes a local gas station and spots a leaking gasoline pump.
    Which one of the following is the MOST appropriate course of action for the firefighter to take?
    A. Stop at the gas station and make sure that the leak is actually gasoline by lighting a match to it.

B. Continue on to work because the gas station attendant will take care of the leak.
  C. Stop at the gas station and tell the gas station attendant to make sure the leak is repaired.
  D. Call the Mayor's Office to complain that the leaking gasoline is polluting the area.

11. A newly appointed firefighter is assigned to go with an experienced firefighter to inspect a paint store. The paint store owner refuses to allow the inspection, saying that he is closing the store early that day and going on vacation. The new firefighter demands rudely that the inspection be allowed, even though it would be permissible to delay it.
Of the following, it would be BEST for the experienced firefighter to
   A. repeat the demand that the inspection be allowed and quote the law to the store owner
   B. tell the new firefighter that it would be best to schedule the inspection after the store owner's vacation
   C. tell the store owner to step aside, and instruct the new firefighter to enter the store and begin the inspection
   D. tell the new firefighter to forget about the inspection because the store owner is uncooperative

12. The picture on the right shows a firefighter standing on a ladder. The firefighter should notice that a dangerous condition exists. Which of the following choices corresponds to the letter in the diagram showing the dangerous condition?
   A. The firefighter's coat is too long for safe climbing of the ladder.
   B. A helmet keeps the firefighter from seeing what is going on.
   C. The firefighter's feet are on the ladder rung.
   D. A ladder rung is missing.

13. A firefighter is ordered to set up a hose on the street  13.___
outside a building in which the second floor is on fire.
The hose should be located about 30 feet from the
building and should be aimed directly at the fire.
Which one of the following diagrams shows how the firefighter should position the hose to aim it at the fire?

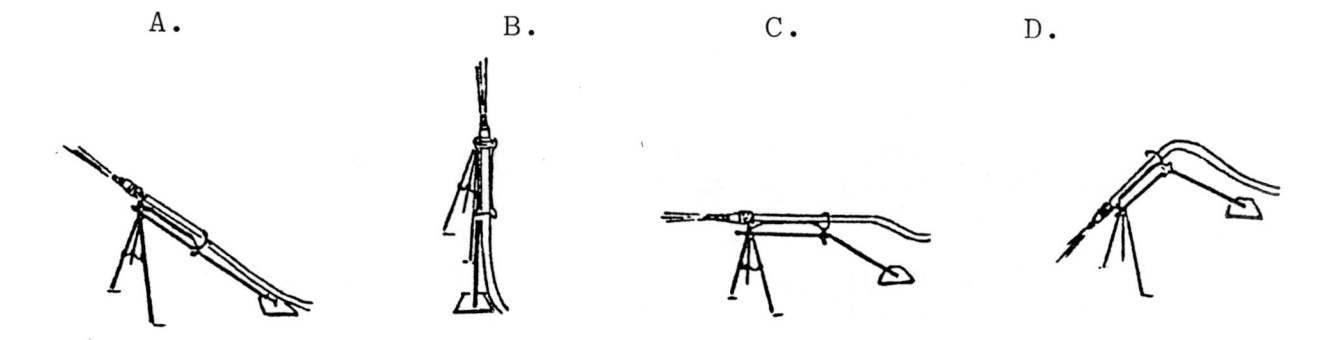

   A.                    B.                    C.                    D.

Questions 14-20.

DIRECTIONS: Questions 14 through 20 are to be answered SOLELY on the basis of the following information.

The portable power saw lets the firefighter cut through various materials so that a fire can be reached. It can be dangerous, however, if it is not properly used or if it has not been inspected and tested to insure that it is in serviceable condition. The parts of the saw should be clean and free of foreign material, especially the exhaust port and spark arrestor, the carburetor enclosure, the cooling fins, the spark plugs, and the V-belt pulley if the saw has one.

The saw should be checked to make sure it has both air and fuel filters. It should never be run without an air filter. The V-belt pulley, if present, must be checked to make sure it is not too tight or too loose. If too loose, it could cause slipping. If too tight, the blade might turn when the engine idles, there might be damage to the clutch bearing, or the motor might stall when the blade is stopped. All nuts, bolts, and screws should be checked for tightness.

The saw may use carbide-tipped blades, aluminum oxide blades, or silicon carbide blades. Carbide-tipped blades should be returned for replacement when two or more tips are broken or missing or when the tips are worn down to the circumference of the blade. Aluminum oxide and silicon carbide blades should be replaced when they are cracked, badly nicked, or when worn down to an eight-inch diameter or less.

5 (#2)

14. The PRINCIPAL reason for inspecting power saws is to make sure that
    A. they are clean
    B. they are in serviceable condition
    C. the pulley is not too tight or too loose
    D. the blades are replaced

15. What does the above passage mean when it says the saw should be kept free of foreign material?
    A. Only American-made parts should be used.
    B. The saw should not be used on material that might damage it.
    C. Both air and fuel filters should be used.
    D. Anything that does not belong on the saw or in it should be removed.

16. Some saws are made to work WITHOUT which one of the following items?
    A. An air filter
    B. A fuel filter
    C. A V-belt pulley
    D. Blades

17. If the V-belt pulley on a power saw is too loose, it is MOST likely to cause
    A. the blade to turn when the engine idles
    B. damage to the clutch bearing
    C. the motor to stall when the blade is stopped
    D. slipping

18. The above passage says that a power saw should never be run without a(n)
    A. air filter
    B. fuel filter
    C. V-belt pulley
    D. blade

19. Which of the following blades should be replaced when two or more tips are missing?
    A. Both aluminum oxide and carbide-tipped blades
    B. Carbide-tipped blades *only*
    C. Both silicon carbide and aluminum oxide blades
    D. Silicon carbide blades *only*

20. Which of the following blades should be replaced when worn down to an eight-inch diameter or less?
    A. Both aluminum oxide and carbide-tipped blades
    B. Carbide-tipped blades *only*
    C. Both silicon carbide and aluminum oxide blades
    D. Silicon carbide blades *only*

21. Fire engines use diesel motors to make them run. Diesel motors have devices called air cleaners which keep dirt from the inside of the motor. To make sure that the air cleaners are cleaned or replaced when necessary, an indicator on the fire engine will display a red color if the air cleaner has become too dirty. Each time the lubricating oil in the motor is changed, or whenever the indicator shows red, the air cleaners must be inspected and cleaned or replaced.

Of the following, the MOST accurate statement concerning air cleaners on fire engine diesel motors is that they should be
A. cleaned every day
B. replaced only when the oil is changed
C. inspected and cleaned only when the oil is changed
D. inspected and cleaned or replaced when the indicator shows red

22. Firefighter Green must check the supply of air tank cylinders at the beginning of each tour of duty. There must be ten air tank cylinders always full of air and ready to be exchanged for used, empty air tank cylinders. At the start of a new tour of duty, Firefighter Green finds that out of twenty cylinders present, only five cylinders are full and ready to be exchanged.
What is the MINIMUM number of used empty cylinders that Firefighter Green must replace with full cylinders?
A. 5     B. 10     C. 15     D. 20

22.___

Questions 23-25.

DIRECTIONS: Questions 23 through 25 are to be answered SOLELY on the basis of the following passage.

Automatic sprinkler systems are installed in many buildings. They extinguish or keep from spreading 96% of all fires in areas they protect. Sprinkler systems are made up of pipes which hang below the ceiling of each protected area and sprinkler heads which are placed along the pipes. The pipes are usually filled with water, and each sprinkler head has a heat sensitive part. When the heat from the fire reaches the sensitive part of the sprinkler head, the head opens and showers water upon the fire in the form of spray. The heads are spaced so that the fire is covered by overlapping showers of water from the open heads.

23. Automatic sprinkler systems are installed in buildings to
A. prevent the build-up of dangerous gases
B. eliminate the need for fire insurance
C. extinguish fires or keep them from spreading
D. protect 96% of the floor space

23.___

24. If more than one sprinkler head opens, the area sprayed will be
A. flooded with hot water
B. overlapped by showers of water
C. subject to less water damage
D. about 1 foot per sprinkler head

24.___

25. A sprinkler head will open and shower water when
    A. it is reached by heat from a fire
    B. water pressure in the pipes gets too high
    C. it is reached by sounds from a fire alarm
    D. water temperature in the pipes gets too low

---

## KEY (CORRECT ANSWERS)

1. B
2. B
3. C
4. A
5. D

6. D
7. D
8. C
9. B
10. C

11. B
12. D
13. A
14. B
15. D

16. C
17. D
18. A
19. B
20. C

21. D
22. A
23. C
24. B
25. A

---

# EXAMINATION SECTION

# TEST 1

DIRECTIONS: Each question or incomplete statement is followed by several suggested answers or completions. Select the one that BEST answers the question or completes the statement. *PRINT THE LETTER OF THE CORRECT ANSWER IN THE SPACE AT THE RIGHT.*

Questions 1-5.

DIRECTIONS: Questions 1 through 5 are to be answered SOLELY on the basis of the following information and map.

A firefighter may be required to assist civilians who seek travel directions or referral to city agencies and facilities.

The following is a map of part of a city, where several public offices and other institutions are located. Each of the squares represents one city block. Street names are as shown. If there is an arrow next to the street name, it means the street is one way only in the direction of the arrow. If there is no arrow next to the street name, two-way traffic is allowed.

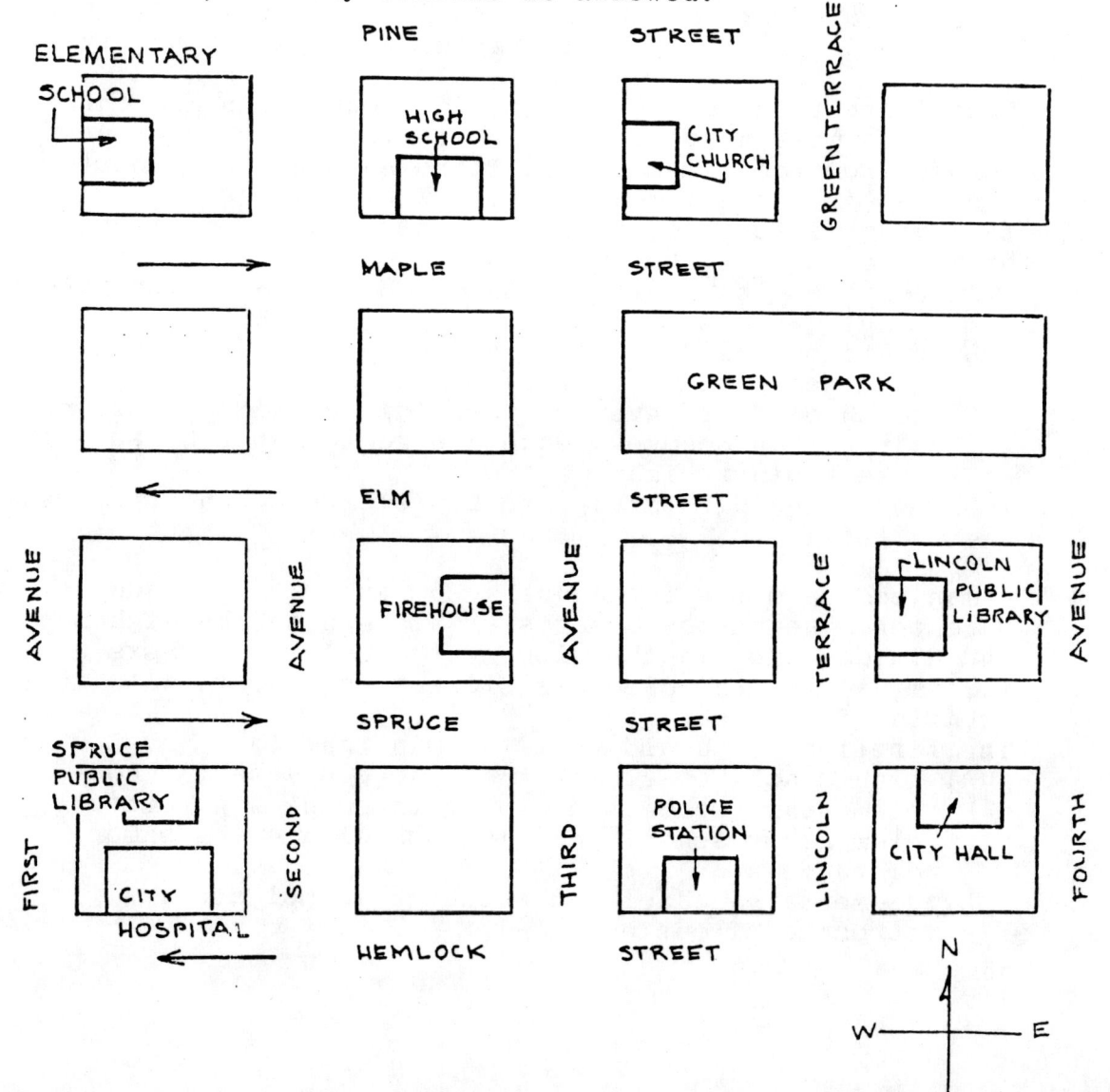

1. A woman whose handbag was stolen from her in Green Park asks a firefighter at the firehouse where to go to report the crime.
   The firefighter should tell the woman to go to the
   A. police station on Spruce St.
   B. police station on Hemlock St.
   C. city hall on Spruce St.
   D. city hall on Hemlock St.

2. A disabled senior citizen who lives on Green Terrace telephones the firehouse to ask which library is closest to her home.
   The firefighter should tell the senior citizen it is the
   A. Spruce Public Library on Lincoln Terrace
   B. Lincoln Public Library on Spruce Street
   C. Spruce Public Library on Spruce Street
   D. Lincoln Public Library on Lincoln Terrace

3. A woman calls the firehouse to ask for the exact location of City Hall.
   She should be told that it is on
   A. Hemlock Street, between Lincoln Terrace and Fourth Ave.
   B. Spruce Street, between Lincoln Terrace and Fourth Ave.
   C. Lincoln Terrace, between Spruce Street and Elm Street
   D. Green Terrace, between Maple Street and Pine Street

4. A delivery truck driver is having trouble finding the high school to make a delivery. The driver parks the truck across from the firehouse on Third Avenue facing north and goes into the firehouse to ask directions.
   In giving directions, the firefighter should tell the driver to go ____ to the school.
   A. north on Third Avenue to Pine Street and then make a right
   B. south on Third Avenue, make a left on Hemlock Street, and then make a right on Second Avenue
   C. north on Third Avenue, turn left on Elm Street, make a right on Second Avenue and go to Maple Street, then make another right
   D. north on Third Avenue to Maple Street, and then make a left

5. A man comes to the firehouse accompanied by his son and daughter. He wants to register his son in the high school and his daughter in the elementary school. He asks a firefighter which school is closest for him to walk to from the firehouse.
   The firefighter should tell the man that the
   A. high school is closer than the elementary school
   B. elementary school is closer than the high school
   C. elementary school and high school are the same distance away
   D. elementary school and the high school are in opposite directions

Questions 6-10.

DIRECTIONS: Questions 6 through 10 are to be answered SOLELY on the basis of the following passage.

Sometimes a fire engine leaving the scene of a fire must back out of a street because other fire engines have blocked the path in front of it. When the fire engine is backing up, each firefighter is given a duty to perform to help control automobile traffic and protect people walking nearby. Before the driver starts to slowly back up the fire engine, all the other firefighters are told the route he will take. They walk alongside and behind the slowly moving fire engine, guiding the driver, keeping traffic out of the street and warning people away from the path of the vehicle. As the fire engine, in reverse gear, approaches the intersection, the driver brings it to a full stop and waits for his supervisor to give the order to start moving again. If traffic is blocking the intersection, two firefighters enter the intersection to direct traffic. They clear the cars and people out of the intersection, making way for the fire engine to back into it. The driver then goes forward, turning into the intersection. Two other firefighters keep cars and people away from the front of the fire engine as it moves. Because of the extra care needed to control cars and protect people in the streets when a fire engine is backing up, it is better to drive a fire engine forward whenever possible.

6. A fire engine is leaving the scene of a fire. The street in front of it is blocked by people and other fire engines. Of the following, it would be BEST for the driver to
    A. put on the siren to clear a path
    B. back out of the street slowly
    C. drive on the sidewalk around the other fire engines
    D. move the other fire engines out of the way

7. Firefighters walk alongside and behind the fire engine when it is backing up in order to
    A. strengthen their legs and stay physically fit
    B. look around the neighborhood for fires
    C. insure that the engine moves slowly
    D. control traffic, protect people, and assist the driver

8. A fire engine going in reverse approaches an intersection blocked with cars and trucks.
   The driver should
    A. go forward and then try to back into the intersection at a different angle
    B. slowly enter the intersection as the firefighters guiding the driver give the signal to move
    C. back up through the intersection without stopping
    D. stop, then enter the intersection only when the supervisor gives the signal to move

9. The above passage states that the two firefighters who first enter the intersection
   A. clear the intersection of cars and people
   B. direct the cars past the fire engine when the engine is in forward gear
   C. see if the traffic signal is working properly
   D. set up barriers to block any traffic

10. The diagram to the right shows a fire engine backing slowly out of Jones Street. The letters indicate where firefighters are standing. Which firefighter is NOT in the correct position?
   Firefighter
   A. D
   B. E
   C. A
   D. C

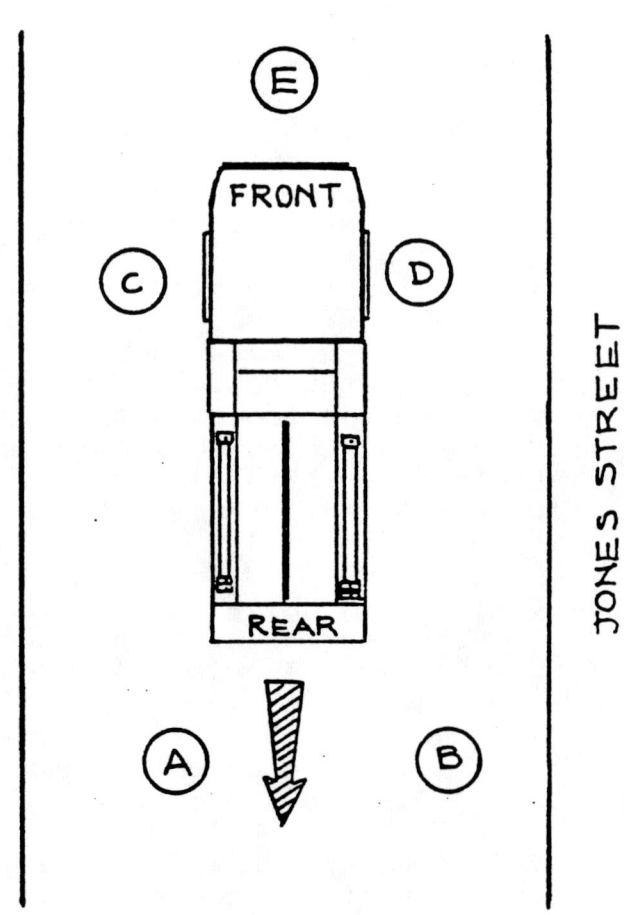

Questions 11-14.

DIRECTIONS: Questions 11 through 14 are to be answered SOLELY on the basis of the following passage.

About 48% of all reported fires are false alarms. False alarms add more risk of danger to firefighters, citizens, and property as well as waste the money and time of the fire department. When the first firefighters are called to a reported fire, they do not know if the alarm is for a real fire or is a false alarm. Until they have made sure that the alarm is false, they must not respond to a new alarm even if a real fire is burning and people's lives and property are in danger. If they do not find a fire or an emergency at the original location, then the firefighters radio the fire department that they have been called to a false alarm. The fire department radios back and tells the firefighters that they are in active service again and tells them where to respond for the next alarm. If that location is far from that of the false alarm, then the distance and the time it takes to get to the new location are increased. This means that firefighters will arrive later to help in fighting the real fire and the fire will have more time to burn. The fire will be bigger and more dangerous just because someone called the firefighters to a false alarm. In addition, each time the firefighters ride to the location of a false alarm, there is additional risk of unnecessary accidents and injuries to them and to citizens.

11. The MAIN point of the above passage is that false alarms
    A. seldom interrupt other activities in the firehouse
    B. occur more often during the winter
    C. are rarely turned in by children
    D. add more risk of danger to life and property

12. When firefighters are called to a false alarm, they must NOT respond to other alarms until they
    A. turn in a written report to the fire department
    B. take a vote and all agree to go
    C. are put back into active service by the fire department
    D. decide on the quickest route

13. Before firefighters get to the location of a reported fire, they
    A. finish eating their lunch at the firehouse
    B. do not know if the alarm is real or false
    C. search the neighborhood for the person who made the report
    D. do not know if the alarm is from an alarm box or telephone

14. The above passage states that false alarms
    A. shorten travel time to real fires
    B. give firefighters needed driving practice
    C. save money on fuel for the fire department
    D. account for about 48% of reported fires

Questions 15-18.

DIRECTIONS: Questions 15 through 18 are to be answered SOLELY on the basis of the following passage.

Fires in vacant buildings are a major problem for firefighters. People enter vacant buildings to remove building material or they damage stairs, floors, doors, and other parts of the building. The buildings are turned into dangerous structures with stairs missing, holes in the floors, weakened walls and loose bricks. Children and arsonists find large amounts of wood, paper, and other combustible materials in the buildings and start fires which damage and weaken the buildings even more. Firefighters have been injured putting out fires in these buildings due to these dangerous conditions. Most injuries caused while putting out fires in vacant buildings could be eliminated if all of these buildings were repaired. All such injuries could be eliminated if the buildings were demolished. Until then, firefighters should take extra care while putting out fires in vacant buildings.

15. The problem of fires in vacant buildings could be solved by
    A. repairing buildings
    B. closing up the cellar door and windows with bricks and cement
    C. arresting suspicious persons before they start the fires
    D. demolishing the buildings

16. Firefighters are injured putting out fires in vacant buildings because
    A. there are no tenants to help fight the fires
    B. conditions are dangerous in these buildings
    C. they are not as careful when nobody lives in the buildings
    D. the water in the buildings has been turned off

17. Vacant buildings often have
    A. occupied buildings on either side of them
    B. safe empty spaces where neighborhood children can play
    C. combustible materials inside them
    D. strong walls and floors that cannot burn

18. While firefighters are putting out fires in vacant buildings, they should
    A. be extra careful of missing stairs
    B. find the children who start the fires
    C. learn the reasons why the fires are set
    D. help to repair the buildings

Questions 19-20.

DIRECTIONS: Questions 19 and 20 are to be answered SOLELY on the basis of the following passage.

Firefighters inspect many different kinds of places to find fire hazards and have them reviewed. During these inspections, the firefighters try to learn as much as possible about the place. This knowledge is useful should the firefighters have to fight a fire at some later date at that location. When inspecting subways, firefighters are much concerned with the effects a fire might have on the passengers because, unless they have been trapped in a subway car during a fire, most subway riders do not think about the dangers involved in a fire in the subway. During a fire, the air in cars crowded with passengers may become intensely hot. The cars may fill with dense smoke. Lights may dim or go out altogether, leaving the passengers in darkness. Ventilation from fans and air conditioning may stop. The train may be stuck and unable to be moved through the tunnel to a station. Fear may send the trapped passengers into a panic. Firefighters must protect the passengers from the fire, heat, and smoke, calm them down, get them out quickly to a safe area, and put out the fire. To do this, firefighters may have to climb from street level down into the subway tunnel to reach a train stopped inside the tunnel. Before actually going on the tracks, they must be sure that the 600 volts of live electricity carried by the third rail is shut off. They may have to stretch fire hose a long distance down subway stairs, on platforms, and along the subway tracks to get the water to the fire and put it out. Subway fires are difficult to fight because of these special problems, but preparing for them in advance can help save the lives of both firefighters and passengers.

19. During a subway fire, a train is stuck in a tunnel. Firefighters have been ordered into the tunnel.
    Before firefighters actually step down on the tracks, they must be sure that
    A. all the passengers have been removed from the burning subway cars to a safe place
    B. they have stretched their fire hose a long distance to put water on the fire
    C. live electricity carried by the third rail is shut off
    D. the train is moved from the tunnel to the nearest station

20. According to the above passage, fire in the subway may leave passengers in subway cars in darkness.
    This occurs MAINLY because
    A. the lights may go out
    B. air in the cars may become very hot
    C. ventilation may stop
    D. people may panic

Questions 21-25.

DIRECTIONS: Questions 21 through 25 concern various forms, reports, or other documents that must be filed according to topic. Listed below are four topics numbered 1 through 4, under which forms, reports, and documents may be filed. In each question, choose the topic under which the form, report, or document concerned should be filed.

   1. Equipment and supplies
   2. Fire prevention
   3. Personnel
   4. Training

21. Under which topic would it be MOST appropriate to file a letter on a heroic act performed by a member of the fire company?
    A. 1          B. 2          C. 3          D. 4

22. Under which topic should a firefighter look for information about the fire company's new portable ladder?
    A. 1      B. 2      C. 3      D. 4

23. Under which topic should a firefighter locate a copy of the fire company's fire prevention building inspection schedule for the current year?
    A. 1      B. 2      C. 3      D. 4

24. Under which topic should a firefighter file a copy of a report on company property which has been damaged?
    A. 1      B. 2      C. 3      D. 4

25. Under which topic should a firefighter be able to locate a roster of firefighters assigned to the company?
    A. 1      B. 2      C. 3      D. 4

# KEY (CORRECT ANSWERS)

1. B
2. D
3. B
4. C
5. A

6. B
7. D
8. D
9. A
10. B

11. D
12. C
13. B
14. D
15. D

16. B
17. C
18. A
19. C
20. A

21. C
22. A
23. B
24. A
25. C

# TEST 2

DIRECTIONS: Each question or incomplete statement is followed by several suggested answers or completions. Select the one that BEST answers the question or completes the statement. *PRINT THE LETTER OF THE CORRECT ANSWER IN THE SPACE AT THE RIGHT.*

1. Firefighters must check gauges on fire engines so that defects are discovered and corrected. Some fire engines are equipped with gauges called *Chargicators*, which indicate whether or not the electrical system is operating properly. When the fire engine's motor is running, the chargicator of a properly operating electrical system will show a reading of 13.5 to 14.2 volts on the scale.
Which one of the following gauges shows a PROPERLY operating electrical system?

1.___

(A) CHARGICATOR

(B) CHARGICATOR

(C) CHARGICATOR

(D) CHARGICATOR

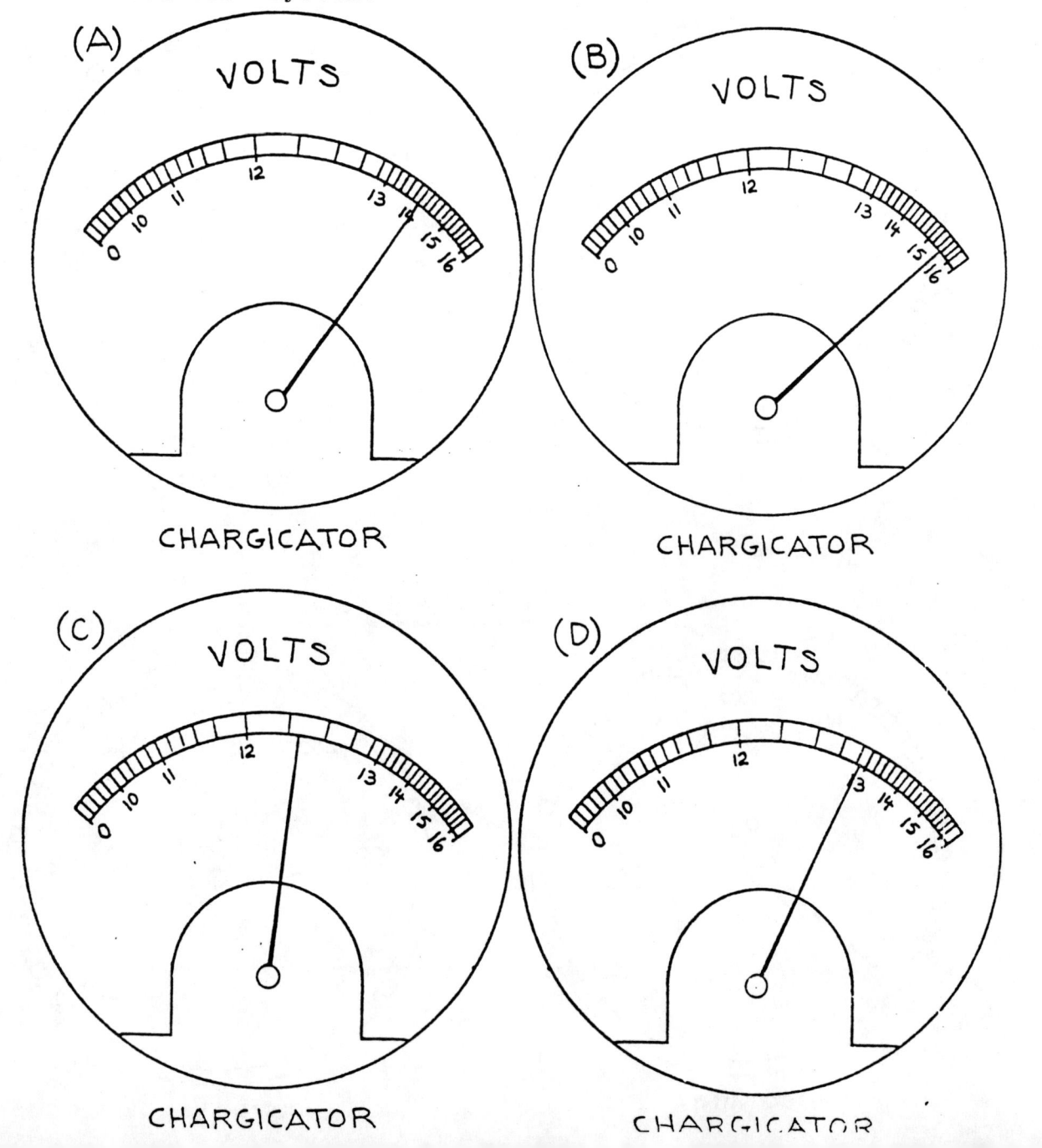

Questions 2-5.

DIRECTIONS: Questions 2 through 5 are to be answered SOLELY on the basis of the following facts and diagrams.

The gauges shown below in Diagrams I and II represent gauges on a fire engine's pump control panel at the scene of a fire. Diagram I gives the readings at 10 A.M., and Diagram II gives the readings at 10:15 A.M. Each diagram has one gauge labeled *Incoming* and one gauge marked *Outgoing*. The *Incoming* gauges show the pressure in pounds per square inch (psi) of the water coming into the pumps on the fire engine from a hydrant. The *Outgoing* gauges show the pressure in pounds per square inch (psi) of the water leaving the pumps on the fire engine. The pumps on the fire engine raise the pressure of the water coming from the hydrant to the higher pressures needed in the fire hoses.

## DIAGRAM I

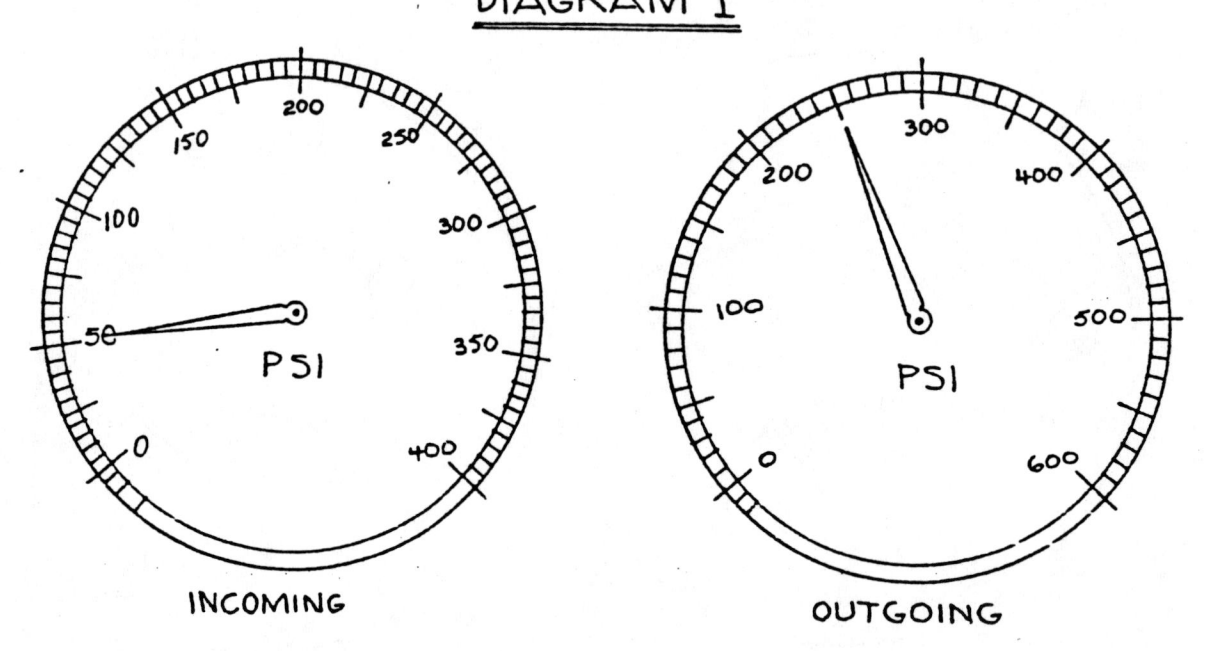

INCOMING    OUTGOING

## DIAGRAM II

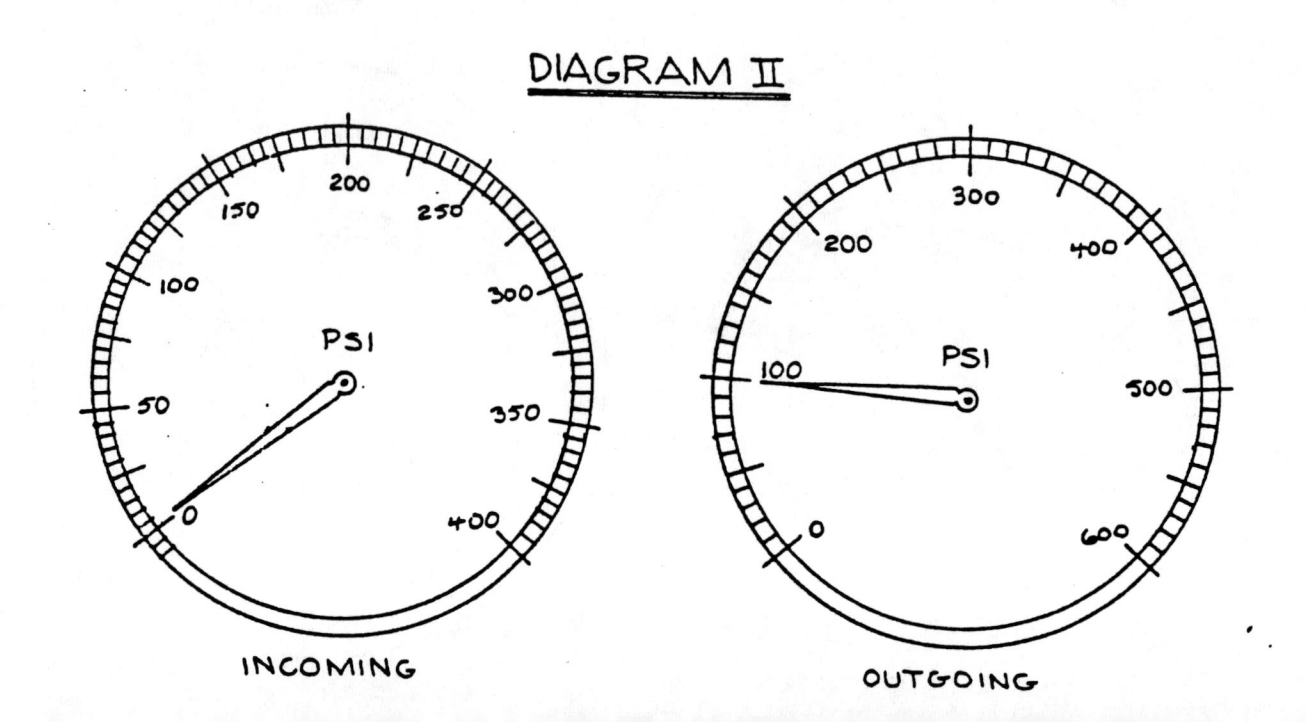

INCOMING    OUTGOING

2. The firefighter looks at the gauges as shown in Diagram I and observes that the pressure, in pounds per square inch (psi), of the water coming into the pumps is MOST NEARLY
   A. 50   B. 250   C. 300   D. 500

3. The firefighter looks at the gauges shown in Diagram I and observes that the pressure, in pounds per square inch (psi), of the water going out of the pumps is MOST NEARLY
   A. 25   B. 50   C. 250   D. 500

4. Diagram II shows the incoming and outgoing water pressure fifteen minutes later.
   By looking at the gauges in Diagram II, the firefighter observes that the water ____ the pumps is ____ psi.
   A. going out of; at 200   B. going out of; at 5
   C. coming into; above 10   D. coming into; below 10

5. The firefighter is able to determine that, between the time of Diagram I and the time of Diagram II, the pressure of the outgoing water from the pumps ____ by ____ psi.
   A. *increased*; 50   B. *decreased*; 150
   C. *decreased*; 45   D. *increased*; 145

Questions 6-11.

DIRECTIONS: Questions 6 through 11 are to be answered SOLELY on the basis of the following information.

In order to extinguish fires, firefighters must pull enough hose from the fire engine to reach the fire. Each length of hose is 50 feet long. The lengths of hose are attached together so that the water can go from the pump on the fire engine to a position where it will extinguish the fire.

6. If the total distance to reach the fire is 50 feet, what is the MINIMUM number of lengths of hose needed?
   A. 1   B. 2   C. 4   D. 4

7. If the total distance to reach the fire is 250 feet, what is the MINIMUM number of lengths of hose needed?
   A. 3   B. 4   C. 5   D. 6

8. If the total distance to reach the fire is 175 feet, what is the MINIMUM number of lengths of hose needed?
   A. 2   B. 3   C. 4   D. 5

9. If the total distance to reach the fire is 125 feet, what is the MINIMUM number of lengths of hose needed?
   A. 2   B. 3   C. 4   D. 5

10. If the total distance to reach the fire is 315 feet, what is the MINIMUM number of lengths of hose needed?
    A. 3   B. 5   C. 6   D. 7

11. If the total distance to reach the fire is 230 feet, what is the MINIMUM number of lengths of hose needed?
    A. 4    B. 5    C. 6    D. 7

Questions 12-13.

DIRECTIONS: Questions 12 and 13 are to be answered SOLELY on the basis of the following passage and diagrams.

Firefighters breathe through an air mask to protect their lungs from dangerous smoke when fighting fires. The air for the mask come from a cylinder which the firefighter wears. A full cylinder contains 45 cubic feet of air when pressurized to 4500 pounds per squar inch.

12. A gauge that firefighters read to tell how much air is left in the cylinder is pictured in the diagram at the right.
    The gauge indicates that the cylinder is
    A. full
    B. empty
    C. more than 3/4 full
    D. less than ½ full

13. A gauge which is part of the cylinder shows the pressure of the air in the cylinder in hundreds of pounds per square inch.
    Which of the following diagrams shows a cylinder which is more than half full?

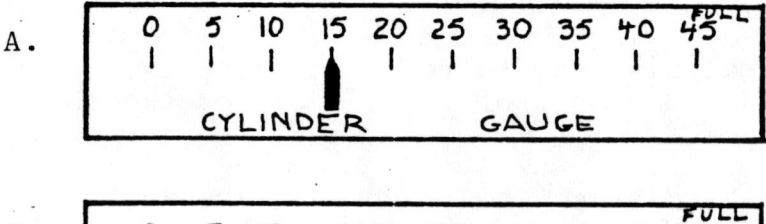

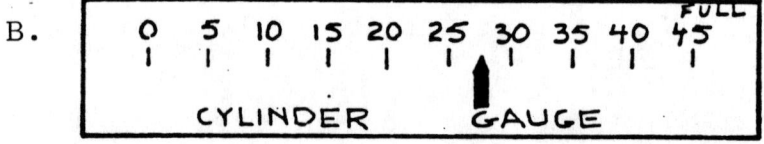

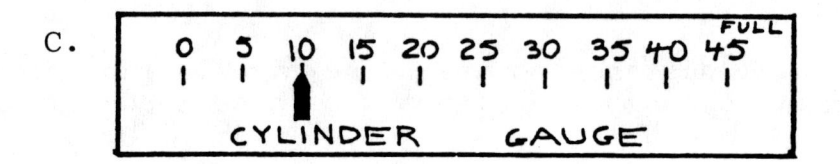

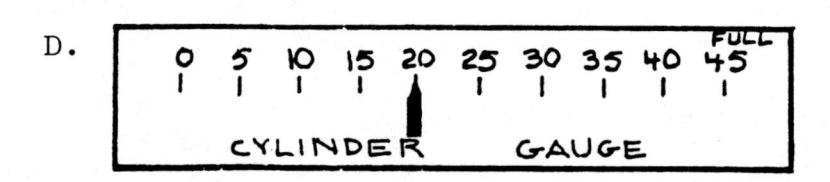

    A. [Cylinder gauge showing arrow at 15]
    B. [Cylinder gauge showing arrow at 25]
    C. [Cylinder gauge showing arrow at 10]
    D. [Cylinder gauge showing arrow at 20]

Questions 14-15.

DIRECTIONS: Questions 14 and 15 are to be answered SOLELY on the basis of the following passage.

The Fire Department uses a firehose nozzle with an automatically adjusting tip. The automatically adjusting nozzle tip keeps the water pressure at the tip constant even though the amount of water being pumped through the hose from the fire engine may vary. A partial loss of water in the hoseline does not result in the stream of water from the nozzle falling short of the target. A partial loss of water is caused by a kink in the hose somewhere between the fire engine pumping the water and the nozzle or by insufficient pressure being supplied by the fire engine pumping water into the hoseline.

The danger of this automatic nozzle is that as the nozzle tip adjusts to maintain constant water pressure, the number of gallons of water per minute flowing out of the nozzle is reduced. When the number of gallons of water per minute flowing from the nozzle is reduced, the nozzle is easier to handle and the stream of water coming from the nozzle appears to be adequate. However, since the number of gallons of flow is reduced, the cooling power of the hose stream will probably not be enough to fight the fire. If a firefighter can physically handle the hoseline alone, the nozzle is not discharging enough water, even though the stream coming out of the nozzle appears adequate. An adequate fire stream requires two firefighters to handle the hoseline.

14. An officer tells a firefighter to check why enough water is not coming out of a hoseline equipped with an automatic nozzle. The firefighter follows the hoseline from the nozzle back to the fire engine pumping the water into the hose but finds no kinks in the hose.
The firefighter should inform the officer that the inadequate flow of water is PROBABLY due to
   A. a defective automatic nozzle
   B. the nozzle stream being aimed in the wrong direction
   C. insufficient pressure being supplied by the fire engine pumping water into the hoseline
   D. the fire engine not being connected to a hydrant

14.___

15. One firefighter alone is easily handling a hoseline equipped with an automatic nozzle. The hoseline's stream is reaching the fire.
According to the above passage, the firefighter should PROPERLY conclude that
   A. being able to handle the hoseline alone indicates extreme strength and excellent physical condition
   B. the stream of water coming from the nozzle is probably not an acceptable firefighting stream because not enough water is flowing
   C. the stream of water coming from the nozzle is adequate and is helping to save water
   D. the automatic nozzle has adjusted itself to provide the proper amount of water to fight the fire

15.___

Questions 16-17.

DIRECTIONS: Questions 16 and 17 are to be answered SOLELY on the basis of the following passage.

Firefighters at times are required to work in areas where the atmosphere contains contaminated smoke. To protect the firefighter from breathing the harmful smoke, a self-contained breathing mask is worn. The mask will supply the firefighter with a limited supply of pure breathing air. This will allow the firefighter to enter the smoke-filled area. The mask is lightweight and compact, which makes it less tiring and easier to move around with. The face mask is designed to give the firefighter the maximum visibility possible. The supply of breathing air is limited, and the rate of air used depends upon the exertion made by the firefighter. Although the mask will protect the firefighter from some types of contaminated smoke, it gives no protection from flame, heat, or heat exhaustion.

16. The rate at which the firefighter breathes the air from the mask will depend upon the
    A. amount of energy used by the firefighter
    B. amount of smoke the firefighter will breathe
    C. color of the flames that the firefighter will enter
    D. color of the heat that the firefighter will enter

17. According to the above passage, the mask will protect the firefighter from some types of
    A. flames            B. smoke
    C. heat              D. heat exhaustion

Questions 18-21.

DIRECTIONS: Questions 18 through 21 are to be answered SOLELY on the basis of the following passage.

In each firehouse, one firefighter is always on housewatch duty. Each 24-hour housewatch tour begins at 9 A.M. each day and is divided into eight 3-hour periods. The firefighter on housewatch is responsible for the correct receipt, acknowledgement, and report of every alarm signal from any source. Firefighters on housewatch are required to enter in the Company Journal the receipt of all alarms, as well as other matters required by Department regulations. All entries by the firefighter on housewatch should be written in blue or black ink. Any entries made by firefighters not on housewatch are made in red ink. Most entries, including receipt of alarms, are recorded in order, starting in the front of the Company Journal on Page 1. Certain types of entries are recorded in special places in the Journal. When high level officers visit the company, those visits are recorded on Page 500. Company training drills and instruction periods are recorded on Page 497. The monthly meter readings of the utility companies which serve the firehouse are recorded on Page 493.

18. A firefighter is asked by the company officer to find out what alarms were received the previous day, August 25, between 1 A.M. and 2 A.M.
    Where in the Company Journal should the firefighter look to obtain this information?
    A. On Page 493
    B. Between Page 1 and Page 492, on the page for August 25
    C. On Page 500
    D. Between Page 497 and Page 500 on the page for August 25

18.___

19. A firefighter on housewatch is asked to find out how much electricity was used in the firehouse between the last two meter readings taken by Con Edison.
    On which one of the following pages of the Company Journal should the firefighter look to find the last two electrical meter readings entered?
    A. 253        B. 493        C. 497        D. 500

19.___

20. A firefighter on housewatch duty is notified by a passing civilian of a rubbish fire around the block. The company responds, extinguishes the rubbish fire, and returns to the firehouse.
    The firefighter on housewatch should
    A. make no entry in the Company Journal of the receipt of the alarm because it was received orally from the civilian
    B. record the alarm in red ink in the Company Journal
    C. record the alarm in blue ink in the Company Journal
    D. ask the civilian to record the alarm in red ink in the Company Journal

20.___

21. The company officer asks the firefighter on housewatch to find out the last date on which the company had a training drill on high-rise building fire operations.
    On which one of the following pages of the Company Journal should the firefighter on housewatch look to find the date of the training drill?
    A. 36        B. 493        C. 497        D. 500

21.___

Questions 22-23.

DIRECTIONS: Questions 22 and 23 are to be answered SOLELY on the basis of the following passage.

Fire Department regulations require that upon receiving an alarm while in the firehouse, the officer of the fire company directs the firefighters to take positions in front of the firehouse. The firefighters warn pedestrians and vehicles that the fire engine is leaving the firehouse. The officer directs the driver of the fire engine to move the fire engine to the front of the firehouse and to stop to check for vehicles and pedestrian traffic. While the fire engine is stopped, the firefighters will get on, and the officer will signal the driver to go to the alarm location.

22. When do the firefighters who were sent to the front of the firehouse actually get on the fire engine?
    A. As the fire engine turns into the street leaving the firehouse
    B. As the fire engine slows down while leaving the firehouse
    C. Inside the firehouse, before the fire engine is moved
    D. After the fire engine has been moved to the front of the firehouse and stopped

23. When responding to an alarm, why are the firefighters sent out of the firehouse before the fire engine?
    To
    A. make sure that the firehouse doors are fully opened
    B. go to the nearest corner to change the traffic signal
    C. warn pedestrians and vehicles that the fire engine is coming out of the firehouse
    D. give the firefighters time to put on their helmets and boots

24. When the engine oil drum in the firehouse is nearly empty, it must be replaced by a new drum full of oil. A firefighter gives the drum a kick. It sounds empty. The firefighter then checks the written log to see how many gallons of oil have been taken out of the drum so far. Checking the written log is
    A. *unnecessary*, since the oil drum sounded empty when the firefighter kicked it
    B. *necessary*, since the log should tell the firefighter exactly how much oil is left
    C. *unnecessary*, since the firefighter should avoid paperwork whenever possible
    D. *necessary*, since the firefighter should always try to keep busy with useful activity

25. The Fire Department provides each firehouse with such basic necessities as electric light bulbs. As the items are used up, new supplies are ordered before the old ones are all gone.
    Of the following, the BEST reason for ordering more electric light bulbs before the old ones are all gone is to
    A. decrease the amount of paperwork a firehouse company must complete
    B. be sure that there are always enough light bulbs on hand to replace those that burn out
    C. make sure that the firehouse has enough electric light bulbs to supply nearby firehouses
    D. decrease the cost of providing electricity to the firehouse

# KEY (CORRECT ANSWERS)

|  |  |  |  |
|---|---|---|---|
| 1. A | | 11. B |
| 2. A | | 12. D |
| 3. C | | 13. B |
| 4. D | | 14. C |
| 5. B | | 15. B |
| | | | |
| 6. A | | 16. A |
| 7. C | | 17. B |
| 8. C | | 18. B |
| 9. B | | 19. B |
| 10. D | | 20. C |

21. C
22. D
23. C
24. B
25. B

# EXAMINATION SECTION

## TEST 1

DIRECTIONS: Each question or incomplete statement is followed by several suggested answers or completions. Select the one that BEST answers the question or completes the statement. *PRINT THE LETTER OF THE CORRECT ANSWER IN THE SPACE AT THE RIGHT.*

Questions 1-8.

DIRECTIONS: Questions 1 through 8 are to be answered SOLELY on the basis of the following Memory Scene 1. Study this scene carefully for five minutes. Then answer Questions 1 through 8. Do not refer back to this scene when answering the questions.

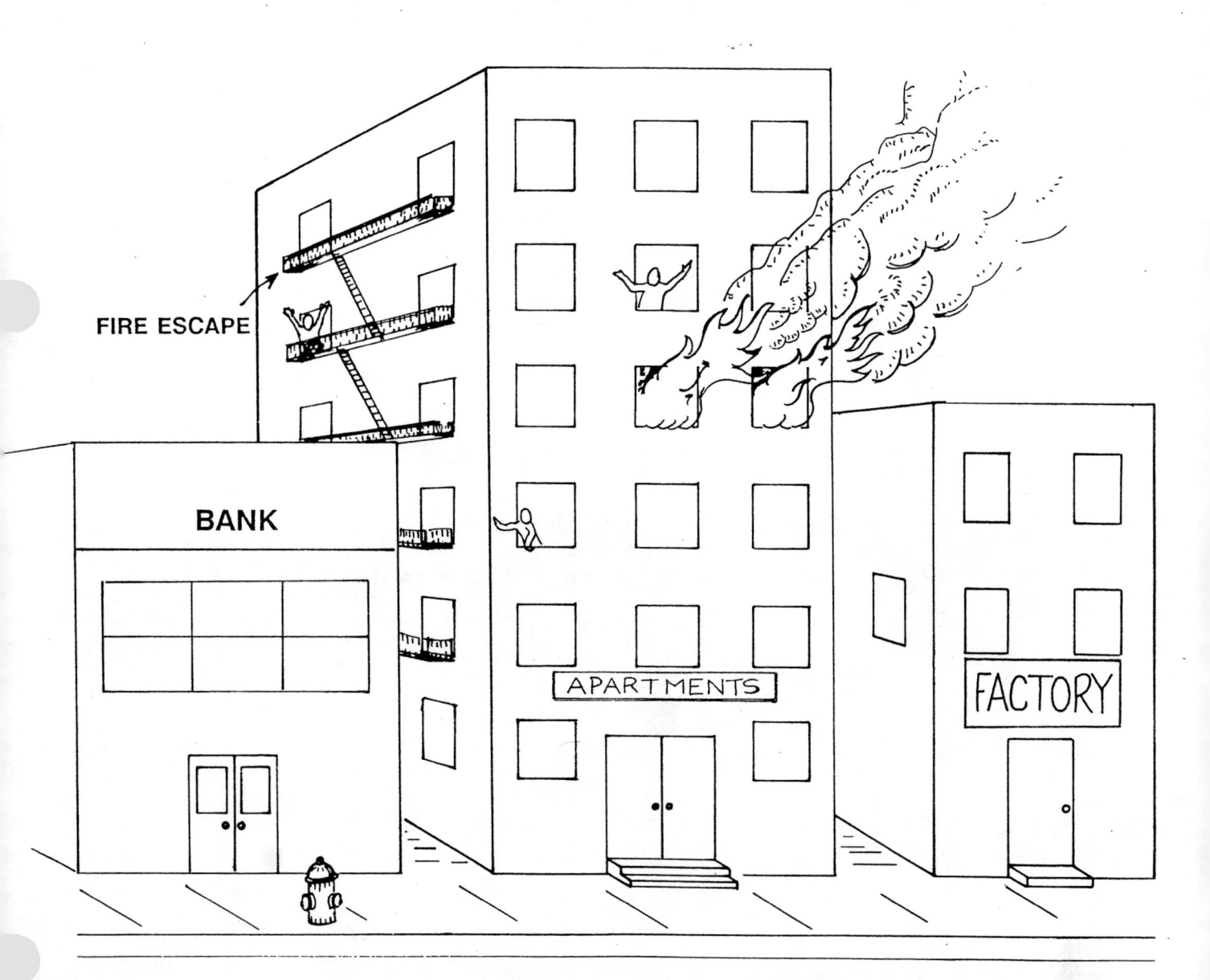

NOTE: THE GROUND FLOOR IS THE FIRST FLOOR.

1. The fire is located on the _____ floor.
   A. first    B. fourth    C. fifth    D. top

2. The smoke and flames are blowing _____ and to the _____.
   A. up; left          B. up; right
   C. down; left        D. down; right

3. There is a person on a fire escape on the _____ floor.
   A. second    B. third    C. fourth    D. fifth

4. Persons are visible in windows at the front of the building on fire on the _____ floors.
   A. second and third      B. third and fifth
   C. fourth and sixth      D. fifth and sixth

5. The person who is CLOSEST to the flames is in a _____ window on the _____ floor.
   A. front; third      B. front; fifth
   C. side; fifth       D. side; third

6. A firefighter is told to go to the roof of the building on fire.
   It would be CORRECT to state that the firefighter can cross directly to the roof from
   A. the roof of the bank
   B. the roof of the factory
   C. either the bank or the factory
   D. neither the bank nor the factory

7. On which side of the building on fire are fire escapes visible?
   A. Left    B. Front    C. Right    D. Rear

8. The hydrant on the sidewalk is
   A. in front of the bank
   B. between the bank and the apartments
   C. in front of the apartments
   D. between the apartments and the factory

Questions 9-16.

DIRECTIONS: Questions 9 through 16 are to be answered on the basis of the following floor plan.
Look at this floor plan of an apartment. It is on the 3rd floor of the building. The floor plan also indicates the public hallway.

Doors are shown as ⌐\⌐   Windows are shown as ▬▬

Doorways are shown as ▬ ▬   Stairs are shown as ▦▦▦

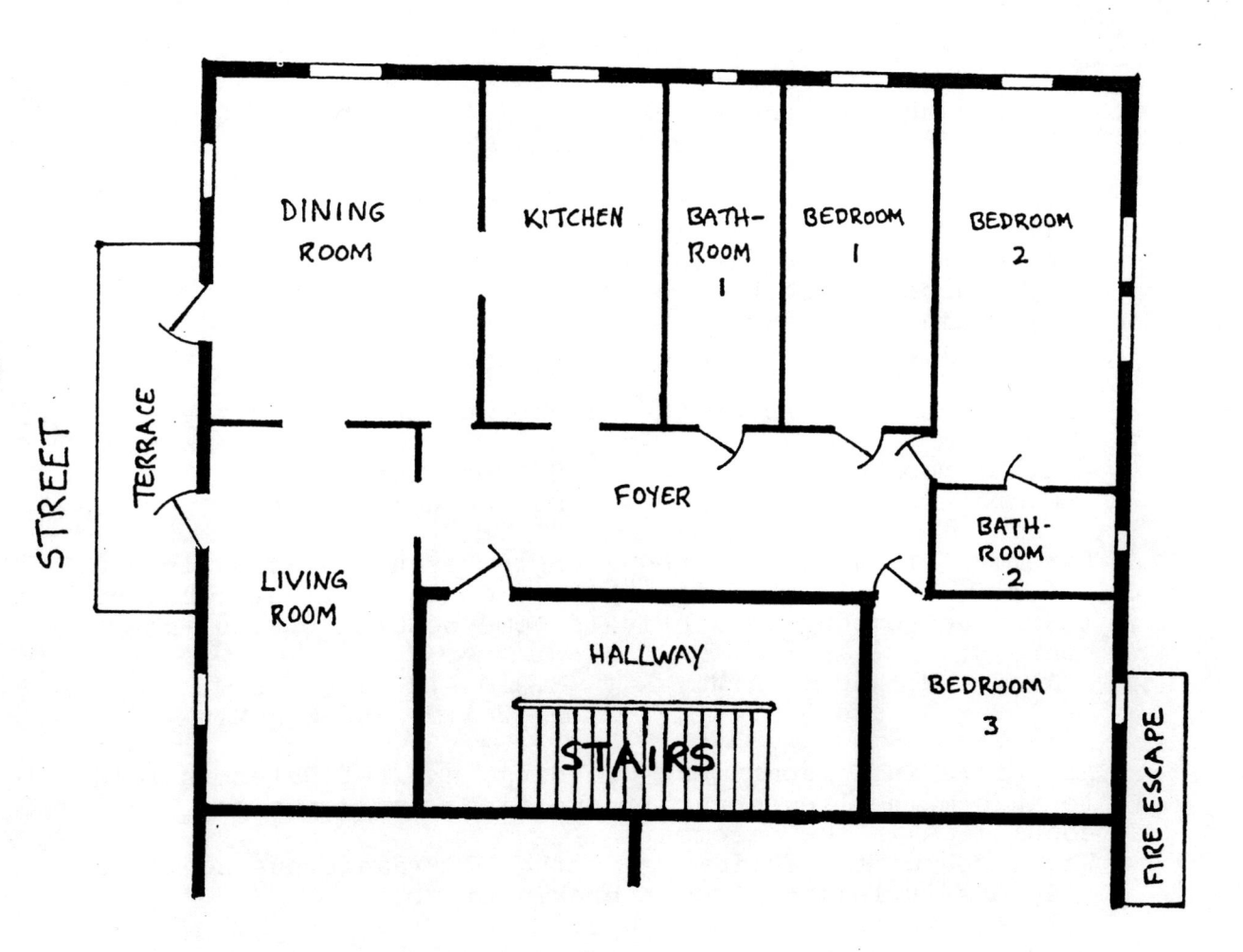

9. Which room is FARTHEST from the fire escape? 9.___
    A. Bedroom 2          B. Bedroom 3
    C. Kitchen            D. Dining room

10. Which one of the following rooms has ONLY one door or doorway? 10.___
    A. Living room        B. Bedroom 1
    C. Kitchen            D. Dining room

11. Which room can firefighters reach DIRECTLY from the fire escape?
    A. Dining room
    B. Living room
    C. Bedroom 1
    D. Bedroom 3

12. Which room does NOT have a door or doorway leading directly to the foyer?
    A. Bathroom 1
    B. Bathroom 2
    C. Bedroom 1
    D. Dining room

13. A firefighter leaving Bathroom 2 would be in
    A. bedroom 1
    B. bedroom 2
    C. bedroom 3
    D. the foyer

14. Firefighters on the terrace would be able to enter directly into which rooms?
    A. Bedroom 1 and bathroom 1
    B. Bedroom 2 and bathroom 2
    C. Dining room and kitchen
    D. Dining room and living room

15. Which rooms have AT LEAST one window on two sides of the building?
    A. Bedroom 2 and dining room
    B. Bedroom 2 and bedroom 3
    C. Dining room and living room
    D. Dining room, bedroom 2, and bedroom 3

16. Firefighters can enter the kitchen directly from the foyer and
    A. bedroom 1
    B. the living room
    C. bathroom 1
    D. the dining room

17. Firefighters are often required to rescue individuals from a fire. The GREATEST possibility of a firefighter having to rescue someone in a private home occurs between the hours of
    A. 7 A.M. and 11 A.M.
    B. 10 A.M. and 2 P.M.
    C. 2 P.M. and 6 P.M.
    D. 2 A.M. and 6 A.M.

18. At a fire in an apartment building, a firefighter is told to inform the lieutenant if she finds any dangerous conditions in the basement.
    Which one of the following is the MOST dangerous condition?
    A. Gas is leaking from a broken pipe.
    B. The sewer pipe is broken.
    C. Water is seeping into the basement.
    D. The electricity has been turned off.

19. Firefighters are required to use portable ladders to rescue people.
    When firefighters are positioning a portable ladder for a rescue, which one of the following would present the GREATEST threat to the firefighters' safety?
    A. A person to be rescued who is standing near an open window

B. Tree branches which are close to the ladder
C. A person to be rescued who is dressed in a long robe
D. Overhead electrical wires which are close to the ladder

20. Firefighters are instructed to notify an officer whenever they attempt to rescue someone who is seriously endangered by fire or smoke. Firefighters respond to a fire in a 6-story apartment building. The fire is in a fourth floor apartment in the front of the building.
Firefighters should notify an officer when they are attempting to rescue
   A. a person who disappears from a smoke-filled window on the fourth floor
   B. a person who is on the roof
   C. three persons on the third floor rear fire escape who appear to be very frightened
   D. two children who are locked in their apartment on the first floor

20.___

21. Firefighters who forcibly enter an apartment on fire may find conditions which indicate that they should immediately search for victims.
Of the following conditions in an apartment on fire, which one would MOST clearly indicate to firefighters that they should immediately search for victims?
   A. There is a pot on the stove.
   B. The apartment door was chain-locked from the inside.
   C. Water is dripping into a pail.
   D. All the windows in the apartment are closed.

21.___

Questions 22-24.

DIRECTIONS: Questions 22 through 24 are to be answered SOLELY on the basis of the following passage.

When there is a fire in a subway train, it may be necessary for firefighters to evacuate people from the trains by way of the tunnels. In every tunnel, there are emergency exit areas which have stairways that can be used to evacuate people to the street from the track area. All emergency exits can be recognized by an exit sign near a group of five white lights.

There is a Blue Light Area which is located every 600 feet in the tunnel. These areas contain a power removal box, a telephone, and a fire extinguisher. Removal of power from the third rail is the first step firefighters must take when evacuating people through tunnels. When a firefighter uses the power removal box to turn off electrical power during evacuation procedures, the firefighter must immediately telephone the trainmaster and explain the reason for the power removal. Communication between the firefighter and the trainmaster is essential. If the trainmaster does not receive a phone call within four minutes after power removal, the power will be restored to the third rail.

22. When evacuating passengers through the subway tunnel, firefighters must FIRST
    A. telephone the trainmaster for assistance
    B. remove electrical power from the third rail
    C. locate the emergency exit in the tunnel
    D. go to the group of five white lights

23. Immediately after using the power removal box to turn off the electrical power, a firefighter should
    A. wait four minutes before calling the trainmaster
    B. begin evacuating passengers through the tunnel
    C. call the trainmaster and explain why the power was turned off
    D. touch the third rail to see if the electrical power has been turned off

24. A group of five white lights in a subway tunnel indicates that
    A. a telephone is available
    B. the electrical power is off in the third rail
    C. a fire extinguisher is available
    D. an emergency exit is located there

25. During a recent day tour with an engine company, Firefighter Sims was assigned to the control position on the hose. The company responded to the following alarms during this tour:
    Alarm 1: At 9:30 A.M., the company responded to a fire on the first floor of an apartment building. At the fire scene, Firefighter Sims pulled the hose from the fire engine and assisted the driver in attaching the hose to the hydrant.
    Alarm 2: At 11:00 A.M., the company responded to a fire on the third floor of a vacant building. Firefighter Sims pulled the hose from the fire engine and went to the building on fire.
    Alarm 3: At 1:00 P.M., the company responded to a fire in a first-floor laundromat. Firefighter Sims pulled the hose from the fire engine and assisted the driver in attaching the hose to the hydrant.
    Alarm 4: At 3:00 P.M., the company responded to a fire on the fourth floor of an apartment building. Firefighter Sims pulled the hose from the fire engine and went to the building on fire.
    Alarm 5: At 5:45 P.M., the company responded to a fire on the second floor of a private house. Firefighter Sims pulled the hose from the fire engine and assisted the driver in attaching the hose to the hydrant.

    The firefighter assigned to the control position assists the driver in attaching the hose to a hydrant when the fire is
    A. in an apartment building    B. above the second floor
    C. in a vacant building        D. below the third floor

## KEY (CORRECT ANSWERS)

| | | | |
|---|---|---|---|
| 1. B | | 11. D | |
| 2. B | | 12. B | |
| 3. D | | 13. B | |
| 4. B | | 14. D | |
| 5. B | | 15. A | |
| 6. D | | 16. D | |
| 7. A | | 17. D | |
| 8. A | | 18. A | |
| 9. D | | 19. D | |
| 10. B | | 20. A | |

21. B
22. B
23. C
24. D
25. D

# TEST 2

DIRECTIONS: Each question or incomplete statement is followed by several suggested answers or completions. Select the one that BEST answers the question or completes the statement. *PRINT THE LETTER OF THE CORRECT ANSWER IN THE SPACE AT THE RIGHT.*

Questions 1-3.

DIRECTIONS: Questions 1 through 3 are to be answered on the basis of the following floor plan and the paragraph which appears on the next page.

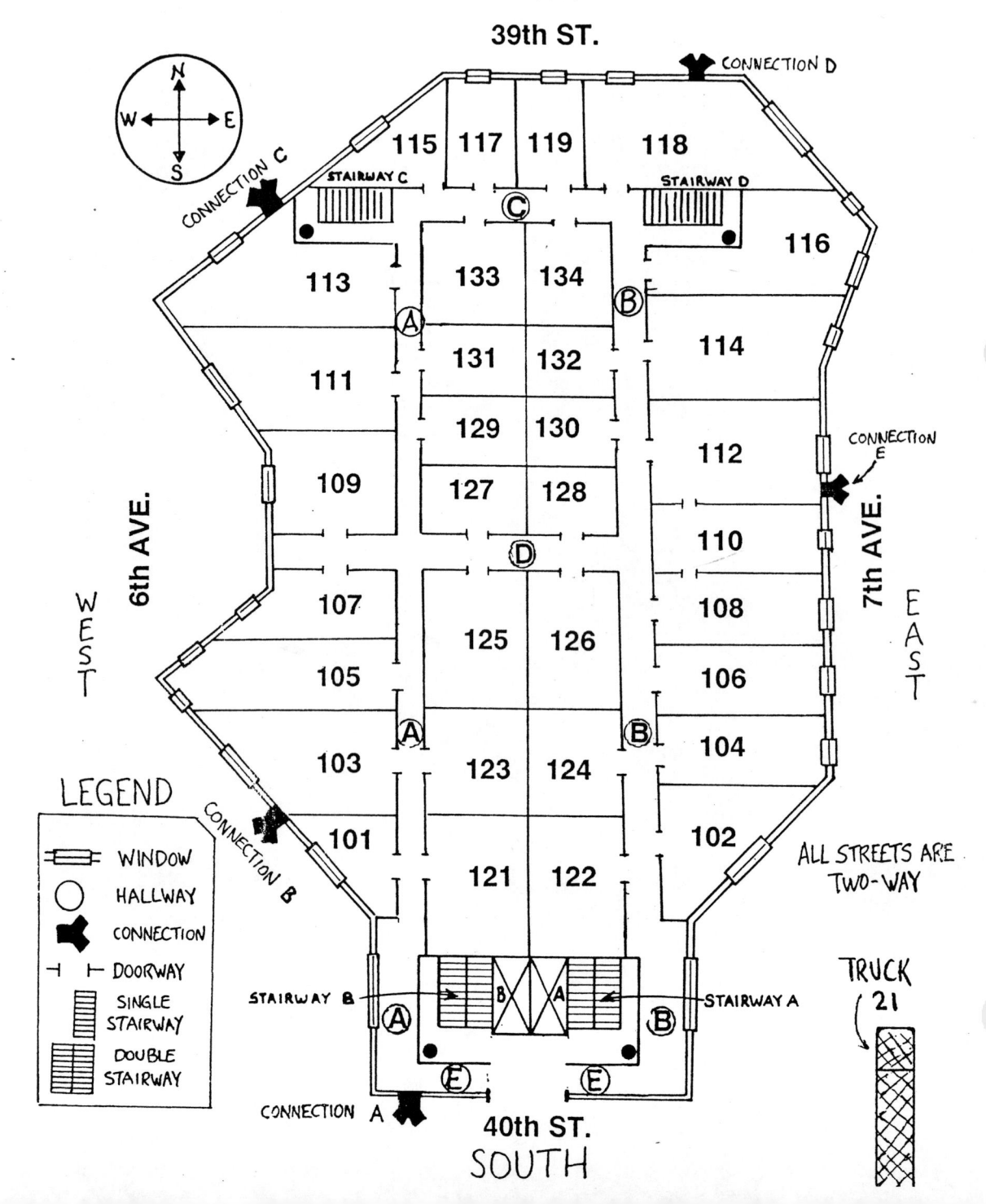

The floor plan represents a typical high-rise office building in midtown. Numbers shown indicate room numbers. The pipe connections for the water supply system are outside the building at street level. Firefighters attach hoses to those connections to send water into the pipes in the building.

Questions 1 through 3 refer to a fire on the 1st floor in Room 111.

1. After fighting the fire in Room 111, firefighters are instructed to go immediately to the east-west hallway in the center of the building and search for victims in that hallway.
   Which one of the following lists ALL of the rooms that the firefighters should search?
   A. 115, 117, 118, 119, 133, and 134
   B. 125, 126, 127, 128, and 129
   C. 107, 109, 125, 126, 127, and 128
   D. 121, 122, 123, 124, 125, and 126

1.___

2. Firefighters are told to search Room 134. They enter the building from 40th Street.
   What is the SHORTEST route for the firefighters to take to reach this room?
   A. West in hallway E, north in hallway A, then east in hallway C
   B. West in hallway E, north in hallway A, east in hallway D, north in hallway B, then west in hallway C
   C. East in hallway E, north in hallway B, then west in hallway C
   D. East in hallway E, north in hallway B, west in hallway D, north in hallway A, then east in hallway C

2.___

3. Firefighters in Truck 21 have been ordered to attach a hose to a connection outside the building. The firefighters cannot use connection A because 40th Street is blocked by traffic.
   What is the FIRST connection the firefighters can drive to? Connection
   A. B        B. C        C. D        D. E

3.___

Questions 4-6.

DIRECTIONS: Questions 4 through 6 are to be answered on the basis of the following passage.

Firefighters often know the appearance and construction features of apartments by recognizing the general features on the outside of the building. The following are some general features of different types of buildings in the city.

1. OLD LAW TENEMENTS:
   Height - 5 to 7 stories
   Width - 25 feet
   Fire Escapes - There will be a rear fire escape if there are two apartments per floor. There will be front and rear fire escapes if there are four apartments per floor.

2. ROW FRAMES:
   Height - 2 to 5 stories
   Width - 20 feet to 30 feet
   Fire Escapes - There will be a rear fire escape if the building is higher than 2 stories.

3. BROWNSTONES:
   Height - 3 to 5 stories
   Width - 20 feet to 25 feet
   Fire Escapes - If the brownstone has been changed from a private home to a multiple dwelling, there will be a rear fire escape. Unchanged brownstones have no fire escapes.

4. Upon arrival at a fire, a firefighter observes that the building is 3 stories high and 25 feet wide. There are fire escapes only in the rear of the building.
   The firefighter should conclude that the building is either a
   A. Row Frame or an unchanged Brownstone
   B. Row Frame or an Old Law Tenement with two apartments per floor
   C. changed Brownstone or an Old Law Tenement with four apartments per floor
   D. Row Frame or a changed Brownstone

5. At another fire, the building is 5 stories high and 25 feet wide. There is a front fire escape.
   The firefighters should conclude that this building has
   A. a rear fire escape because the building is a Row Frame higher than two stories
   B. a rear fire escape because the building is an Old Law Tenement with four apartments per floor
   C. no rear fire escape because the building is a Brownstone that has been changed into a multiple dwelling
   D. no rear fire escape because the building has a front fire escape

6. At another fire, the building is 4 stories high and 30 feet wide. The building has no front fire escape.
   The firefighter should conclude that the building is a(n)
   A. Row Frame which has no rear fire escape
   B. Old Law Tenement which has four apartments per floor
   C. Row Frame which has a rear fire escape
   D. Brownstone which has been changed from a private home to a multiple dwelling

Questions 7-9.

DIRECTIONS: Questions 7 through 9 are to be answered on the basis of the following passage.

Firefighters use 2-way radios to alert other firefighters of dangerous conditions and of the need for help. Messages should begin with *MAY DAY* or *URGENT*. *MAY DAY* messages have priority over *URGENT* messages. Following is a list of specific emergencies and the messages which should be sent.

*MAY DAY* Messages:
1. When a collapse is probable in the area where the firefighters are working: *MAY DAY - MAY DAY, collapse probable, GET OUT*.
2. When a collapse has occurred in the area where the firefighters are working: *MAY DAY - MAY DAY, collapse occurred*. The firefighter should also give the location of the collapse. If there are trapped victims, the number and condition of the trapped victims is also given.
3. When a firefighter appears to be a heart attack victim: *MAY DAY - MAY DAY, CARDIAC*. The location of the victim is also given.
4. When anyone has a serious, life-threatening injury: *MAY DAY - MAY DAY*. The firefighter also describes the injury and gives the condition and the location of the victim.

Messages:
1. When anyone has a less serious injury which requires medical attention (for example, a broken arm): *URGENT - URGENT*. The firefighter also gives the type of injury and the location of the victim.
2. When the firefighters should leave the building and fight the fire from the outside: *URGENT - URGENT, back out*. The firefighter also indicates the area to be evacuated.
3. *URGENT* messages should also be sent when firefighters' lives are endangered due to a drastic loss of water pressure in the hose.

7. Firefighters are ordered to extinguish a fire on the third floor of an apartment building. As the firefighters are operating the hose on the third floor, the stairway collapses and cuts the hose.
What message should the firefighters send?
A. URGENT - URGENT, back out
B. URGENT - URGENT, we have a loss of water on the third floor
C. MAY DAY - MAY DAY, collapse occurred on third floor stairway
D. MAY DAY - MAY DAY, collapse probable, GET OUT

7.____

8. Two firefighters on the second floor of a vacant building are discussing the possibility of the floor's collapse. One of the firefighters clutches his chest and falls down. What message should the other firefighter send?
    A. MAY DAY - MAY DAY, firefighter collapse on the second floor
    B. MAY DAY - MAY DAY, CARDIAC on the second floor
    C. URGENT - URGENT, firefighter unconscious on the second floor
    D. URGENT - URGENT, collapse probable on the second floor

9. A firefighter has just decided that a collapse of the third floor is probable when he falls and breaks his wrist. What is the FIRST message he should send?
    A. URGENT - URGENT, broken wrist on the third floor
    B. MAY DAY - MAY DAY, broken wrist on the third floor
    C. MAY DAY - MAY DAY, collapse probable, GET OUT
    D. URGENT - URGENT, back out, third floor

Questions 10-11.

DIRECTIONS: Questions 10 and 11 are to be answered on the basis of the following information and the diagram which appears on the next page.

An 8-story apartment building has scissor stairs beginning on the first floor and going to the roof. Scissor stairs are two separate stairways (Stairway A and Stairway B) that criss-cross each other and lead to opposite sides of the building on each floor. Once a person has entered either stairway, the only way to cross over to the other stairway on any floor is by leaving the stairway and using the hallway on that floor. A person entering Stairway A, which starts on the east side of the building on the first floor, would end up on the west side of the building on the second floor, and back on the east side on the third floor. Similarly, a person entering Stairway B, which starts on the west side of the building on the first floor, would end up on the east side of the building on the second floor, and back on the west side on the third floor.

The apartment building has one water pipe for fighting fires. This pipe runs in a straight line near the stairway on the east side of the building from the first floor to the roof. There are water outlets for this pipe on each floor.

Both of the following questions involve a fire in an apartment on the west side of the 6th floor.

## SCISSOR STAIRS

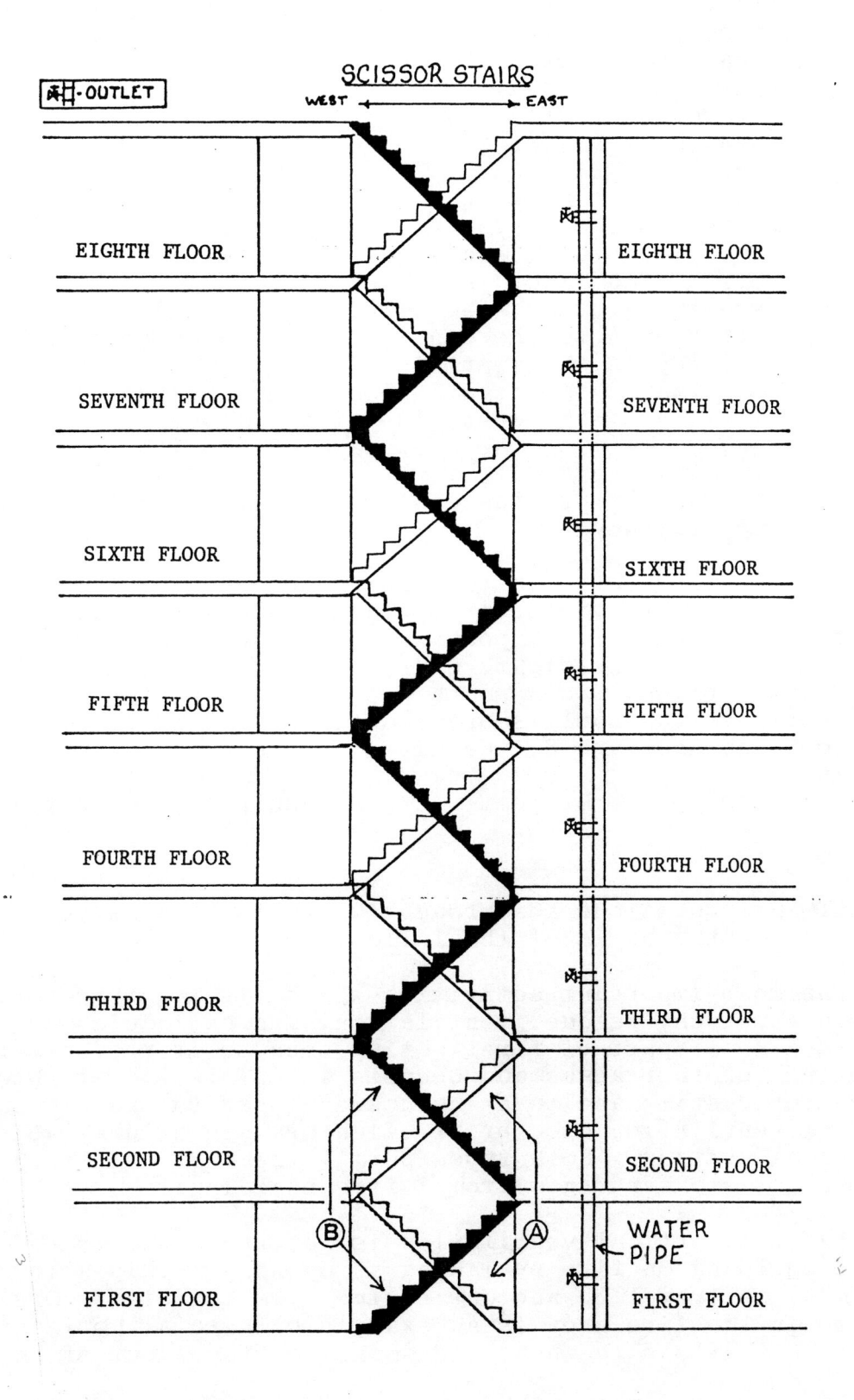

🀫 - OUTLET

WEST ← → EAST

EIGHTH FLOOR — EIGHTH FLOOR
SEVENTH FLOOR — SEVENTH FLOOR
SIXTH FLOOR — SIXTH FLOOR
FIFTH FLOOR — FIFTH FLOOR
FOURTH FLOOR — FOURTH FLOOR
THIRD FLOOR — THIRD FLOOR
SECOND FLOOR — SECOND FLOOR
FIRST FLOOR — FIRST FLOOR

Ⓑ   Ⓐ

WATER PIPE

10. Firefighters are ordered to connect a hose to the nearest outlet below the fire. Upon reaching this outlet, they find that it is not usable.
Where is the next available outlet?
\_\_\_\_ floor near Stairway \_\_\_\_.
   A. 5th; B    B. 3rd; A    C. 4th; B    D. 4th; A

11. A firefighter working on the west side of the 7th floor is ordered to search for victims on the west side of the 8th floor. The door leading to the stairway on the west side of the 7th floor is jammed shut.
To reach the victims, the firefighter should take
   A. Stairway A to the 8th floor, and then go across the hallway to the west side of the floor
   B. Stairway B to the 8th floor, and then go across the hallway to the west side of the floor
   C. the hallway to the east side of the 7th floor and go up Stairway A
   D. the hallway to the east side of the 7th floor and go up Stairway B

12. Firefighters refer to the four sides of a building on fire as *exposures*. The front of the fire building is referred to as Exposure 1. Exposures 2, 3, and 4 follow in clockwise order. Firefighters are working at a building whose front entrance faces south. A firefighter who is in the center of the roof is ordered to go to Exposure 3.
To reach Exposure 3, the direction in which he must walk is
   A. east    B. west    C. south    D. north

Questions 13-17.

DIRECTIONS: Questions 13 through 17 are to be answered SOLELY on the basis of the following passage.

The most important activities which firefighters perform at fires are search, rescue, ventilation, and extinguishment. Ventilation is a vital part of firefighting because it prevents fire from spreading to other areas and because it enables firefighters to search for victims and to bring hoses closer to the fire area. Two types of ventilation used by firefighters are natural venting and mechanical venting. Both types permit the vertical and horizontal movement of smoke and gas from a fire building.

Natural vertical ventilation is generally performed on the roof of the building on fire by making an opening. This allows the heat and smoke to travel up and out of the fire building. Opening windows in the fire area is an example of natural horizontal ventilation. This allows the heat and smoke to travel out of the windows.

Mechanical ventilation takes place when mechanical devices, such as smoke ejectors or hoses with nozzles, are used to remove heated gases from an area. A smoke ejector might be used in a cellar fire when smoke has traveled to the far end of the cellar, creating a heavy smoke condition that cannot be removed naturally. The smoke ejector would be brought into the area to draw the smoke out of the cellar. A nozzle is used with a hose to create a fine spray of water. When directed towards an open window, the water spray pushes smoke and heated gases out of the window.

Extinguishment means bringing a hose to the fire and operating the nozzle to put water on the fire. The proper positioning of hoses is essential to firefighting tactics. Most lives are saved at fires by the proper positioning of hoses.

At each fire, firefighters must use the quickest and best method of extinguishment. There are times when an immediate and direct attack on the fire is required. This means that the hose is brought directly to the fire itself. A fire in a vacant lot, or a fire in the entrance of a building, calls for an immediate and direct attack on the fire.

It is generally the ladder company that is assigned the tasks of venting, search, and rescue while the engine company performs the task of extinguishment.

13. Ventilation performed at the roof is GENERALLY _____ ventilation.
    A. mechanical vertical
    B. natural vertical
    C. natural horizontal
    D. mechanical horizontal

14. When an immediate and direct attack on the fire is required, the hose is
    A. positioned between the building on fire and the building which the fire might spread to
    B. brought to a window in order to push smoke and gases out
    C. brought to the roof to push the smoke and gases out
    D. brought directly to the fire itself

15. Ladder companies are GENERALLY assigned the tasks of
    A. extinguishment, rescue, and search
    B. extinguishment, venting, and search
    C. venting, search, and rescue
    D. venting, rescue, and extinguishment

16. MOST lives are saved at fires by
    A. a systematic search
    B. the proper positioning of hoses
    C. the proper performance of ventilation
    D. the use of nozzles for ventilation and extinguishment

17. Ventilation enables firefighters to
    A. bring hoses to the fire and search for victims
    B. create a fine spray of water
    C. use a nozzle to remove smoke and gases
    D. use an ejector to draw smoke out of an area

Questions 18-19.

DIRECTIONS: Questions 18 and 19 are to be answered SOLELY on the basis of the following passage.

A new firefighter learns the following facts about his company's response area: All the factories are located between 9th Avenue and 12th Avenue, from 42nd Street to 51st Street; all the apartment buildings are located between 7th Avenue and 9th Avenue, from 47th Street to 51st Street; all the private houses are located between 5th Avenue and 9th Avenue, from 42nd Street to 47th Street; and all the stores are located between 5th Avenue and 7th Avenue, from 47th Street to 51st Street.

The firefighter also learns that the apartment buildings are all between 4 and 6 stories; the private houses are all between 1 and 3 stories; the factories are all between 3 and 5 stories; and the stores are all either 1 or 2 stories.

18. An alarm is received for a fire located on 8th Avenue between 46th Street and 47th Street.
    A firefighter should assume that the fire is in a
    A. private house between 1 and 3 stories
    B. private house between 4 and 6 stories
    C. factory between 3 and 5 stories
    D. factory between 4 and 6 stories

19. The company responds to a fire on 47th Street between 6th Avenue and 7th Avenue.
    The firefighter should assume that he would be responding to a fire in a(n)
    A. store of either 1 or 2 stories
    B. factory between 3 and 5 stories
    C. apartment building between 4 and 6 stories
    D. private house between 4 and 6 stories

Questions 20-25.

DIRECTIONS: Questions 20 through 25 are to be answered on the basis of the following information and the diagram which appears on the next page.

At three o'clock in the morning, a fire alarm is received for the area shown in the diagram. A train loaded with highly flammable material is on fire. The entire area is surrounded by a ten-foot-high fence. At the time of the fire, Gate A is open and Gates B, C, and D are locked.

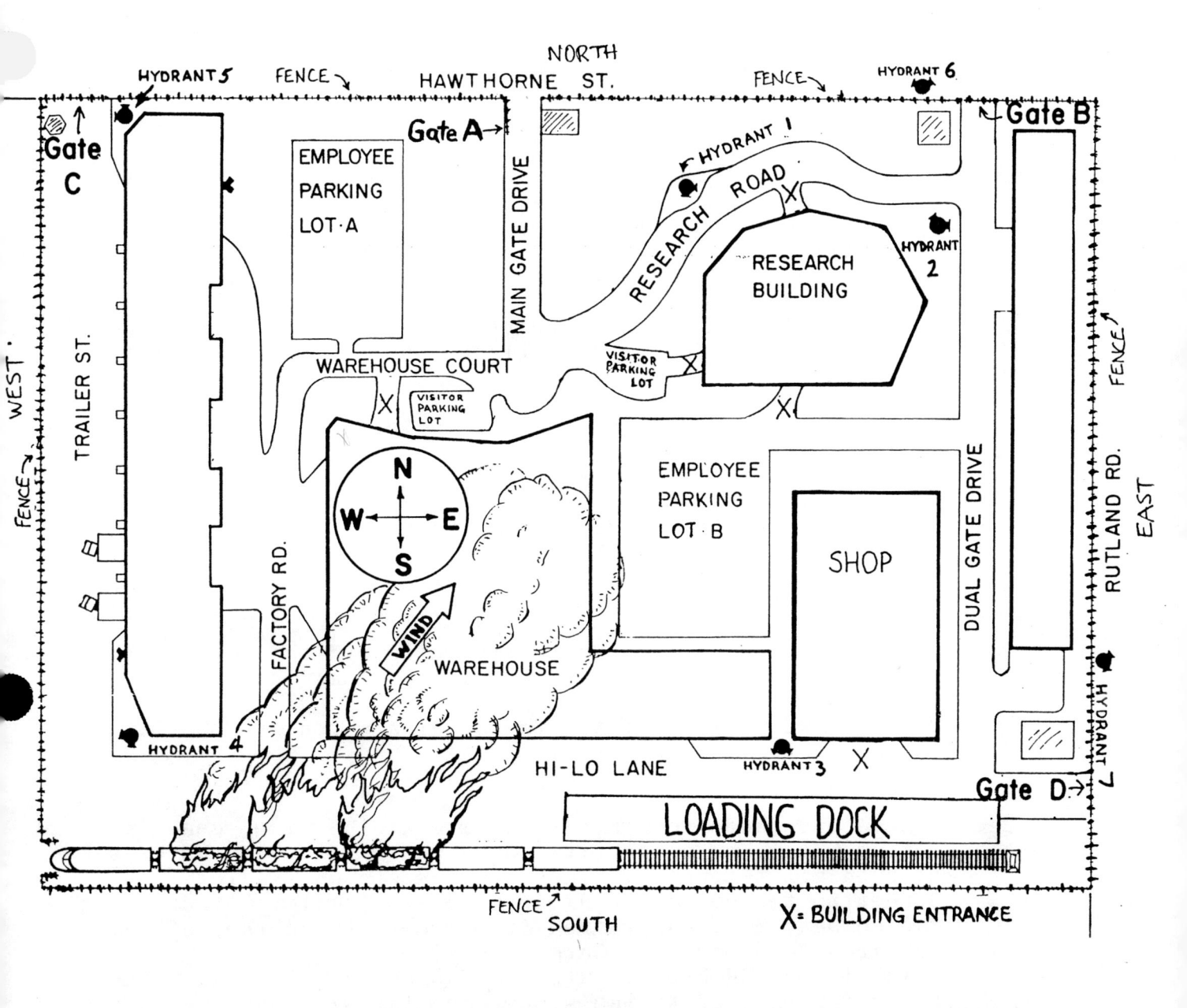

20. The first engine company arrives at the fire scene. The security guard at Gate A informs the firefighters of the location of the fire. Firefighter Jensen knows the area. He should inform the lieutenant that the way to drive to a hydrant that is as close to the fire as possible without passing through the smoke and flames is by going
    A. south on Main Gate Drive, east on Research Road, south on Dual Gate Drive, and west on Hi-Lo Lane to hydrant 3
    B. south on Main Gate Drive, west on Warehouse Court, south on Factory Road, and west on Hi-Lo Lane to hydrant 4
    C. south on Main Gate Drive and east on Research Road to hydrant 1
    D. east on Hawthorne Street and south on Rutland Road to hydrant 7

21. Firefighters at Employee Parking Lot A are ordered to drive their truck to the fence outside Gate D. Which of the following is the SHORTEST route the firefighters could take from Warehouse Court?
    A. South on Factory Road, then west on Hi-Lo Lane, and north on Trailer Street
    B. East on Research Road, and south on Dual Gate Drive
    C. North on Main Gate Drive, east on Hawthorne Street, and south on Rutland Road
    D. North on Main Gate Drive, west on Hawthorne Street, south on Trailer Street, and west on Hi-Lo Lane

22. The first ladder company arrives at the fire scene. As they are driving north on Rutland Road, firefighters see the fire through Gate D. They cut the locks and enter Gate D. The lieutenant orders a firefighter to go on foot from Gate D to the Research Building and to search it for occupants.
    The entrance to the Research Building which is CLOSEST to this firefighter is
    A. connected to the Visitor Parking Lot
    B. located on Research Road
    C. connected to Parking Lot B
    D. located on Dual Gate Drive

23. The second engine company to arrive is ordered to attach a hose to a hydrant located outside of the fenced area and then to await further orders.
    The hydrant outside of the fenced area which is CLOSEST to the flames is hydrant
    A. 6        B. 3        C. 4        D. 7

24. The second ladder company to arrive at the fire scene is met at Gate C by a security guard who gives them the keys to open all the gates. They drive south on Trailer Street to the corner of Hi-Lo Lane and Trailer Street. The company is then ordered to drive to the corner of Research Road and Dual Gate Drive.
    Which is the SHORTEST route for the company to take without being exposed to the smoke and flames?
    A. East on Hi-Lo Lane, north on Factory Road, and east on Warehouse Court to Research Road
    B. East on Hi-Lo Lane and north on Dual Gate Drive
    C. North on Trailer Street, east on Hawthorne Street, and south on Dual Gate Drive
    D. North on Trailer Street, east on Hawthorne Street, south on Main Gate Drive, and east on Research Road

25. The heat from the fire in the railroad cars ignites the warehouse on the other side of Hi-Lo Lane. The officer of the first ladder company orders two firefighters who are on the west end of the loading dock to break the windows on the north side of the warehouse.

Of the following, the SHORTEST way for the firefighters to reach the northwest corner of the warehouse without passing through the smoke and flames is to go
- A. east on Hi-Lo Lane, north on Dual Gate Drive, and then west on Research Road to the entrance on Warehouse Court
- B. west on Hi-Lo Lane, north on Factory Road, and then east on Warehouse Court to the Visitor Parking Lot on Warehouse Court
- C. east on Hi-Lo Lane, north on Rutland Road, west on Hawthorne Street, and then south on Main Gate Drive to the Visitor Parking Lot on Warehouse Court
- D. east on Hi-Lo Lane, north on Dual Gate Drive, west on Hawthorne Street, and then south on Main Gate Drive to the entrance on Warehouse Court

---

# KEY (CORRECT ANSWERS)

| | |
|---|---|
| 1. C | 11. C |
| 2. C | 12. D |
| 3. D | 13. B |
| 4. D | 14. D |
| 5. B | 15. C |
| 6. C | 16. B |
| 7. C | 17. A |
| 8. B | 18. A |
| 9. C | 19. A |
| 10. C | 20. A |

21. C
22. C
23. D
24. C
25. A

# EXAMINATION SECTION
# TEST 1

DIRECTIONS: Each question or incomplete statement is followed by several suggested answers or completions. Select the one that BEST answers the question or completes the statement. *PRINT THE LETTER OF THE CORRECT ANSWER IN THE SPACE AT THE RIGHT.*

1. When attempting to rescue a person trapped at a window, firefighters frequently use an aerial ladder with a rotating base. The rotating base allows the ladder to move up and down and from side to side. In a rescue situation, the ladder should be placed so that both sides of the ladder rest fully on the window sill after it has been raised into position.
Which one of the following diagrams shows the PROPER placement of the rotating base in relation to the window where the person is trapped?

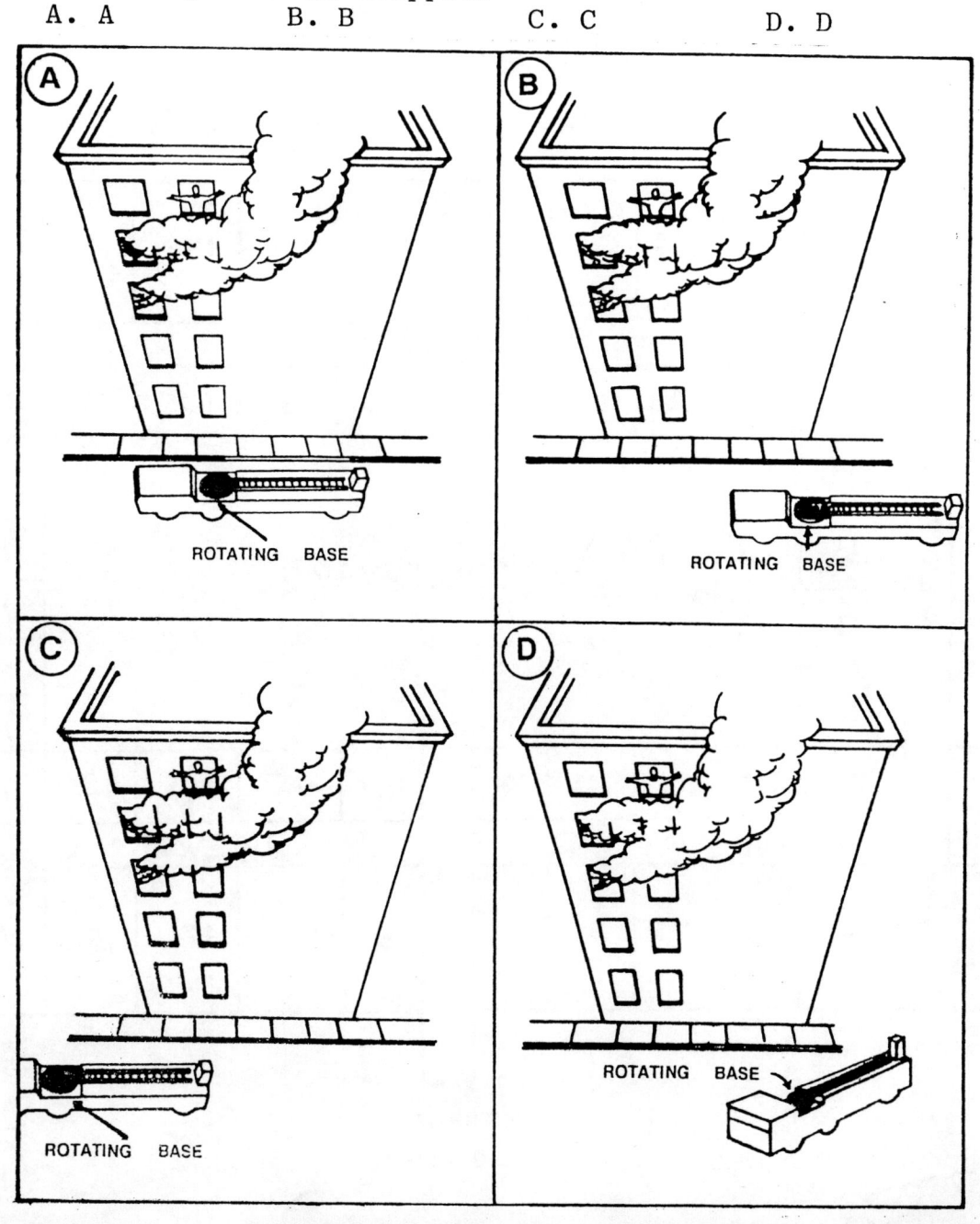

   A. A     B. B     C. C     D. D

1.____

Questions 2-6.

DIRECTIONS: Questions 2 through 6 are to be answered on the basis of the following floor plan and information.

Since many children may need to be rescued in the event of a school fire, city firefighters must become familiar with the floor layouts of public schools. Firefighters can develop this familiarity by conducting training drills at the schools.

A ladder company and an engine company recently conducted a drill at Pierce High School. The firefighters determined that the room layout is the same on all floors.

Several days after the drill, the ladder and the engine companies report to a fire at Pierce High School in classroom 304, which is on the third floor. The fire has spread into the hallway in front of Room 304, blocking the hallway.

NORTH

## PIERCE HIGH SCHOOL

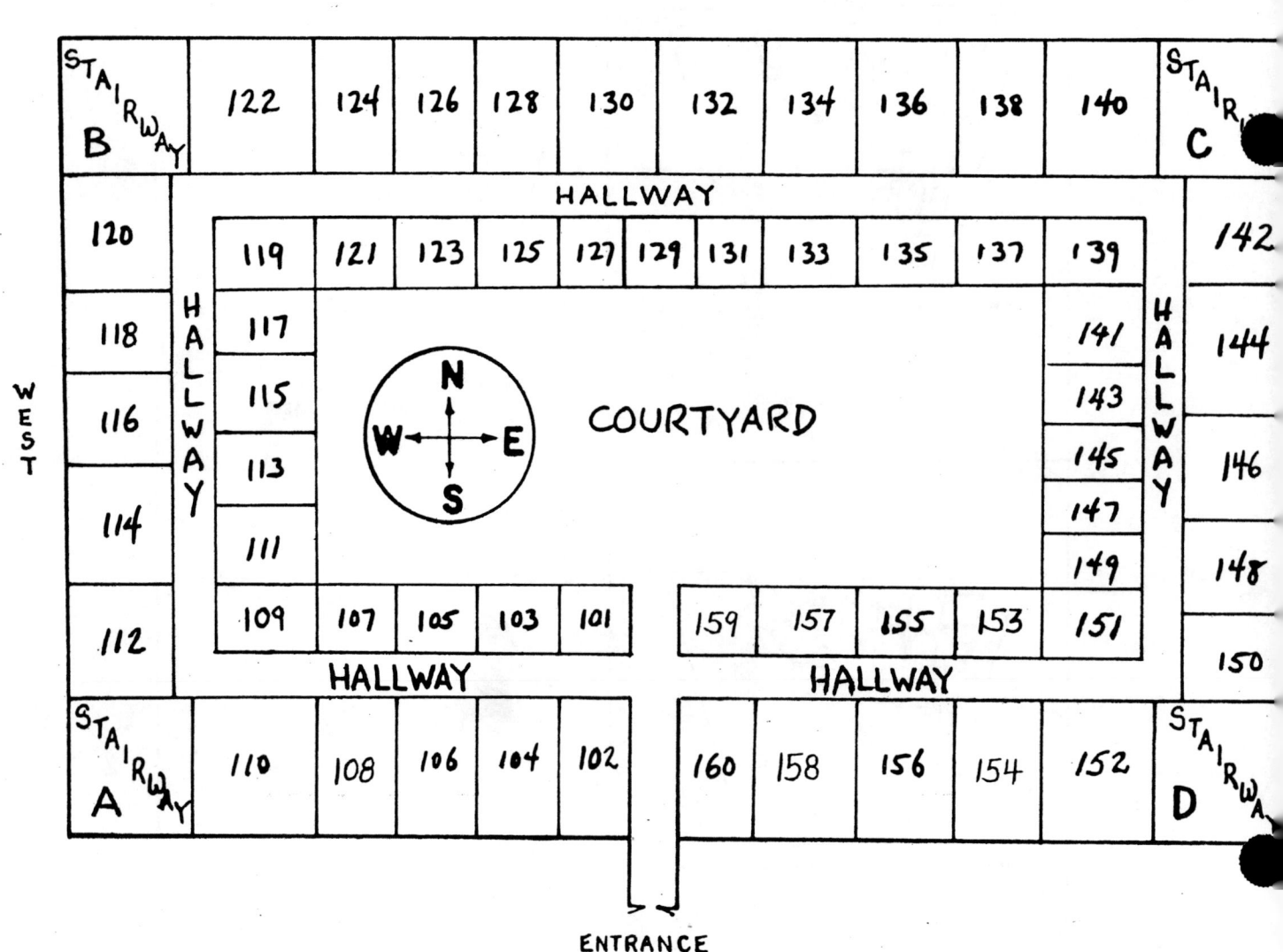

| STAIRWAY B | 122 | 124 | 126 | 128 | 130 | 132 | 134 | 136 | 138 | 140 | STAIRWAY C |
|---|---|---|---|---|---|---|---|---|---|---|---|

HALLWAY

| 120 | 119 | 121 | 123 | 125 | 127 | 129 | 131 | 133 | 135 | 137 | 139 | 142 |
| 118 | 117 |   |   |   |   |   |   |   |   |   | 141 | 144 |
| 116 | 115 |   |   |   |   |   |   |   |   |   | 143 | 146 |
| 114 | 113 |   | COURTYARD |   |   |   |   |   |   |   | 145 | 148 |
| 112 | 111 |   |   |   |   |   |   |   |   |   | 147 | 150 |
|   | 109 |   |   |   |   |   |   |   |   |   | 149 |   |

WEST (left side) — HALLWAY (left interior) — HALLWAY (right interior)

| 109 | 107 | 105 | 103 | 101 | 159 | 157 | 155 | 153 | 151 |

HALLWAY — HALLWAY

| STAIRWAY A | 110 | 108 | 106 | 104 | 102 | 160 | 158 | 156 | 154 | 152 | STAIRWAY D |

ENTRANCE
SOUTH

2. A firefighter is instructed to search for victims in the southwest area of the third floor. He wants to search as many rooms as possible and start his search as close to the fire as possible without passing through the fire. From the street, the firefighter should use his ladder to enter Room
   A. 302  B. 306  C. 312  D. 352

3. A firefighter goes to the third floor by way of the southwest building stairway. In Room 317, he finds a child who has been overcome by smoke. Upon returning to the hallway, he finds that the stairway he came up is now blocked by fire hoses.
   Which is the CLOSEST stairway that the firefighter can use to bring the child to the street level?
   A. A  B. B  C. C  D. D

4. Fire has spread from Room 304 to the room directly across the hall. As a result of heavy smoke, firefighters are ordered to break the windows of this room from the closest room on the floor above.
   Which room should the firefighters go to?
   A. 403  B. 305  C. 313  D. 413

5. The fire is in Rooms 303 and 305. Firefighters are told to go to rooms in the north corridor facing the courtyard that are directly opposite 303 and 305.
   Which rooms should the firefighters go to?
   A. 323 and 325
   B. 326 and 328
   C. 333 and 335
   D. 355 and 357

6. Another fire breaks out in Room 336, blocking the entire hallway. Firefighters have brought a hose up the northeast stairway to fight this fire. Another hose must be brought up another stairway so that firefighters can approach the fire from the same direction.
   What is the CLOSEST stairway that the firefighters could use?
   A. A  B. B  C. C  D. D

Questions 7-8.

DIRECTIONS: Questions 7 and 8 are to be answered on the basis of the following passage.

The firefighter who is assigned to the roof position at a fire in a Brownstone building should perform the following steps in the order given:

I. Go to the roof using one of the following ways:
   (a) First choice - The aerial ladder
   (b) Second choice - An attached building of the same height as the fire building
   (c) Third choice - A rear fire escape
   (d) Fourth choice - A thirty-five foot portable ladder

II. Upon arrival at the roof, look around to determine if any people are trapped who cannot be seen from the street.
   (a) If a trapped person is observed, notify the officer and the driver that a life-saving rope rescue is required. While waiting for assistance to conduct this rescue, assure the victim that help is on the way and proceed to Step III.
   (b) If no trapped persons are visible, proceed directly to Step III.

III. Remove the cover from the opening in the roof.
   (a) If there is no smoke or very little smoke coming from the opening, report to the officer for further orders.
   (b) If heavy smoke comes from the opening, proceed to Step IV.

IV. Remove the glass from the skylight.

7. Firefighters arriving at a fire in a Brownstone are using the aerial ladder to make an immediate rescue. The firefighter assigned to the roof position should go to the roof of the building on fire by
   A. a 35-foot portable ladder
   B. a rear fire escape
   C. an attached building of the same height
   D. the inside stairway of the fire building

8. The firefighter assigned to the roof position at a fire in a Brownstone arrives at the roof and finds that no persons are trapped. He then removes the roof cover from the opening in the roof.
   Which one of the following steps should be performed next? He should _____ is coming from the roof opening.
   A. remove the glass from the skylight if heavy smoke
   B. remove the glass from the skylight if no smoke
   C. go to the top floor to assist in the search for trapped persons if heavy smoke
   D. report to the officer if heavy smoke

Questions 9-10.

DIRECTIONS: Questions 9 and 10 are to be answered on the basis of the following passage.

Firefighters are often required to remove people who are trapped in elevators. At this type of emergency, firefighters perform the following steps in the order given:

1. Upon entering the building, determine the location of the elevator involved.
2. Reassure the trapped occupants that the Fire Department is on the scene and that firefighters are attempting to free them.
3. Determine if there are any injured people in the elevator.

4. Determine if all the doors from the hallways into the elevator shaft are closed.
5. If all the doors are closed, call for an elevator mechanic.
6. Wait until a trained elevator mechanic arrives before attempting to remove any trapped persons from the elevator, unless they can be removed through the door to the hallway. However, firefighters must remove the trapped persons by any safe method if any one of the following conditions exists:
    (a) There is a fire in the building
    (b) Someone in the elevator is injured
    (c) The people trapped in the elevator are in a state of panic.

9. Firefighters arrive at an elevator emergency in an office building. When they arrive, a maintenance man directs them to an elevator which is stuck between the fourth and fifth floors. He informs the firefighters that there is a young man in the elevator who apparently is calm and unhurt.
Which one of the following steps should the firefighter perform NEXT?
    A. Determine if the young man is injured.
    B. Reassure the young man that the Fire Department is on the scene and that firefighters are attempting to free him.
    C. Check to make sure that all the doors to the elevator and hallways are closed.
    D. Call for an elevator mechanic and await his arrival.

10. Firefighters are called to an elevator emergency at a factory building. The freight elevator has stopped suddenly between floors. The sudden stop caused heavy boxes to fall on the elevator operator, breaking his arm. Upon arrival, the firefighters determine the location of the elevator. They tell the trapped operator that they are on the scene, are aware of his injury, and are attempting to free him. They determine that all the hallway doors leading into the elevator shaft are closed.
The firefighters' NEXT step should be to
    A. call for an ambulance and wait until it arrives
    B. remove the trapped person through the door to the hallway
    C. call for an elevator mechanic
    D. remove the trapped person by any safe method

11. The preferred order of actions for firefighters to take when removing a victim from an apartment on fire is as follows:
    1. First choice - Remove the victim to the street level through the public hallway.
    2. Second choice - Remove the victim to the street level by the fire escape.

3. Third choice - Remove the victim to the street level using either a portable ladder or an aerial ladder.
4. Fourth choice - Lower the victim to the street level with a life-saving rope.

Firefighters answering an alarm are not able to use the entrance to a building on fire to reach a victim on the third floor because there is a fire in the public hallway. The victim is standing at the front window of an apartment on fire which has a fire escape. A firefighter places a portable ladder against the building, climbs the ladder, and enters the window where the victim is standing. The firefighter is carrying the life-saving rope and a 2-way radio. The radio allows her to communicate with the firefighter who operates the aerial ladder.
The firefighter should then remove this victim from the fire apartment by using the
   A. fire escape             B. aerial ladder
   C. portable ladder       D. life-saving rope

12. Firefighters must regularly inspect office buildings to determine whether fire prevention laws have been obeyed. Some of these fire prevention laws are as follows:
DOORS: Doors should be locked as follows:
  1. Doors on the ground floor may be locked on the street side to prevent entry into the stairway.
  2. Doors in office buildings that are less than 100 feet in height may be locked on the stairway side on each floor above the ground floor.
  3. Doors in office buildings that are 100 feet or more in height may be locked on the stairway side except for every fourth floor.

The doors in an office building which is less than 100 feet in height may be locked on the stairway side
   A. on all floors including the ground floor
   B. on all floors above the ground floor
   C. except for every fourth floor
   D. on all floors above the fourth floor

13. SIGNS: Signs concerning stairways should be posted in the following manner:
  1. A sign shall be posted near the elevator on each floor, stating *IN CASE OF FIRE, USE STAIRS UNLESS OTHERWISE INSTRUCTED*. The sign shall contain a diagram showing the location of the stairs and the letter identification of the stairs.
  2. Each stairway shall be identified by an alphabetical letter on a sign posted on the hallway side of the stair door.
  3. Signs indicating the floor number shall be attached to the stairway side of each door.
  4. Signs indicating whether re-entry can be made into the building, and the floors where re-entry can be made, shall be posted on the stairway side of each door.

Which one of the following CORRECTLY lists the information which should be posted on the stairway side of a door? A sign will indicate the
- A. floor number, whether re-entry can be made into the building, and the floors where re-entry can be made
- B. alphabetical letter of the stairway, whether re-entry can be made into the building, and the floors where re-entry can be made
- C. alphabetical letter of the stairway and the floor number
- D. alphabetical letter of the stairway, the floor number, whether re-entry can be made into the building, and the floors where re-entry can be made

14. Every firefighter must know the proper first aid procedures for treating injured people when there is a subway fire. In general, anyone suffering from smoke inhalation or heat exhaustion should be removed to fresh air and given oxygen immediately. Heart attack victims should be kept calm and should receive oxygen and medical attention immediately. Persons suffering from broken bones should not be moved until a splint is applied to the injury. However, in a situation where there is a smoky fire in the subway and the passengers needing immediate first aid are in danger from the fire, firefighters must first evacuate the passengers and perform first aid later, regardless of the injury.
The PROPER first aid procedure for a man who has apparently suffered a heart attack on the station platform is to
- A. have the man take the next train to the nearest hospital
- B. remove the man to the street and administer oxygen
- C. turn off the electrical power and evacuate the man through the tunnel
- D. keep the man calm and administer oxygen

14.___

Questions 15-16.

DIRECTIONS: Questions 15 and 16 are to be answered SOLELY on the basis of the following passage.

A firefighter is responsible for a variety of duties other than fighting fires. One such duty is housewatch.

A firefighter's primary responsibility during housewatch is to properly receive alarm information. This enables firefighters to respond to alarms for fires and emergencies. The alarms are received at the firehouse by one of the following methods: computer teleprinter messages, Fire Department telephone or verbal alarm. The computer teleprinter and the telephone are used to alert the fire companies. These two types of alarms are transmitted by a dispatcher from a central communication office to the firehouse closest to the fire. The verbal alarm occurs when someone comes to the firehouse or stops the fire truck on the street to report a fire. Once an alarm has been received, the firefighter on housewatch duty alerts the rest of the firefighters to respond to the alarm.

Other housewatch responsibilities include keeping the appearance of the housewatch area neat and orderly, keeping the front of the firehouse clear of all vehicles and obstructions, and receiving telephone calls and visitors with complaints about fire hazards. The firefighter on housewatch duty also keeps an accurate and complete record of all administrative matters in a journal.

15. The methods a dispatcher uses to transmit alarms to the firehouse are the
    A. computer teleprinter, Fire Department telephone, and verbal alarm
    B. verbal alarm and computer teleprinter
    C. Fire Department telephone and verbal alarm
    D. computer teleprinter and Fire Department telephone

16. The PRIMARY responsibility of a firefighter on housewatch duty is to
    A. properly assign firefighters to specific duties
    B. properly receive alarm information
    C. keep the housewatch area neat and orderly
    D. write all important information in the company journal

Questions 17-18.

DIRECTIONS: Questions 17 and 18 are to be answered SOLELY on the basis of the following passage.

One duty of a firefighter on housewatch is to ensure that the computer teleprinter is working properly. A company officer should be notified immediately of any equipment problems. The firefighter on housewatch should check on the amount of paper in the teleprinter and should refill it when necessary. The firefighter should also check the selector panel on the computer. This selector panel has a series of buttons which are used by the firefighter to let the dispatcher know that an alarm has been received and that the fire company is responding. These buttons have lights. To check that the computer is functioning properly, the firefighter should press the button marked *test* and then release the button. If the computer lights go on, and then go off after the *test* button has been released the computer is working properly. In addition, the light next to the *test* button should always be blinking.

17. In order to check that the selector panel of the computer is working properly, the firefighter on housewatch duty presses the button marked *test*, and then releases the button.
    The firefighter should conclude that the computer is working properly if the
    A. computer lights stay on
    B. computer lights keep blinking
    C. computer lights go on and then off
    D. *test* light stays on

18. A firefighter on housewatch duty notices that the teleprinter is almost out of paper.
    In this situation, the firefighter should
    A. test the computer panel by pushing the *test* button
    B. notify the officer to replace the paper
    C. place a new supply of paper in the teleprinter
    D. notify the dispatcher that the paper is being changed

Questions 19-20.

DIRECTIONS: Questions 19 and 20 are to be answered SOLELY on the basis of the following passage.

Following is a list of rules for fire extinguishers which are required in different types of public buildings in the city:

Rule 1: Hospitals, nursing homes, hotels, and motels must have one 2½ gallon water extinguisher for every 2500 square feet, or part thereof, of floor area on each floor.

Rule 2: Stores with floor areas of 1500 square feet or less must have one 2½ gallon water extinguisher. Stores with floor areas of over 1500 square feet must have one 2½ gallon water extinguisher for every 2500 square feet, or part thereof, of floor area on each floor.

Rule 3: Kitchens must have one 2½ gallon foam extinguisher or one 5 pound dry chemical extinguisher for every 1250 square feet, or part thereof, of floor area on each floor. For kitchen areas, this rule is in addition to Rules 1 and 2.

19. A firefighter is inspecting a one-story nursing home which has a total of 3000 square feet of floor area. This includes a kitchen, which is 1500 square feet in area, in the rear of the floor.
    Of the following, the firefighter should conclude that the nursing home should be equipped with
    A. 1 water extinguisher and 1 foam extinguisher
    B. 1 water extinguisher and 1 dry chemical extinguisher
    C. 2 water extinguishers and 2 foam extinguishers
    D. 2 foam extinguishers and 1 dry chemical extinguisher

20. A firefighter is inspecting a store which has two floors. The first floor has 2600 square feet. The second floor has 1450 square feet.
    The store should be equipped with AT LEAST
    A. two 2½ gallon water extinguishers, one for each floor
    B. three 2½ gallon water extinguishers, two for the first floor and one for the second floor
    C. two 2½ gallon foam extinguishers, one for each floor
    D. two 2½ gallon extinguishers, either foam or water, one for each floor

21. Firefighters from the first arriving ladder company work in teams while fighting fires in private homes. The inside team enters the building through the first floor entrance and then searches the first floor for victims. The outside team uses ladders to enter upper level windows for a quick search of the bedrooms on the second floor and above. The assignments for the members of the outside team are as follows:

    <u>Roof person</u> - This member places a ladder at the front porch and enters the second floor windows from the roof of the porch.

    <u>Outside vent person and driver</u> - These members work together and place a portable ladder at a window on the opposite side of the house from which the roof person is working. However, if the aerial ladder can be used, the outside vent person and driver climb the aerial ladder in the front of the house and the roof person places a portable ladder on the left side of the house.

In order to search all four sides of a private home on the upper levels, firefighters from the second arriving ladder company place portable ladders at the sides of the house not covered by the first ladder company, and enter the home through the upper level windows.

The second ladder company to arrive at a fire in a 2-story private home sees the aerial ladder being raised to the front porch roof.

In this situation, the firefighters should place their portable ladders to the

    A. left and right sides of the house since there is a front porch
    B. rear and right sides of the house since the aerial ladder is being used
    C. rear and left sides of the house since there is a front porch
    D. left and right sides of the house since the aerial ladder is being used

22. The priority for the removal of a particular victim by aerial ladder depends on the following conditions:

If two victims are at the same window and are not seriously endangered by spreading fire, the victim who is easier to remove is taken down the ladder first and helped safely to the street. In general, the term *easier to remove* refers to the victim who is more capable of being moved and more able to cooperate. After the easier removal is completed, time can be spent on the more difficult removal.

If there are victims at two different windows, the aerial ladder is first placed to remove the victims who are the most seriously endangered by the fire. The ladder is then placed to remove the victims who are less seriously exposed to the fire.

Assume that you are working at a fire and that there are a total of three victims at two windows. Victims #1 and #2 are at the same window, which is three floors above the fire and shows no evidence of heat or smoke. Victim #1 is a disabled, 23-year-old male, and Victim #2 is a 40-year-old woman. Victim #3, a 16-year-old male, is at a window of the apartment on fire. From your position in the street, you can see heavy smoke coming from this window and flames coming out of the window next to it. Which one of the following is the PROPER order for victim removal?
Victim
- A. #3, #2, #1
- B. #1, #2, #3
- C. #1, #3, #2
- D. #3, #1, #2

Questions 23-24.

DIRECTIONS: Questions 23 and 24 are to be answered SOLELY on the basis of the following passage.

The four different types of building collapses are as follows:

1. <u>Building Wall Collapse</u> - An outside wall of the building collapses but the floors maintain their positions.
2. <u>Lean-to Collapse</u> - One end of a floor collapses onto the floor below it. This leaves a sheltered area on the floor below.
3. <u>Floor Collapse</u> - An entire floor falls to the floor below it but large pieces of machinery in the floor below provide spaces which can provide shelter.
4. <u>Pancake Collapse</u> - A floor collapses completely onto the floor below it, leaving no spaces. In some cases, the force of this collapse causes successive lower floors to collapse.

23. The MOST serious injuries are likely to occur at _____ collapses.
    - A. pancake
    - B. lean-to
    - C. floor
    - D. building wall

24. Of the following, a floor collapse is MOST likely to occur in a
    - A. factory building
    - B. private home
    - C. apartment building
    - D. hotel

25. Many subway tunnels contain a set of three rails used for train movement. The subway trains run on two rails. The third rail carries electricity and is the source of power for all trains. Electricity travels from the third rail through metal plates called contact shoes which are located near the wheels on every train car. Electricity then travels through the contact shoes into the train's motor. Firefighters must be very careful when operating near the third rail because contact with the third rail can result in electrocution.

From the above, it is apparent that the source of power for subway trains is the
- A. third rail
- B. contact shoes
- C. motor
- D. metal plates

---

## KEY (CORRECT ANSWERS)

1. A
2. B
3. B
4. A
5. A

6. D
7. C
8. A
9. B
10. C

11. A
12. B
13. A
14. D
15. D

16. B
17. C
18. C
19. C
20. B

21. B
22. A
23. A
24. A
25. A

---

# TEST 2

DIRECTIONS: Each question or incomplete statement is followed by several suggested answers or completions. Select the one that BEST answers the question or completes the statement. *PRINT THE LETTER OF THE CORRECT ANSWER IN THE SPACE AT THE RIGHT.*

Questions 1-5.

DIRECTIONS: Questions 1 through 5 are to be answered SOLELY on the basis of the following passage.

Firefighters receive an alarm for an apartment fire on the fourth floor of a 14-story housing project at 1191 Park Place. One firefighter shouts the address as the other firefighters are getting on the fire truck. Knowledge of the address helps the firefighters decide which equipment to pull off the fire truck when they reach the fire scene.

The firefighters know where the water outlets are located in the building on fire. There is an outlet in every hallway. Firefighters always attach the hose at the closest outlet on the floor below the fire.

As they arrive at 1191 Park Place, three firefighters immediately take one length of hose each and go into the building. Since an officer has been told by the dispatcher that two children are trapped in the rear bedroom, the officer and two firefighters begin searching for victims and opening windows immediately upon entering the apartment on fire.

As in all housing project fires, the roof person goes to the apartment above the apartment on fire. From this position, he attaches a tool to a rope in order to break open the windows of the apartment on fire. From this position, the roof person could also make a rope rescue of a victim in the apartment on fire.

1. A firefighter shouted the address of the fire when the alarm was received so that the firefighters would
   A. know which equipment to take from the truck at the fire scene
   B. be more alert when they arrived at the fire
   C. be prepared to make a rope rescue
   D. know that two children were reported to be trapped

2. The hose should be attached to an outlet on the
   A. floor above the fire     B. ground floor
   C. fire floor     D. floor below the fire

1.\_\_\_

2.\_\_\_

3. Because of the information given to the officer by the dispatcher, the officer and two firefighters
   A. entered the apartment above the fire for a rope rescue
   B. began immediately to search for victims and to open windows
   C. opened all the windows before the hose was moved in
   D. attached a hose and moved to the origin of the fire

4. The roof person broke the windows of the apartment on fire with a(n)
   A. axe while leaning out of the windows
   B. axe attached to the end of a rope
   C. tool while standing on the roof
   D. tool attached to a rope

5. The PROPER location for a rescue by the roof person at a fire in a housing project is the
   A. hallway
   B. apartment below the apartment on fire
   C. apartment above the apartment on fire
   D. fire escape

6. Firefighters may have to use tools to force open an entrance door. Before the firefighters use the tools, they should turn the doorknob to see if the door is unlocked. If the door is locked, one firefighter should use an axe and the other firefighter should use a halligan tool. This tool is used to pry open doors and windows. Firefighters must take the following steps in the order given to force open the door:
   I. Place the prying end of the halligan tool approximately six inches above or below the lock. If there are two locks, the halligan tool should be placed between them.
   II. Tilt the halligan tool slightly downward so that a single point on the prying end is at the door's edge.
   III. Strike the halligan tool with the axe until the first point is driven in between the door and the door frame.
   IV. Continue striking with the axe until the door and frame are spread apart and the lock is broken.
   V. Apply pressure toward the door and the door will spring open.

   Firefighters respond to a fire on the second floor of a 3-story apartment building. Two firefighters, one equipped with an axe and the other with a halligan tool, climb the stairs to the apartment on fire. They see that there are two locks on the apartment door.
   The firefighters should now
   A. place the prying end of the halligan tool about six inches above or below the locks
   B. turn the doorknob to determine whether the door is locked
   C. tilt the halligan tool towards the floor before striking
   D. place the prying end of the halligan tool between the locks

7. You are a firefighter who is inspecting a building for violations. You must perform the following steps in the order given:
   I. Find the manager of the building and introduce yourself.
   II. Have the manager accompany you during the inspection.
   III. Start the inspection by checking the Fire Department permits which have been issued to the building. The permits are located in the office of the building.
   IV. Inspect the building for violations of the Fire Prevention Laws. Begin at the roof and work down to the basement or cellar.
   V. As you inspect, write on a piece of paper any violations you find and explain them to the building manager.

   You are inspecting a supermarket. After entering the building, you identify yourself to the store manager and ask him to come along during the inspection.
   Which one of the following actions should you take NEXT?
   A. Start inspecting the supermarket, beginning at the basement.
   B. Start inspecting the supermarket, beginning at the roof.
   C. Ask to see the Fire Department permits which have been issued to the supermarket.
   D. Write down any violations which are seen while introducing yourself to the manager.

Questions 8-9.

DIRECTIONS: Questions 8 and 9 are to be answered SOLELY on the basis of the following passage.

Engine company firefighters are responsible for putting water on a fire and extinguishing it. To do this properly, they should perform their tasks in the following order:

   I. Once an apartment door has been forced open, the engine company officer orders the driver to start the flow of water through the hose.
   2. As the water starts to flow into the hose, it pushes trapped air ahead of it. To clear this air from the hose, the nozzle is pointed away from the fire area, opened, and then closed before water starts to flow from it. This is done to prevent a rush of fresh air from the hose which will intensify the fire.
   3. When the fire is found, the nozzle is directed at the ceiling to allow water to rain down on the fire. As the fire becomes smaller, the nozzle is aimed directly at the burning object.

8. When engine company firefighters enter an apartment where there is a fire, the occupant takes the firefighters to a fire in the bedroom.
   Once air has been cleared from the hose, the firefighter operating the nozzle should

A. wait for the ladder company to open the door
B. aim water directly onto the bed
C. spray the water across the floor
D. direct the water at the ceiling and allow it to rain down on the fire

9. After the locked door at an apartment fire has been forced open and water starts to flow into the hose, the firefighter operating the nozzle sees an intense fire just inside the apartment doorway.
She should then point the nozzle
   A. away from the fire    B. directly at the fire
   C. at any burning object  D. at the apartment floor

10. When a leak occurs in an oil pipeline, the Fire Department dispatcher sends a message for specific companies to respond to the leak. There is a letter code on the message indicating the possible location of the leak. After a firefighter reads the letter code on the message, the following steps are performed in the order given to properly close the valves on the pipeline:
  I. The firefighter looks up the alarm assignment card which gives the location of the valve.
  II. The firefighter makes sure that a short wrench and a long wrench are placed on the fire truck.
  III. Upon arrival at the location of the valve, the firefighter removes the steel valve cover with the short wrench.
  IV. The long wrench is then used to completely close the valve.

A firefighter receives a message from the dispatcher about a leak in an oil pipeline. After noting the letter code on the message, the firefighter should
  A. give the alarm card immediately to the officer in charge
  B. make sure the proper wrenches for closing the valve have been placed on the fire apparatus
  C. look up the alarm assignment card to determine the location of the valve
  D. remove the steel valve cover

11. When administering first aid to a person who is severely bleeding, firefighters should perform the following steps in the order given:
  I. Direct pressure
    (a) Press a dressing directly on the wound
  II. Elevation
    (a) Lift the injured body part above the heart level, while continuing direct pressure. This will slow down the movement of blood to the wound.
    (b) Never elevate a body part if it might be fractured.
    (c) If the bleeding continues while the injured body part is elevated and is receiving direct pressure, pressure should be applied to an artery or other pressure point.

A firefighter arrives at an automobile accident and finds a woman who is bleeding severely from a cut just above the ankle. She also has a fracture of the upper arm.
After placing a dressing on the ankle wound, the firefighter should NEXT
   A. apply pressure to a pressure point to stop the bleeding
   B. elevate the upper arm and apply direct pressure to it
   C. apply direct pressure to an artery in the arm
   D. apply direct pressure to the leg while elevating it

12. One firefighter of the first company to arrive at a fire in a private house is assigned to the roof position. During the beginning stages of a fire, the roof person is part of a team which enters and searches the building for victims.
The roof person's duties are performed in the following order:
   I. Climb a portable ladder to the front porch roof, break a window, and enter the building through this opening if there is no victim in immediate danger visible at another window. If there is such a victim, place the ladder at that window.
   II. If there is no front porch, use the portable extension ladder at a side of the house.
   III. Enter the house after breaking a window.

The roof person at a fire in a private house sees a boy at a top floor window on the right side of the house. There is a porch in the front of the house.
The roof person should now place the portable ladder at the
   A. front of the porch
   B. top floor front window
   C. top floor window, right side of the house
   D. top floor window, left side of the house

13. The following is a description of the actions taken by the outside vent person (O.V.) at different types of fires:
   <u>Fire 1</u>: At a fire at 3:00 A.M. on the third floor of a 5-story apartment building, the O.V. climbed the fire escape to break the windows in the fire area.
   <u>Fire 2</u>: At a fire at 1:00 P.M. on the fourth floor of a 4-story apartment building, the O.V. went to the roof to assist the firefighter assigned to the roof position.
   <u>Fire 3</u>: At a fire at 2:00 P.M. on the third floor of a 3-story factory building, the O.V. went to the roof to assist the firefighter assigned to the roof position.
   <u>Fire 4</u>: At a fire at 6:00 A.M. on the first floor of a 2-story clothing store, the O.V. broke the first floor windows from the outside of the building.

Fire 5: At a fire at 1:00 A.M. on the fifth floor of a 5-story apartment building, the O.V. went to the roof to assist the firefighter assigned to the roof position.

A firefighter should conclude that the O.V. assists the firefighter assigned to the roof position when the fire
A. is in an apartment building
B. occurs at night
C. is located on the top floor of the building
D. is in a commercial building

14. Firefighters perform both vertical and horizontal ventilation. In vertical ventilation, an opening is made on the upper levels of the fire building so that the natural air currents can assist in the removal of smoke and heated gases. In horizontal ventilation, windows are opened on the same level as the fire to allow fresh air into the fire area.
A ladder company recently responded to the following fires at different 6-story apartment buildings and performed the actions indicated:
Fire 1: At a fire in a mattress in a second floor apartment, firefighters immediately opened the roof door. After water began flowing through the hose, firefighters opened the windows in the apartment. The fire was quickly extinguished.
Fire 2: At a fire in the top floor bedroom, firefighters cut a hole in the roof as soon as possible and then used the water from the hose to shatter the windows. The fire was quickly extinguished.
Fire 3: At an apartment fire on the second floor, firefighters broke the windows in the apartment as the hose was being brought from the street. The fire spread before water could be applied to the fire.

Based upon the types of ventilation performed at the three fires, which one of the following statements is CORRECT?
A. Vertical ventilation must be performed by opening the roof door.
B. Horizontal ventilation should be delayed until firefighters are ready to apply water to the fire.
C. Horizontal ventilation must be performed before vertical ventilation.
D. Vertical ventilation must be delayed until water is applied to the fire.

Questions 15-16.

DIRECTIONS: Questions 15 and 16 are to be answered on the basis of the following passage.

A newly appointed firefighter is studying the proper use of foam, water, or dry chemicals to extinguish a fire. The firefighter looks over past fire reports to see whether any patterns exist.

Fire 1: Gasoline fire near a car was extinguished by foam.
Fire 2: Fire in a television set with a disconnected power cord was extinguished by water.
Fire 3: Fire in a fuse box of a private home was extinguished by dry chemicals.
Fire 4: Oil fire near an oil burner in a private home was extinguished by foam.
Fire 5: Fire near the electrical rail at a subway was extinguished by dry chemicals.
Fire 6: Fire involving an electric range was extinguished by dry chemicals.
Fire 7: Fire in the front seat of an automobile was extinguished by water.

15. The firefighter should conclude that dry chemicals are used to extinguish fires which involve
    A. automobiles
    B. private homes
    C. oil and gasoline
    D. live electrical equipment

16. The firefighter should conclude that foam is used to extinguish
    A. car fires
    B. oil and gasoline fires
    C. stove fires
    D. electrical fires

17. In situations where there is no fire, firefighters must make immediate rescue attempts when they come upon persons in danger.
Which one of the following persons to be rescued is in the GREATEST danger?
A
    A. sleeping baby inside a car that has a leaking gasoline tank
    B. woman inside an elevator stuck on the 33rd floor
    C. teenage boy drifting on a lake in a boat
    D. woman confined to a wheelchair is locked in her apartment

18. Firefighters are inspecting a furniture factory. During the inspection, they find employees smoking cigarettes in various areas.
In which area does smoking pose the GREATEST danger of causing a fire?
    A. Employee lounge
    B. Woodworking shop
    C. A private office
    D. A rest room

19. Firefighters should observe the sidewalk and street area in front of the firehouse and inform the officer of any conditions that may cause a significant delay when fire trucks must go out in response to an alarm.
Which one of the following conditions should the firefighters report to the officer?
    A. A car is stopped in front of the firehouse for a red light.
    B. People are standing and talking in front of the firehouse.

C. A truck is parked in front of the firehouse.
D. There is a small crack in the sidewalk in front of the firehouse.

20. Which of the following conditions observed by a firefighter inspecting an automobile repair garage is the MOST dangerous fire hazard?
     A. A mechanic is repairing a hole in a half-filled gas tank while smoking a cigarette.
     B. A heater is being used to heat the garage.
     C. A mechanic is changing a tire on a van while smoking a pipe.
     D. There is no fire extinguishing equipment in the garage.

21. During a fire prevention inspection, a firefighter may find a condition which could be the immediate cause of death in the event of a fire.
    Which one of the following conditions in a restaurant is the MOST dangerous?
     A. Blocked exit doors
     B. A crack in the front door
     C. A window that does not open
     D. A broken air conditioning system

22. It is very important to get fresh air into a closed area that is filled with gas or smoke.
    In which one of the following situations should such an action be taken FIRST?
    A(n)
     A. smell of gas coming through an open apartment window
     B. unoccupied car with the motor running
     C. strong odor coming from a closed refrigerator
     D. gas leak in the closed basement of an occupied building

23. A firefighter who is assigned to the roof position at a fire must notify the officer of dangerous conditions which can be seen from the roof.
    Which one of the following conditions is the MOST dangerous?
     A. The roof is sagging and may collapse because of the fire on the top floor.
     B. Rubbish is visible on the roof of the building next door.
     C. The stairway to the roof of the building has poor lighting.
     D. An automobile accident in the street is causing a traffic jam.

24. Firefighters must often deal with people who need medical assistance. In life-threatening situations, firefighters must perform first aid until an ambulance arrives. In less serious situations, firefighters should make the person comfortable and wait for the ambulance personnel to give first aid.

A firefighter should give first aid until an ambulance arrives when a person
  A. appears to have a knee injury
  B. is bleeding heavily from a stomach wound
  C. has bruises on his head
  D. has a broken ankle

25. At a fire on the west side of the third floor of a 10-story office building, a firefighter is responsible for rescuing trapped persons by means of the aerial ladder. The trapped person who is in the most dangerous location should be removed first.
Of the following, the firefighter should FIRST remove the trapped person who is
  A. on the rear fire escape on the east side of the second floor
  B. on the roof
  C. at a window on the west side of the fourth floor
  D. at a window on the tenth floor

---

## KEY (CORRECT ANSWERS)

1. A
2. D
3. B
4. D
5. C

6. B
7. C
8. D
9. A
10. C

11. D
12. C
13. C
14. B
15. D

16. B
17. A
18. B
19. C
20. A

21. A
22. D
23. A
24. B
25. C

# FIRE SCIENCE
## EXAMINATION SECTION

Questions 1-10. Booklet/Floor Plan

Firefighters must be able to find their way in and out of buildings that are filled with smoke. They must learn the floor plan quickly for their own safety and to help fight the fire and remove victims.

Look at this floor plan of an apartment. There is an apartment on each side of this one. It is on the <u>fifth floor</u> of the building.

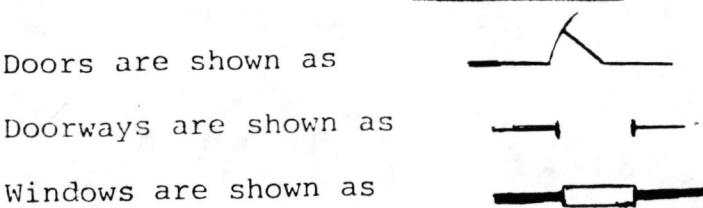

Doors are shown as

Doorways are shown as

Windows are shown as

You will have 5 minutes to memorize this floor plan. Then you will be asked to answer some questions about it without looking at it.

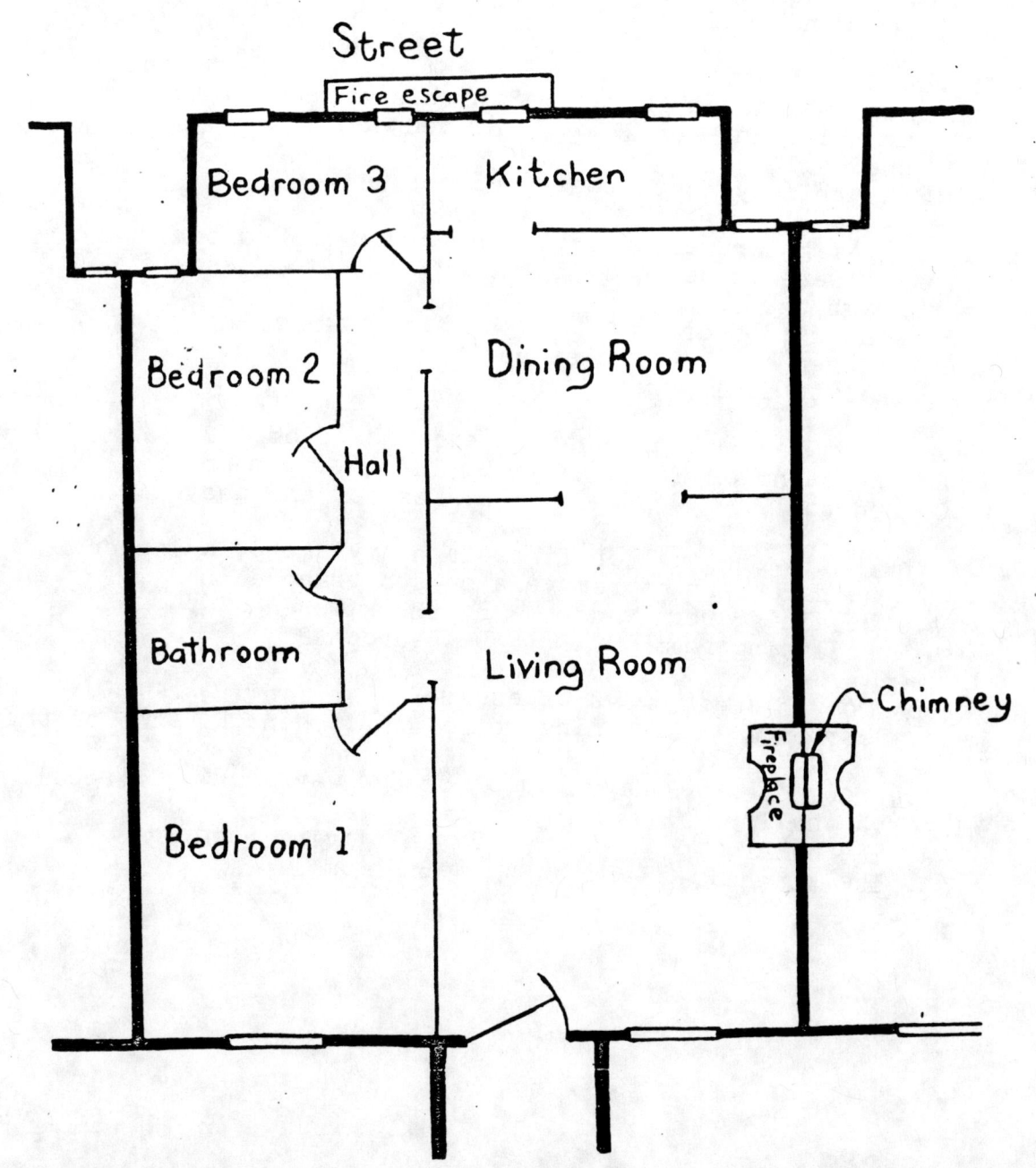

Questions 1-10.  **Visual Recall**

DIRECTIONS: Questions 1 through 10 test your ability to recall the details of the floor plan you have just studied. Each question or statement is followed by four choices. For each question, choose the one BEST answer (A,B,C,or D). Then *PRINT THE LETTER OF THE CORRECT ANSWER IN THE SPACE AT THE RIGHT.*

1. *Which* room has NO doors that can be closed?  1. \_\_\_\_
    A. Bedroom 1          B. Living room
    C. Dining room       D. None of these

2. *Which* room is FARTHEST from the bathroom?  2. \_\_\_\_
    A. Bedroom 3          B. Living room
    C. Dining room       D. Kitchen

3. If there is a fire in the living room, firefighters entering from the fire escape should bring a hose in through  3. \_\_\_\_
    A. the kitchen window    B. the hall
    C. the window of bedroom 2    D. any one of the above

4. It would be MOST important to check for a fire in the apartment next door if a fire in this apartment were in  4. \_\_\_\_
    A. the kitchen        B. bedroom 3
    C. the hall
    D. the chimney above the fireplace

5. If a firefighter were rescuing a person in bedroom 2 and the fire were in bedroom 3, the *safest* way of escape would be through the  5. \_\_\_\_
    A. window of bedroom 2     B. hall and living room
    C. kitchen to the fire escape
    D. hall to dining room window

6. *Which* room has *only one* way of escaping from it?  6. \_\_\_\_
    A. The bathroom       B. The living room
    C. Bedroom 2           D. None of the above

7. If the hall were full of fire and heavy smoke, a ladder would be necessary to remove a person trapped in  7. \_\_\_\_
    A. the dining room      B. the kitchen
    C. the living room      D. bedroom 2

8. *Which* room has *four* ways of escape?  8. \_\_\_\_
    A. Bedroom 1    B. Dining room    C. Kitchen    D. None of them

9. *Which* room does NOT have a door or doorway leading directly into the hall?  9. \_\_\_\_
    A. The bathroom       B. The living room
    C. The kitchen         D. Bedroom 1

10. Of the following, the SHORTEST way from the fire escape to   10. ____
    the kitchen is through
    A. bedroom 3, hall, and dining room
    B. bedroom 2, hall, and dining room
    C. bedroom 1, living room, and dining room
    D. the living room and dining room

---

# KEY (CORRECT ANSWERS)

| | | | | |
|---|---|---|---|---|
| 1. | C | | 6. | A |
| 2. | D | | 7. | D |
| 3. | A | | 8. | B |
| 4. | D | | 9. | C |
| 5. | B | | 10. | A |

# EXAMINATION SECTION
## TEST 1

DIRECTIONS: Each question or incomplete statement is followed by several suggested answers or completions. Select the one that BEST answers the question or completes the statement. *PRINT THE LETTER OF THE CORRECT ANSWER IN THE SPACE AT THE RIGHT.*

1. In an effort to discourage the sending of false alarms and to help apprehend those guilty of this practice, it is suggested that the handles of fire alarm boxes be covered with a dye which would stain the hand of a person sending an alarm, and which would not wash off for 24 hours. The dye would be visible only under an ultraviolet light.
Of the following, the CHIEF objection to such a device is that it would
   A. require funds that can be better used for other purposes
   B. have no effect on false alarms transmitted by telephone
   C. discourage some persons from sending alarms for real fires
   D. punish the innocent as well as the guilty

1.___

2. Of the following, the MAIN difficulty in the way of obtaining accurate information about the causes of fire is that
   A. firemen are too busy putting out fires to have time for investigation of the causes of fires
   B. most people have little knowledge about fire hazards
   C. fires destroy much of the evidence which would indicate the causes of the fires
   D. fire departments are more interested in fire prevention than in investigating fires that have already occurred

2.___

3. In case of a fire in a U.S. Mail Box, the Fire Department recommends that an extinguishing agent which smothers the fire, such as carbon tetrachloride, should be used.
Of the following, the MOST likely reason for NOT recommending the use of water is that
   A. water is not effective on fires in small tightly enclosed spaces
   B. someone might have mailed chemicals that could explode in contact with water
   C. water may damage the mail untouched by fire so that it could not be delivered
   D. the smothering agent can be put on the fire faster than water can be

3.___

4. A man found an official Fire Department badge and gave it to his young son to use as a toy.
The man's action was *improper* MAINLY because
   A. it is disrespectful to the fire department to use the badge in this manner
   B. the boy may injure himself playing with the badge
   C. an effort should have been made first to locate the owner of the badge before giving it to the boy
   D. the badge should have been returned to the fire department

5. Two firemen, on their way to report for duty early one morning, observe a fire in a building containing a supermarket on the street level and apartments on the upper stories. One fireman runs to a street alarm box two blocks away and sends an alarm.
The latter fireman should then
   A. return to the building which is on fire and help evacuate the tenants
   B. remain at the fire alarm box in order to direct the first fire company that arrives to the location of the fire
   C. look for a telephone in order to call his own fire company and explain that he and his company will be late in reporting for duty
   D. look for a telephone in order to call the Health Department and request that an inspector be sent to the supermarket to examine the food involved in the fire

6. At a recent five-alarm fire in County A, several companies from County B were temporarily assigned to occupy the quarters and take over the duties of companies engaged in fighting the fire.
The MAIN reason for relocating the companies was to
   A. protect the firehouses from robbery or vandalism which might occur if they were left vacant for a long period
   B. provide for speedy response to the fire if additional companies are required
   C. give the companies an opportunity to become familiar with the problems of the area
   D. provide protection to the area in the event other fires should occur

7. A fireman on duty who answers a departmental telephone should give his name and rank
   A. at the start of the conversation, as a matter of routine
   B. only if asked for this information by the caller
   C. only if the caller is a superior officer
   D. only if the telephone message requires the fireman to take some action

8. While performing a routine inspection of a factory building, a fireman is asked a question by the plant manager about a matter which is under the control of the Health Department and about which the fireman has little knowledge.
In this situation, the BEST of the following courses of action for the fireman to take is to
   A. answer the question to the best of his ability
   B. tell the manager that he is not permitted to answer the question because it does not relate to a Fire Department matter
   C. tell the manager that he will refer the question to the Health Department
   D. suggest to the manager that he communicate with the Health Department about the matter

9. Automatic fire extinguishing sprinkler systems sometimes are not effective on fires accompanied by explosions, CHIEFLY because
   A. these fires do not generate enough heat to start sprinkler operations
   B. the pipes supplying the sprinklers are usually damaged by the explosion
   C. fires in explosive materials usually cannot be extinguished by water
   D. sprinkler heads are usually clogged by dust created by the explosion

10. When a fire occurs in the vicinity of a railroad system, there is the possibility that water from the fireman's hose streams will flood underground portions of the railway lines through sidewalk gratings.
Of the following methods of reducing this danger, the one that would be generally MOST suitable is for the officer in command to order his men to
   A. use fewer hose lines and smaller quantities of water than they would ordinarily
   B. attack the fire from positions which are distant from the sidewalk gratings
   C. cover the sidewalk gratings with canvas tarpaulins
   D. advise the railroad dispatcher to re-route trains

11. When responding to alarms, fire department apparatus generally follows routes established in advance.
The one of the following which would be the LEAST valid justification for this practice is that
   A. motorists living in the area become familiar with these routes and tend to avoid them
   B. the likelihood of collision between two pieces of fire department apparatus is reduced
   C. the fastest response generally is obtained
   D. road construction, road blocks, detours, and similar conditions can be avoided

12. An off-duty fireman sees, from a distance, a group of teenage boys set fire to a newspaper and toss the flaming pages into an open window of a building which is being torn down.
In this situation, the FIRST action which should be taken by the fireman is to
   A. send a fire alarm from the closest street alarm box
   B. chase the boys and attempt to catch one of them
   C. investigate whether a fire has been started
   D. call the police from the closest police alarm box or telephone

13. When responding to an alarm, officers are not to talk to chauffeurs driving the apparatus except to give orders or directions.
Of the following, the BEST justification for this rule is that it
   A. gives the officer an opportunity to make preliminary plans for handling the fire problem
   B. enables the chauffeur to concentrate on driving the apparatus
   C. maintains the proper relationship between the ranks while on duty
   D. permits the officer to observe the chauffeur's skill, or lack of skill, in driving the apparatus

14. The approved method of reporting a fire by telephone in the city is FIRST to dial the
   A. central headquarters of the fire department
   B. county headquarters of the fire department
   C. local fire station house
   D. telephone operator

15. Doors in theatres and other places of public assembly usually open outward.
The MAIN reason for this requirement is, in the event of fire, to
   A. provide the widest possible passageway for escape of the audience
   B. prevent a panic-stricken audience from jamming the doors in a closed position
   C. indicate to the audience the safe direction of travel
   D. prevent unauthorized persons from entering the building

16. Some gas masks provide protection to the user by filtering out from the air certain harmful gases present in the atmosphere.
A mask of this type would NOT be suitable in an atmosphere containing
   A. heavy, black smoke
   B. a filterable gas under pressure
   C. insufficient oxygen to sustain life
   D. more than one filterable harmful gas

17. Fire prevention inspections should be conducted at
    irregular hours or intervals.
    The BEST justification for this irregularity is that
    it permits the firemen to
    A. make inspections when they have free time
    B. see the inspected establishments in their normal
       condition and not in their *dressed-up* condition
    C. avoid making inspections at times which would be
       inconvenient for the inspected establishments
    D. concentrate their inspectional activities on those
       establishments which present the greatest fire
       hazard

18. Firemen are instructed to turn on the gas supply to a
    house which was turned off by them during a fire.
    Of the following, the MOST important reason for this
    prohibition is that
    A. the fire may have made the gas meters inaccurate
    B. unburned gas may escape from open gas jets
    C. the utility company's employees may object to fire-
       men performing their work
    D. firemen should not do anything which is not directly
       related to extinguishing fires

19. A fireman, in uniform, performing inspectional duty,
    comes upon a group of young men assaulting a policeman.
    The fireman goes to the aid of the policeman and, in
    the course of the struggle, receives some minor injuries.
    The action of the fireman in this situation was
    A. *proper*, chiefly because members of the uniformed
       forces must *stick together*
    B. *improper*, chiefly because people in the neighborhood,
       as a result, might refuse to cooperate with the fire
       department's various programs
    C. *proper*, chiefly because all citizens have an obliga-
       tion to assist policemen in the performance of their
       duty
    D. *improper*, chiefly because the fire department lost
       the services of the fireman while he was recovering
       from his injuries

20. Members of the fire department may not make a speech on
    fire department matters without the approval of the fire
    commissioner. Requests for permission must be accom-
    panied by a copy or summary of the speech.
    The MAIN reason for this requirement is to
    A. determine whether the member is engaged in political
       activities which are forbidden
    B. reduce the chance that the public will be misinformed
       about fire department policies or procedures
    C. provide the department with a list of members who can
       serve in the department's speakers' bureau
    D. provide the department with information about the
       off-duty activities of the members

21. For a fireman to straddle a hose line while holding the nozzle and directing water on fires is a
    A. *good* practice, mainly because better balance is obtained by the fireman
    B. *poor* practice, mainly because the fireman directing the hose may trip over the hose
    C. *good* practice, mainly because better control over the hose line is obtained
    D. *poor* practice, mainly because the hose might whip about and injure the fireman

22. Fireman are required to wear steel-reinforced innersoles inside their rubber boots.
    The MAIN purpose of these innersoles is to
    A. make the boots more durable and long-lasting
    B. protect the fireman's feet from burns from smoldering objects or embers
    C. protect the fireman's feet from injury from falling objects
    D. protect the fireman's feet from nails or other sharp objects

23. Promoting good relations with the public is an important duty of every member of the fire department.
    Of the following, the BEST way for a fireman to promote good public relations generally is to
    A. become active in civic and charitable organizations
    B. be well-dressed, clean, and neat on all occasions
    C. write letters to newspapers explaining the reasons for departmental procedures
    D. perform his duties with efficiency, consideration, and courtesy

24. Fireman are advised to avoid wearing rings on their fingers.
    The MAIN reason for this advice is that the rings have a tendency to
    A. be damaged during operations at fires
    B. scratch persons receiving first aid treatment
    C. catch on objects and injure the wearer
    D. scratch furniture and/or other valuable objects

25. Suppose that you are a fireman on housewatch duty when a civilian enters the firehouse. He introduces himself as a Canadian fireman visiting the country to study American firefighting methods. He asks you for permission to ride on the fire apparatus when it responds to alarms in order to observe operations at first hand.
    You know that it is against departmental policy to permit civilians to ride apparatus without written permission from headquarters.
    In this situation, you should

A. refuse the request but suggest that he follow the apparatus in his own car when it responds to an alarm
B. call headquarters and request permission to permit the visitor to ride the apparatus
C. refuse the request and suggest that he apply to headquarters for permission
D. refuse the request and suggest that he should return the next time that the fire department holds open house

## KEY (CORRECT ANSWERS)

1. C
2. C
3. C
4. D
5. B

6. D
7. A
8. D
9. B
10. C

11. A
12. C
13. B
14. D
15. B

16. C
17. B
18. B
19. C
20. B

21. D
22. D
23. D
24. C
25. C

# TEST 2

DIRECTIONS: Each question or incomplete statement is followed by several suggested answers or completions. Select the one that BEST answers the question or completes the statement. *PRINT THE LETTER OF THE CORRECT ANSWER IN THE SPACE AT THE RIGHT.*

1. Suppose that a factory has stored within it a number of substances.
   If the owner asked you which of the following is MOST likely to constitute a fire hazard, you would reply
   A. sodium chloride
   B. calcium chloride
   C. chromium
   D. silicon dioxide
   E. absorbent cotton

   1.___

2. Vertical openings such as dumbwaiters, elevators, and chutes are the bane of a firefighting force.
   This condition arises MAINLY because the existence of such openings in a burning building facilitates
   A. accidental falls
   B. generation of gases
   C. spread of the fire
   D. the perpetration of arson
   E. collapse of wall supports

   2.___

3. Suppose that a neighbor, knowing that you are a fireman, were to ask you whether there is more hazard in the use of kerosene than gasoline at ordinary room temperature.
   You should reply that there is MORE hazard in the use of
   A. *kerosene*, because it gives off dangerous quantities of explosive vapors which are lighter than air
   B. *gasoline*, because gasoline vapor may flow along the floor and be ignited at a long distance from its point of origin
   C. *kerosene*, because its flash point is very low
   D. *gasoline*, particularly because when ignited it burns
   E. *kerosene*, because its vapors are not easily detected by the sense of smell and yet may be present in dangerous quantities

   3.___

4. Steel supporting beams in buildings often are surrounded by a thin layer of concrete to keep the beams from becoming hot and collapsing during a fire.
   The one of the following statements which BEST explains how collapse is prevented by this arrangement is that concrete
   A. becomes stronger as its temperature is increased
   B. acts as an insulating material
   C. protects the beam from rust and corrosion
   D. reacts chemically with steel at high temperatures

   4.___

5. It has been suggested that property owners should be charged a fee each time the fire department is called to extinguish a fire on their property.
Of the following, the BEST reason for *rejecting* this proposal is that
   A. delay in calling the fire department may result
   B. many property owners don't occupy the property they own
   C. property owners may resent such a charge as they pay real estate taxes
   D. it may be difficult to determine on whose property a fire started

6. A fireman inspecting buildings in a commercial area came to one whose outside surface appeared to be of natural stone. The owner told the fireman that it was not necessary to inspect his building as it was *fireproof*. The fireman, however, completed his inspection of the building.
Of the following, the BEST reason for continuing the inspection is that
   A. stone buildings catch fire as readily as wooden buildings
   B. the fire department cannot make exceptions in its inspection procedures
   C. the building may have been built of imitation stone
   D. interiors and contents of stone buildings can catch fire

7. From the viewpoint of fire safety, the CHIEF advantage of a foam rubber mattress compared to a cotton mattress is that the foam rubber mattress
   A. is slower burning
   B. generates less heat when burning
   C. does not smolder
   D. is less subject to water damage

8. The one of the following methods of storing large piles of coal which is UNDESIRABLE because it increases the danger of spontaneous heating is
   A. making the pile compact by use of a roller
   B. storing the coal on smooth, solid ground
   C. covering the sides and top of the pile with road tar
   D. mixing coal of various sizes in one pile

9. After a fire has been extinguished, every effort should be made to determine how the fire started.
Of the following, the CHIEF reason for determining the origin of the fire is to
   A. reduce the amount of damage caused by the fire
   B. determine how the fire should have been fought
   C. eliminate causes of fire in the future
   D. explain delays in fighting the fire
   E. improve salvage operations

10. A partially filled gasoline drum is a more dangerous fire hazard than a full one.
Of the following, the BEST justification for this statement is that
   A. a partially filled gasoline drum contains relatively little air
   B. gasoline is difficult to ignite
   C. when a gasoline drum is full, the gasoline is more explosive
   D. gasoline vapors are more explosive than gasoline itself
   E. air is not combustible

11. Chief officers shall instruct their aides that, when transmitting particulars of a fire, they shall include the fact that foods are involved if the fire involves premises where foodstuffs are sold or stored.
Of the following, the BEST justification for this regulation is that, when foodstuffs are involved in a fire,
   A. the fire may reach serious proportions
   B. police protection may be desirable to prevent looting
   C. relatively little firefighting equipment may be needed
   D. there is a strong likelihood of arson
   E. inspection to detect contamination may be desirable

12. The one of the following circumstances concerning a fire which indicates MOST strongly the possibility of arson is that
   A. there was a heavy charring of wood around the point of origin of the fire
   B. three fires apparently broke out simultaneously in different parts of the building
   C. the heat was so intense that glass in the building became molten and fused
   D. when the firemen arrived, the smoke was very heavy
   E. the fire apparently started in an oil-soaked mop

13. As a fireman, you may be assigned to inspect buildings for fire hazards.
The one of the following MOST appropriately used for fire-retardant coating of wood is
   A. varnish          B. shellac          C. wood stain
   D. lacquer          E. white wash

14. A fireman taking some clothing to a dry cleaner in his neighborhood, noticed that inflammable cleaning fluid was stored in a way which created a fire hazard. The fireman called this to the attention of the proprietor, explaining the danger involved.
This method of handling the situation was
   A. *bad*; the fireman should not have interfered in a matter which was not his responsibility

B. *good*; the proprietor would probably remove the hazard and be more careful in the future
C. *bad*; the fireman should have reported the situation to the fire inspector's office without saying anything to the proprietor
D. *good*; since the fireman was a customer, he should treat the proprietor more leniently than he would treat other violators
E. *bad*; the fireman should have ordered the proprietor to remove the violation immediately and issued a summons

15. A fireman caught a civilian attempting to re-enter a burning building despite several warnings to stay outside of the fire lines. The civilian insisted frantically that he must save some very valuable documents from the fire. The fireman then called a policeman to remove civilian.
The fireman's action was
   A. *wrong*; it is bad public relations to order people about
   B. *right*; the fireman is charged with the responsibility of protecting lives
   C. *wrong*; the fireman should have explained to the civilian why he should not enter the building
   D. *right*; civilians must be excluded from the fire zone
   E. *wrong*; every person has a right to risk his own life as he sees fit

16. The one of the following combustible materials whose tendency to spontaneous heating is very slight is
   A. lamp black     B. fish meal     C. cotton seed
   D. waste paper    E. roofing felt

Questions 17-19.

DIRECTIONS: Questions 17 through 19, inclusive, are based on the following paragraph.

*A flameproof fabric is defined as one which, when exposed to small sources of ignition, such as sparks or smoldering cigarettes, does not burn beyond the vicinity of the source of ignition. Cotton fabrics are the materials commonly used that are considered most hazardous. Other materials, such as acetate rayons and linens, are somewhat less hazardous, and woolens and some natural silk fabrics, even when untreated, are about the equal to the average treated cotton fabric insofar as flame spread and ease of ignition are concerned. The method of application is to immerse the fabric in a flameproofing solution. The container used must be large enough so that all the fabric is thoroughly wet and there are no folds which the solution does not penetrate.*

17. According to the above paragraph, a flameproof fabric is one which
    A. is unaffected by heat and smoke
    B. resists the spread of flames when ignited
    C. burns with a cold flame
    D. cannot be ignited by sparks or cigarettes
    E. may smolder but cannot burn

18. According to the above paragraph, woolen fabrics which have not been flameproofed are as likely to catch fire as _____ fabrics.
    A. *treated* silk         B. *treated* acetate rayon
    C. *untreated* linen      D. *untreated* synthetic
    E. *treated* cotton

19. In the method described above, the flameproofing solution is BEST applied to the fabric by _____ the fabric.
    A. sponging      B. spraying      C. dipping
    D. brushing      E. sprinkling

20. The daily peak time for the number of fires in the city, in general,
    A. varies from day to day
    B. is about 9 A.M.
    C. is at about 5 P.M.
    D. is at about 1 A.M.
    E. varies from season to season

21. The sharp increase in the annual dollar fire loss in the United States during and immediately following World War II was due MAINLY to the
    A. increase in population
    B. marketing of new products with high fire hazard
    C. pressure of war production
    D. greater concentration of property values
    E. higher valuation of property

22. The real problem in fire prevention and protection in the presence of radioactive isotopes is based on the fact that the radioactivity of an element or compound
    A. is not diminished by change of the compound by fire or explosion
    B. increases directly as the intensity of fire in establishments using them
    C. causes a compound to vaporize, melt, or oxidize more readily
    D. is reduced significantly if control by means of suitable sprays or extinguishers is immediately applied
    E. increases with the decrease in the size of the radioactive particle

23. The MOST prolific structural cause of fire-spread in non-fireproof hotels, other than that of unprotected vertical openings, is
    A. inadequate auxiliary appliances and alarm systems
    B. unprotected horizontal openings
    C. poorly protected storage of paints, oils, wastes, and volatile mixtures
    D. inadequately protected linen and furniture storage rooms
    E. large dining areas, cocktail lounges, etc., with combustible decorations

24. Of the following metals, the one which is LEAST acceptable as a non-sparking metal for tools is
    A. hardened copper     B. bronze
    C. brass               D. copper alloys

25. Of the heating defects responsible for hotel fires, the MAJOR defect is
    A. defective flues         B. overheated appliances
    C. defective appliances    D. inadequate clearance

---

# KEY (CORRECT ANSWERS)

1. D
2. C
3. B
4. B
5. A

6. D
7. C
8. D
9. C
10. D

11. E
12. B
13. E
14. B
15. B

16. A
17. B
18. E
19. C
20. C

21. C
22. A
23. B
24. C
25. A

# FIRE SCIENCE
## EXAMINATION SECTION

DIRECTIONS FOR THIS SECTION:
Each question or incomplete statement is followed by several suggested answers or completions. Select the one that BEST answers the question or completes the statement. *PRINT THE LETTER OF THE CORRECT ANSWER IN THE SPACE AT THE RIGHT.*

## **TEST 1**

1. When fighting fires in passenger airplanes, firemen usually attempt to rescue passengers and crew before putting out the flames.
   To accomplish the rescue, it is usually BEST to approach the burning airplane from the side
   A. where the fire is hottest
   B. where the generators are located
   C. where the reserve gas tanks are located
   D. which is nearest the fire apparatus
   E. where the doors are located

2. As soon as the engine pulled up to the scene of the fire, a fireman, axe in hand, jumped off, ran to the door, and broke it in.
   The action of this fireman was
   A. *wise;* he prepared the way for the hose men to move in
   B. *unwise;* he should have broken a window
   C. *wise;* speed is important in the rescue of fire victims
   D. *unwise;* he should have tried the door first to see if it was unlocked
   E. *unwise;* he should have first tried to locate the owner

3. Fire fighters generally try to confine a fire to its point of origin.
   Of the following, the MOST important result of doing this is that
   A. property damage is minimized
   B. shorter hose lines are required
   C. immediate risks to fire forces are reduced
   D. fewer firemen are needed on the fire fighting forces
   E. damage to fire equipment is reduced

4. Suppose you, a newly assigned fireman, are shown how to do a certain task by your lieutenant. You start the job but as you progress you encounter many difficulties.
   Of the following, the MOST desirable step for you to take at this time is to
   A. ask your lieutenant to suggest an easier way of doing the job
   B. speak to your lieutenant about your difficulties
   C. continue the task as well as you can
   D. stop what you are doing and do something else
   E. ask one of the older members for instructions

5. The one of the following statements about electric fuses that is MOST valid is that they
   A. should never be replaced by coins
   B. may be replaced by coins for a short time if there are no fuses available
   C. may be replaced by coins provided that the electric company is notified

D. may be replaced by coins provided that care is taken to avoid overloading the circuit
E. may be replaced only by a licensed electrician

6. A principal of an elementary school made a practice of holding fire drills on the last Friday of each month, just before normal dismissal.
In general, conducting fire drills according to a regular schedule, is
   A. *good;* pupils are more cooperative when fire drills result in early dismissal
   B. *bad;* fire drills should not be expected
   C. *good;* panic is avoided if the pupils know that there isn't a fire
   D. *bad;* holding fire drills once or twice a term is sufficient
   E. *good;* teachers can plan to finish their lessons before the fire drill

7. It has been observed that persons in a burning building generally attempt to escape through the means provided for normal entry and exit.
Of the following, the MOST likely reason for this is that
   A. people generally feel safer in groups
   B. people usually don't know the location of fire exits
   C. emergency exits are not easily reached
   D. the use of emergency exits requires physical dexterity
   E. people tend to behave in accordance with their habits

8. A fireman inspecting a small retail store for hazardous fire conditions is told by the owner that the whole inspection procedure is a waste of time and money.
Of the following, the BEST action for the fireman to take is to
   A. question the owner to prove to him how little he knows about the problem
   B. explain to the owner the benefits of the inspection program
   C. curtly tell the owner that he is entitled to his opinions and continue the inspection
   D. ask the owner if he can suggest a better way of preventing fires
   E. continue the inspection without answering the owner

9. The officer in charge of operations at a fire has the responsibility for "sizing up" or evaluating the fire situation.
Of the following factors, the one which would have LEAST influence on the "size up" is the
   A. time of fire      B. contents of the building on fire
   C. insurance coverage  D. amount of smoke
   E. height of the building on fire

10. When searching burning houses, firemen usually pay particular attention to closets and the space under beds and furniture.
Of the following, the MOST important reason for this practice is that *often*
   A. information about the cause of the fire may be found there
   B. children try to hide from danger in those places
   C. dogs and cats are forgotten in the excitement

D. people mistake closet doors for exits
E. valuable possessions may be found there
11. When fighting fires, it is MOST important for a fireman to realize that in the winter
    A. the water supply is more plentiful
    B. cold water is more effective than warm water in putting out fires
    C. snow conditions may delay fire apparatus
    D. water in hose lines not in use may freeze
    E. many fires are caused by heating equipment
12. Suppose you are a fireman making an inspection of a factory. During the inspection, the factory manager asks you a technical question which you cannot answer.
    Of the following, the BEST procedure for you to follow is to
    A. tell him you are not there to answer his questions but to make an inspection
    B. guess at the answer so that he won't doubt your competency
    C. tell him you don't know the answer but that you will look it up and notify him
    D. give him the title of a textbook that probably would contain the information
    E. change the subject by asking him a question
13. While performing building inspections, a fireman finds a janitor in the basement checking for a gas leak by holding a lighted match to the gas pipes.
    Of the following, the fireman's FIRST action *should be* to
    A. reprimand the janitor for endangering life and property
    B. explain the hazards of this action to the janitor
    C. report the janitor to his superior as incompetent
    D. tell the janitor to put out the match
    E. issue a summons for this action
14. A fireman has complained to his lieutenant about drafts from loosely fitting windows in the bunk area of the firehouse. Several weeks pass and the condition has not been corrected.
    Of the following, the MOST appropriate action for the fireman to take at this time is to
    A. ask the captain whether the lieutenant has reported his complaint
    B. ask his lieutenant how the matter is coming along
    C. circulate a petition among the other members of the company to have this condition corrected
    D. write to the office of the Chief of the Department about the matter
    E. write to the Uniformed Firemen's Association about the matter
15. In answering an alarm, it is found that the fire has been caused by "smoking in bed," setting fire to the mattress. The man is safe but the mattress is blazing.
    After putting out the flames, the mattress should be
    A. turned over and left on the bed
    B. immediately ripped open and the stuffing examined
    C. taken into the bathroom and soaked in the tub
    D. taken to the street below and the stuffing examined
    E. thoroughly soaked in place by means of a hose stream

TEST 1

16. As a probationary fireman, you get an idea for improving     16. ...
    equipment maintenance and mention it to an older member.  At
    the next company inspection, your superior officer publicly
    praises this man for his excellent suggestion but it is
    your idea.
    The action you should take in this situation is to
       A. tell the other members of the company the whole story
          after the inspection
       B. ask for advice from another older member
       C. forget about the incident since this man will probably
          be helpful to you in return
       D. do nothing about it but next time make your suggestions
          to your superior officer
       E. warn the older man that you won't permit him to get
          away with stealing your idea
17. The first rule of hosemen is to place themselves in the     17. ...
    line of travel of a fire whenever possible.
    Of the following, the MOST valid reason for this rule is
    that
       A. danger to firemen from heat and smoke is reduced
       B. shorter hose lines are necessary
       C. the opportunity to control the fire is increased
       D. danger to fire equipment is reduced
       E. life-saving rescues are facilitated
18. Of the following types of fires, the one which presents     18. ...
    the GREATEST danger from poisonous gas fumes is a fire in
    a warehouse storing
       A. drugs         B. groceries        C. cotton cloth
       D. paper         E. unfinished furniture
19. Fires in prisons and mental hospitals are particularly      19. ...
    dangerous to life CHIEFLY because their inmates *usually*
       A. live under crowded conditions
       B. live in locked rooms
       C. ignore fire safety regulations
       D. deliberately start fires
       E. cannot be trusted with fire extinguishers
20. In fighting fires, use the smallest amount of water suf-    20. ...
    ficient to put out the fire.
    In general, this advice is
       A. *good;* MAINLY because it will conserve the water supply
       B. *bad;* MAINLY because it will increase the danger of the
          fire spreading
       C. *good;* MAINLY because it will require the use of fewer
          hose lines
       D. *bad;* MAINLY because it will take longer to put out the
          fire
       E. *good;* MAINLY because it will reduce water damage
21. The Fire Department has criticized the management of        21. ...
    several hotels for failure to call the Fire Department
    promptly when fires are discovered.
    The MOST probable reason for this delay by the management
    is that
       A. fire insurance rates are affected by the number of
          fires reported
       B. most fires are extinguished by the hotels' staff be-
          fore the Fire Department arrives
       C. hotel guests frequently report fires erroneously

4

D. it is feared that hotel guests will be alarmed by the arrival of fire apparatus
E. many fires smolder for a long time before they are discovered

22. A fireman, taking some clothing to a dry cleaner in his neighborhood, noticed that inflammable cleaning fluid was stored in a way which created a fire hazard. The fireman called this to the attention of the proprietor, explaining the danger involved.
This method of handling the situation was
    A. *bad;* the fireman should not have interfered in a matter which was not his responsibility
    B. *good;* the proprietor would probably remove the hazard and be more careful in the future
    C. *bad;* the fireman should have reported the situation to the fire inspector's office without saying anything to the proprietor
    D. *good;* since the fireman was a customer, he should treat the proprietor more leniently than he would treat other violators
    E. *bad;* the fireman should have ordered the proprietor to remove the violation immediately and issued a summons

23. Traditionally firemen have attacked fires with solid streams of water from hose lines. A current development in fire fighting is to break up the solid water stream as it leaves the hose nozzle into a large number of tiny droplets, called a fog stream.
Of the following claimed advantages of a solid stream, as compared to a fog stream, the one that is MOST valid is that a solid stream
    A. has greater cooling effect per gallon of water
    B. causes less water damage
    C. results in less drain on the water supply
    D. involves less risk of walls collapsing
    E. can be used at a greater distance from the fire

24. A fireman caught a civilian attempting to re-enter a burning building despite several warnings to stay outside of the fire lines. The civilian insisted frantically that he must save some very valuable documents from the fire. The fireman then called a policeman to remove the civilian. The fireman's action was
    A. *wrong;* it is bad public relations to order people about
    B. *right;* the fireman is charged with the responsibility of protecting lives
    C. *wrong;* the fireman should have explained to the civilian why he should not enter the building
    D. *right;* civilians must be excluded from the fire zone
    E. *wrong;* every person has a right to risk his own life as he sees fit

25. A lieutenant orders a fireman to open the windows in a room filled with smoke. He starts with the window nearest the entrance and follows the wall around the room until all the windows are opened. The MOST important reason for using this procedure is that he can
    A. avoid stumbling over furniture
    B. breathe the fresher air near the walls

C. locate unconscious persons at the same time
D. avoid the weakened floor in the middle of the room
E. find his way back to the entrance

# TEST 2

1. Spontaneous combustion may be the reason for a pile of oily rags catching fire.
   In general, spontaneous combustion is the *direct* result of
   A. application of flame
   B. falling sparks
   C. intense sunlight
   D. chemical action
   E. radioactivity

2. In general, firemen are advised not to direct a solid stream of water on fires burning in electrical equipment.
   Of the following, the MOST logical reason for this instruction is that
   A. water is a conductor of electricity
   B. water will do more damage to the electrical equipment than the fire
   C. hydrogen in water may explode when it comes in contact with electric current
   D. water will not effectively extinguish fires in electrical equipment
   E. water may spread the fire to other circuits

3. The height at which a fireboat will float in still water is determined CHIEFLY by the
   A. weight of the water displaced by the boat
   B. horsepower of the boat's engines
   C. number of propellers on the boat
   D. curve the bow has above the water line
   E. skill with which the boat is maneuvered

4. When firemen are working at the nozzle of a hose they usually lean forward on the hose.
   The MOST likely reason for taking this position is that
   A. the surrounding air is cooled, making the firemen more comfortable
   B. a backward force is developed which must be counteracted
   C. the firemen can better see where the stream strikes
   D. the firemen are better protected from injury by falling debris
   E. the stream is projected further

5. In general, the color and odor of smoke will BEST indicate
   A. the cause of the fire
   B. the extent of the fire
   C. how long the fire has been burning
   D. the kind of material on fire
   E. the exact seat of the fire

6. As a demonstration, firemen set up two hose lines identical in every respect except that one was longer than the other. Water was then delivered through these lines from one pump and it was seen that the stream from the longer hose line had a shorter "throw."
   Of the following, the MOST valid explanation of this difference in "throw" is that the
   A. air resistance to the water stream is proportional to the length of hose

B. time required for water to travel through the longer hose is greater than for the shorter one
C. loss due to friction is greater in the longer hose than in the shorter one
D. rise of temperature is greater in the longer hose than in the shorter one
E. longer hose line probably developed a leak at one of the coupling joints

7. Of the following toxic gases, the one which is MOST dangerous because it cannot be seen and has no odor is
   A. ether          B. carbon monoxide     C. chlorine
   D. ammonia        E. cooking gas

8. You are visiting with some friends when their young son rushes into the room with his clothes on fire. You immediately wrap him in a rug and roll him on the floor.
   The MOST important reason for your action is that the
   A. flames are confined within the rug
   B. air supply to the fire is reduced
   C. burns sustained will be third degree, rather than first degree
   D. whirling action will put out the fire
   E. boy will not suffer from shock

9. A fireman discovers a man bleeding moderately from a gash wound about 1 1/2" long in his right arm.
   Of the following, the FIRST action this fireman should take is to
   A. apply a tourniquet between the wound and the heart
   B. permit the bleeding to continue for a while in order to cleanse the wound
   C. give the injured man a blood transfusion
   D. apply pressure at the nearest pressure point between the wound and the heart
   E. apply pressure directly to the wound with compress

10. In treating burns, the LEAST important of the following goals is to
    A. prevent blistering      B. prevent infection
    C. relieve pain            D. prevent shock
    E. prevent tissue damage

11. One purpose of building inspections is to enable the Fire Department to plan its operations before a fire starts.
    This statement is
    A. *incorrect;* no two fires are alike
    B. *correct;* many fire-fighting problems can be anticipated
    C. *incorrect;* fires should be prevented, not extinguished
    D. *correct;* the Fire Department should have detailed plans for every possible emergency
    E. *incorrect;* fires are not predictable

12. A recent study showed that false alarms occur mostly between noon and 1 P.M., and between 3 and 10 P.M. The MOST likely explanation of these results is many false alarms are sent by
    A. school children    B. drunks      C. mental defectives
    D. arsonists          E. accident victims

13. A superintendent of a large apartment house discovered a fire in a vacant apartment. After notifying the Fire Department, he went to the basement and shut off the central

7

air conditioning system. In so doing, the superintendent acted
- A. *wisely;* escape of gas fumes from the air conditioning system was prevented
- B. *unwisely;* the fire would have been slowed down by the cooling effect of the air conditioning
- C. *wisely;* the air conditioning system was protected from damage by the fire
- D. *unwisely;* the air conditioning system would have expelled smoke from the building
- E. *wisely;* spread of the fire by means of a forced draft was prevented

14. Large woolen blankets are unsatisfactory as emergency life nets CHIEFLY because they usually are
    - A. too small to catch a falling person
    - B. difficult to grasp since they have no handles
    - C. difficult to maneuver into position
    - D. not circular in shape as are regular life nets
    - E. not tensile enough to hold falling bodies

15. Fires can be fought most effectively from close range. Of the following, the CHIEF obstacle preventing firemen from getting close to fires is the
    - A. heat of the fire
    - B. height of most city buildings
    - C. distance from the hydrants of most fires
    - D. inaccessible location of most fires
    - E. wide area covered by the fire

16. While in training school, your class assists at a fire. After the fire is under control, an older fireman, who has no authority over you, tells you that he was watching you perform your tasks. He suggests certain changes in your methods.
    Of the following, your BEST course of action is to
    - A. thank him for his advice and tell him you will use it when you find yourself in difficulty
    - B. discuss the changes he proposes with him and then take the action which seems best to you
    - C. listen to his analysis of the situation and follow his advice
    - D. thank him for his advice and bring up his suggestions at the next class session
    - E. listen to him, thank him courteously, but ignore his suggestions

17. A member of a fire rescue company discovers an injured man at the foot of the stairway on the third floor of a burning building. The man, who fell down the stairs, complains of pains in his back. The fire is a considerable distance away, in the cellar, but the area is rapidly filling with smoke.
    Of the following, the BEST course for the fireman to follow is to
    - A. give the injured man first aid on the spot and leave him there
    - B. carefully carry the injured man to safety
    - C. stay with the injured man to make certain that the fire doesn't reach him

D. find his officer and ask for instructions
E. go for medical assistance

18. Listed below are five operating characteristics of most automatic sprinkler systems.
The one characteristic of those listed which is LEAST desirable is that automatic sprinkler systems
    A. operate only in the fire zone
    B. go into operation soon after a fire starts
    C. operate in the midst of high heat and smoke
    D. continue operating after the fire is extinguished
    E. operate in inaccessible places

18. ...

Questions 19-22.
DIRECTIONS: Questions 19 through 22 inclusive are based on the following paragraph.

Ventilation, as used in fire fighting operations, means opening up a building or structure in which a fire is burning to release the accumulated heat, smoke and gases. Lack of knowledge of the principles of ventilation on the part of firemen may result in unnecessary punishment due to ventilation being neglected or improperly handled. While ventilation itself extinguishes no fires, when used in an intelligent manner, it allows firemen to get at the fire more quickly, easily and with less danger and hardship.

19. According to the above paragraph, the MOST important result of failure to apply the principles of ventilation at a fire may be
    A. loss of public confidence
    B. disciplinary action       C. waste of water
    D. excessive use of equipment   E. injury to firemen

19. ...

20. It may be inferred from the above paragraph that the CHIEF advantage of ventilation is that it
    A. eliminates the need for gas masks
    B. reduces smoke damage
    C. permits firemen to work closer to the fire
    D. cools the fire
    E. enables firemen to use shorter hose lines

20. ...

21. Knowledge of the principles of ventilation, as defined in the above paragraph, would be LEAST important in a fire in a
    A. tenement house   B. grocery store   C. ship's hold
    D. lumberyard       E. office building

21. ...

22. We may conclude from the above paragraph that, for the well-trained and equipped fireman, ventilation is
    A. a simple matter            B. rarely necessary
    C. relatively unimportant     D. a basic tool
    E. sometimes a handicap

22. ...

Questions 23-25.
DIRECTIONS: Questions 23 through 25 are based on the following paragraph.

A fire of undetermined origin started in the warehouse shed of a flour mill. Although there was some delay in notifying the Fire Department, they practically succeeded in bringing the fire under control when a series of dust explosions occurred which caused the fire to spread and the main building was destroyed. The Fire Department's efforts were considerably handicapped because it was undermanned, and the water pressure in the vicinity was inadequate.

23. From the information contained in the above paragraph, it     23. ...
    is MOST accurate to state that the cause of the fire was
       A. suspicious      B. unknown         C. accidental
       D. arson           E. spontaneous combustion
24. In the fire described above, the MOST important cause of     24. ...
    the fire spreading to the main building was the
       A. series of dust explosions
       B. delay in notifying the Fire Department
       C. inadequate water pressure     D. lack of manpower
       E. wooden construction of the building
25. In the fire described above, the Fire Department's efforts   25. ...
    were handicapped CHIEFLY by
       A. poor leadership              B. out-dated apparatus
       C. uncooperative company employees
       D. insufficient water pressure   E. poorly trained men

# TEST 3

1. The MOST important reason for having members of the Fire      1. ...
   Department wear uniforms is to
      A. indicate the semi-military nature of the Fire Department
      B. build morale and esprit de corps of members
      C. identify members on duty to the public and other members
      D. provide clothing suitable for the work performed
2. Of the following types of fires, the one which is likely      2. ...
   to have the LEAST amount of damage from water used in extinguishment is a fire in a(n)
      A. rubber toy factory        B. retail hardware store
      C. outdoor lumber yard       D. furniture warehouse
3. When fighting fires involving unevenly piled goods, it is     3. ...
   particularly important that the water streams penetrate
   all parts of the goods exposed to the fire.
   The position of hose nozzle which will provide maximum
   water penetration is
      A. above the fire    B. to the side away from the wind
      C. on level with the fire
      D. to the side facing the wind
4. In cases of suspected arson, it is important that firemen     4. ...
   engaged in fighting the fire remember conditions that
   existed at the time of their arrival. Particular attention
   should be given to all doors and windows.
   The MAIN justification for this statement is that knowledge
   of the condition of the doors and windows may indicate
      A. where the fire started    B. who set the fire
      C. the best way to ventilate the building
      D. that someone wanted to prevent extinguishment
5. While visiting the lounge of a hotel, a fireman discovers     5. ...
   a fire which apparently has been burning for some time and
   is rapidly spreading.
   Of the following, the FIRST action for him to take is to
      A. find the nearest fire extinguisher and attempt to put
         out the fire
      B. notify the desk clerk of the fire
      C. send an alarm from the nearest street alarm box

TEST 3

    D. run throughout the hotel and warn all occupants to evacuate the building

6. A fireman inspecting buildings in a commercial area, came to one whose outside surface appeared to be of natural stone. The owner told the fireman that it was not necessary to inspect his building as it was "fireproof." The fireman, however, completed his inspection of the building. Of the following, the BEST reason for continuing the inspection is that 6. ...
    A. stone buildings catch fire as readily as wooden buildings
    B. the Fire Department cannot make exceptions in its inspection procedures
    C. the building may have been built of imitation stone
    D. interiors and contents of stone buildings can catch fire

7. The one of the following which is LEAST valid as a reason for the Fire Department to investigate the causes of fire is to 7. ...
    A. determine whether the fire was the result of arson
    B. estimate the amount of loss for insurance purposes
    C. gather information useful in fire prevention
    D. discover violations of the Fire Prevention Code

8. While on duty at a fire, a probationary fireman receives an order from his lieutenant which appears to conflict with the principles of fire-fighting taught at the fire school. Of the following, the BEST course of action for the fireman to take is to follow the order *and*, at a convenient time, after the fire, to 8. ...
    A. discuss the apparent inconsistency with his lieutenant
    B. discuss the apparent inconsistency with another officer
    C. mention this apparent inconsistency in an informal discussion group
    D. ask a more experienced fireman about the apparent inconsistency

9. When fighting fires on piers, the Fire Department frequently drafts salt water from the harbor. The CHIEF advantage of using harbor water instead of relying on water from street mains is that harbor water is 9. ...
    A. less likely to cause water damage
    B. available in unlimited quantities
    C. more effective in extinguishing fires due to its salt content
    D. less likely to freeze in low temperatures due to its salt content

10. Firemen always try to keep to a minimum the amount of water used in extinguishing a fire without reducing the effectiveness of their operation. Of the following reasons for firemen using water sparingly, the LEAST valid is that the use of excess water may 10. ...
    A. dangerously overload a building and cause its collapse
    B. flood the subway system or damage other public utilities
    C. damage the contents of the building on fire
    D. dangerously reduce the water supply of the city

11. A fireman on duty at a theatre who discovers standees obstructing aisles should *immediately* 11. ...
    A. report the situation to his superior officer

        B. order the standees to move out of the aisles
        C. ask the theatre manager to correct the situation
        D. issue a summons to the usher assigned to that area
12. At a fire on the fourth floor of an apartment house, the first engine company to arrive advanced a hose line up the stairway to the third floor before charging the hose with water.
    The MAIN reason that the firemen delayed charging their line is that an empty line
        A. is less likely to whip about and injure firemen
        B. is easier to carry        C. won't leak water
        D. is less subject to damage
13. Suppose the owner of a burning tenement building complains that, although the fire is located on the first floor, firemen are chopping holes in the roof.
    Of the following, the MOST appropriate reason you can give for their action is that the fire can be fought MOST effectively by permitting
        A. smoke and hot gases to escape
        B. firemen to attack the fire from above
        C. firemen to gain access to the building through the holes
        D. immediate inspection of the roof area for extension of the fire
14. The Fire Department always endeavors to purchase the best apparatus and equipment and maintain them in the best condition.
    The MAIN justification for this policy is that
        A. public confidence in the department is increased
        B. failure of equipment at a fire may have serious consequences
        C. replacement of worn out parts is often difficult
        D. the dollar cost to the department is less in the long run
15. The one of the following statements about smoke which is MOST accurate is that smoke is
        A. irritating but not dangerous in itself
        B. irritating and dangerous only because it may reduce the oxygen content of the air breathed
        C. dangerous because it may reduce the oxygen content of the air breathed and often contains toxic gases
        D. dangerous because it supports combustion
16. Suppose that you are a fireman making a routine inspection of a rubber goods factory. During the inspection you discover some minor violation of the Fire Prevention Code. When you call these violations to the attention of the factory owner, he becomes annoyed and tells you that he is the personal friend of high officials in the Fire Department and the city government.
    Under these circumstances, the BEST of the following courses for you to follow is to
        A. summon a policeman to arrest the owner for attempting to intimidate a public official performing his duty
        B. make a very thorough inspection and serve summonses for every possible violation of the Fire Prevention Code

12. ...

13. ...

14. ...

15. ...

16. ...

C. ignore the owner's remarks and continue the inspection in your usual manner
   D. try to obtain from the owner the names and positions of his friends

17. It has been suggested that property owners should be charged a fee each time the Fire Department is called to extinguish a fire on their property.
    Of the following, the BEST reason for rejecting this proposal is that
    A. delay in calling the Fire Department may result
    B. many property owners don't occupy the property they own
    C. property owners may resent such a charge as they pay real estate taxes
    D. it may be difficult to determine on whose property a fire started

18. Standpipe systems of bridges in the city all are the dry pipe type. A dry pipe system has no water in the pipes when not in use; when water is required, it is necessary first to pump water into the system
    The MAIN reason for using a dry standpipe system is to *prevent*
    A. corrosion of the pipes
    B. freezing of water in the pipes
    C. waste of water through leakage
    D. strain on the pumps

19. Assume that you are a fireman on your way home after completing your tour of duty. Just as you are about to enter the subway, a man runs up to you and reports a fire in a house located five blocks away. You recognize the man as a simple-minded but harmless person who frequently loiters around fire houses and at fires.
    Of the following, the BEST action for you to take is to
    A. run to the house to see if there really is a fire
    B. call in an alarm from a nearby telephone
    C. ignore the report because of the man's mental condition
    D. call the police and ask that a radio patrol car investigate the report

20. Sometimes a piece of apparatus is ready to leave the fire station before all members are completely dressed and equipped. In order to avoid delay, these firemen finish dressing on the way to the fire.
    This practice, although sometimes necessary, is *undesirable* MAINLY because
    A. a poor impression is made on the public
    B. the firemen are not able to size up the situation as they approach the fire
    C. the possibility of dropping equipment from the moving apparatus is increased
    D. the danger of injury to the firemen is increased

21. When operating at a pier fire, firemen usually avoid driving their apparatus onto the pier itself.
    The MAIN reason for this precaution is to reduce the possibility that the apparatus will be
    A. delayed in returning to quarters
    B. driven off the end of the pier

C. destroyed by a fire that spreads rapidly
D. in the way of the firemen

22. Pumpers recently purchased by the Fire Department are equipped with enclosed cabs. In the past, Fire Department apparatus was the open type, with no cab or roof.
The MAIN advantage of the *enclosed cab* is that it provides
    A. additional storage space for equipment
    B. a place of shelter for firemen operating in an area of radioactivity
    C. protection for firemen from weather conditions and injury
    D. emergency first aid and ambulance facilities

23. Heavy blizzards greatly increase the problems and work of the Fire Department.
When such a situation occurs, the fire commissioner could *reasonably* be expected to
    A. order members of the Fire Department to perform extra duty
    B. limit parking on city streets
    C. station firemen at fire alarm boxes to prevent the sending of false alarms
    D. prohibit the use of kerosene heaters

24. Regulations of the Fire Department require that when placing hose on a fire wagon care should be taken to avoid bending the hose at places where it had been bent previously.
The MOST important reason for this requirement is that repeated bending of the hose at the same places will cause
    A. kinks in the hose at those places
    B. weakening of the hose at those places
    C. discoloration of the hose at those places
    D. dirt to accumulate and clog the hose at those places

25. While fighting a fire in an apartment when the occupants are not at home, a fireman finds a sum of money in a closet.
Under these circumstances, the fireman should turn over the money to
    A. a responsible neighbor
    B. the desk sergeant of the nearest police station
    C. the superintendent of the apartment house
    D. his superior officer

# TEST 4

1. The leather fire helmet is an important item in a fireman's safety equipment.
In the maintenance of the helmet, it is considered a *GOOD* practice to use
    A. shoe polish on the helmet   B. neatsfoot oil on the helmet
    C. paint remover on the helmet
    D. fast drying, high gloss, synthetic enamel on the helmet

2. A dry-pipe sprinkler system is generally *NOT* considered acceptable protection for an occupancy utlizing flammable liquids *MAINLY* because
    A. corrosion tends to weaken these systems
    B. water is a poor extinguishing agent for flammable liquids
    C. the systems are too expensive for the purpose
    D. a fast spreading fire may be out of control by the time water arrives

Test 4

3. Providing clearance around unprotected steel columns in storage occupancies is a practice which is GENERALLY
   A. *desirable*, chiefly because the quantity of combustibles stored is reduced
   B. *undesirable*, chiefly because flue-like conditions will prevail
   C. *desirable*, chiefly because it will allow water from sprinklers to keep the column wet
   D. *undesirable*, chiefly because stock can topple if not supported

4. In the event of a failure in the electric power supply to a section of the city, each of the following would be expected to remain in service EXCEPT the
   A. voice alarm system
   B. street boxes
   C. public telephones
   D. traffic signal lights

5. Assume that an officer must order a vehicle moved over a hose line. He has the choice of moving the vehicle over the line before or after it is charged.
   *Generally*, he should choose to move the vehicle over the line when it is
   A. *charged*, chiefly because there is less tendency for the vehicle wheels to separate the jacket from the rubber lining
   B. *uncharged*, chiefly because there is less tendency for the hose to burst when the vehicle wheels compress it
   C. *charged*, chiefly because there is less chance of hose butts becoming deformed from the weight of the vehicle
   D. *uncharged*, chiefly because there is less chance of interfering with the functioning of an operational hose stream

6. Jacking up or moving a stalled elevator in an upward direction is a practice NOT generally recommended chiefly because
   A. civilians trapped in the elevator may panic
   B. the car may become activated and move upward suddenly
   C. the car safety may come free, permitting the car to fall
   D. slackened cables may slip off the hoisting sheaves or winding drums

7. Where a back draft explosion condition is a possibility at a fire scene, the one of the following which would generally be the MOST appropriate *initial* action to take is to
   A. cause appropriate ventilation of the fire area
   B. force entry below the fire area from the rear of the structure
   C. require two lines to enter simultaneously and cover one another
   D. open front and rear and have lines make a determined advance to the fire area

8. Where a storefront has been protected by overhead steel rolling-curtain security doors and unusual delay is anticipated in opening these doors, it would generally be LEAST appropriate for a fire officer to
   A. operate from the roof or floor above
   B. gain access to the interior via the cellar
   C. telephone the store owner to bring the necessary keys
   D. breach partitions on either side of the store

9. A pool of gasoline forms on a highway after a gasoline tank truck spill. The time it would take for this pool of gasoline to burn itself out would depend MOST on the
   A. shape of the pool
   B. type of gasoline involved
   C. temperature of the gasoline when spilled
   D. depth of the pool

15

Test 4/KEYS

10. During a firefighting operation, a fireman's eye is accidentally burned by a chemical.
The one of the following *USUALLY* recommended as first aid procedure in such a case is
    A. covering the eye with pads dipped in sodium bicarbonate
    B. wrapping ice in a sterile bandage and placing it over the eye
    C. flushing the eye with fresh clean water
    D. taking no action other than removing the member from the scene

10. ..

## KEYS (CORRECT ANSWERS)

| TEST 1 | TEST 2 | TEST 3 | TEST 4 |
|---|---|---|---|
| 1. E | 1. D | 1. C | 1. D |
| 2. D | 2. A | 2. C | 2. D |
| 3. A | 3. A | 3. A | 3. C |
| 4. B | 4. B | 4. D | 4. D |
| 5. A | 5. D | 5. B | 5. A |
| 6. B | 6. C | 6. D | 6. C |
| 7. E | 7. B | 7. B | 7. A |
| 8. B | 8. B | 8. A | 8. C |
| 9. C | 9. E | 9. B | 9. D |
| 10. B | 10. A | 10. D | 10. C |
| 11. D | 11. B | 11. C | |
| 12. C | 12. A | 12. B | |
| 13. D | 13. E | 13. A | |
| 14. B | 14. E | 14. B | |
| 15. D | 15. A | 15. C | |
| 16. D | 16. D | 16. C | |
| 17. C | 17. B | 17. A | |
| 18. A | 18. D | 18. B | |
| 19. B | 19. E | 19. B | |
| 20. E | 20. C | 20. D | |
| 21. D | 21. D | 21. C | |
| 22. B | 22. D | 22. C | |
| 23. E | 23. B | 23. A | |
| 24. B | 24. A | 24. B | |
| 25. E | 25. D | 25. D | |

# FIRE SCIENCE
## EXAMINATION SECTION
## TEST 1

*Test 1*

DIRECTIONS: Questions 1 through 25 test judgment in situations that a firefighter might meet on the job. Read the question or statement. Each question or statement is followed by four choices. For each question, choose the one BEST answer (A, B, C or D). THEN, PRINT THE LETTER OF THE CORRECT ANSWER IN THE SPACE AT THE RIGHT.

1. Which of these makes the BEST exit door from a large public building? A     1. ...
   A. door that opens out         B. sliding door
   C. revolving door              D. door that opens in
2. The BEST way to delay the spread of a fire from one room     2. ...
   to the next is to
   A. put a hole through the wall between the two rooms
   B. close all windows in both rooms
   C. remove all furniture from both rooms
   D. close the door between the rooms
3. In which of the following one-story buildings would there     3. ...
   most likely be a need for rescue work during a fire? A(n)
   A. high school with 70 students     B. store with 30 customers
   C. nursing home with 70 residents
   D. office building with 70 workers
4. Fires in industrial plants are likely to cause more     4. ...
   damage at night when they are closed than during the day
   when they are open because
   A. it takes firefighters longer to travel to the fire
      at night
   B. fires are noticed sooner during work hours
   C. more arsonists work at night
   D. fire smolders longer when it is cooler
5. Firefighters are getting ready to leave the scene after a     5. ...
   fire when a reporter stops one of them and starts asking
   for details about the fire. The firefighter should tell
   the reporter
   A. that firefighters are not allowed to talk to reporters
   B. to speak to the firefighter's supervisor
   C. to call for an appointment at the firehouse
   D. to check with other reporters at the fire who might
      know the details
6. A firefighter becomes trapped in a third-floor apartment     6. ...
   when the stairs leading to the apartment catch fire. There
   is no fire escape. The BEST thing for the firefighter to do
   is
   A. call for a portable ladder and escape through a window
   B. do nothing until help arrives
   C. jump from a window as quickly as possible
   D. move up to the next floor and wait to be rescued
7. When firefighters give first aid to an unconscious person,     7. ...
   there are several things to check for. Which of the following is NOT one of them?
   A. Are the person's legs twisted in a way which might show
      that bones may be broken?
   B. Is the person breathing?

C. Is there an open container of poison nearby?
D. Did the person try to commit suicide?

8. Mirrors can sometimes be a problem when firefighters are fighting a fire. *Most likely*, this is for the reason that
   A. firefighters may see the fire in the mirror and aim a hose at the mirror instead of at the fire itself
   B. mirrors are expensive and the owner will be angry if one is broken
   C. mirrors are usually heavy so firefighters have to be careful that a mirror doesn't fall on them
   D. mirrors shining on fires make them hotter

9. A firefighter went to work the day after spraining an ankle while playing football. Even though in pain, the firefighter did not want to stay home because he felt needed on the job.
   The *MAIN* reason the firefighter should have stayed home is that the firefighter
   A. should know that no one is that necessary
   B. should get medical attention
   C. might not be able to do his share of the work at a bad fire
   D. was injured off duty and his medical expenses should not be paid by the department

10. Pet dogs sometimes save their masters' lives by waking them up when there is a fire in the house.
    The *most probable* reason that dogs detect fire before their masters is that
    A. dogs are more used to fires than their masters are
    B. dogs are more sensitive to smoke than their masters
    C. dogs always sense danger    D. fires make dogs thirsty

11. During an inspection of a building, it is *least likely* that a firefighter would need to check the
    A. number and location of fire extinguishers
    B. storage areas for combustible material
    C. location of the main electric control switch
    D. location of public washrooms

12. *Which* of these types of fires is *most likely* to have been started on purpose? A fire in a(n)
    A. frying pan         B. mailbox
    C. child's bedroom    D. attic

13. A firefighter chopping a hole in a roof to let smoke out of a building would probably be in *least* danger from the smoke when chopping with the wind blowing
    A. from the firefighter's left
    B. toward the firefighter's face
    C. toward the firefighter's back
    D. from the firefighter's right

14. More firefighters' hands are hurt in summer than in winter.
    That is, *most probably*, for the reason that
    A. things they handle stay hot longer in summer
    B. their hands sweat and things slip more easily in summer
    C. fires burn hotter in summer
    D. they are more likely to remove their protective gloves in summer

Test 1

15. Normally, firefighters try to get as close as possible to the fire they are fighting in order to
    A. find out what started the fire
    B. aim their hoses more accurately
    C. use as little hose as possible
    D. avoid working in thick smoke

16. *Which* of these items would firefighters be *least likely* to need when putting out a fire at the scene of an automobile accident on a city street?
    A. portable ladder          B. portable fire extinguisher
    C. stretcher                D. hose

17. During a fire, a firefighter searching an apartment for victims finds an unconscious woman on her bed.
    It would probably be BEST for the firefighter to *first*
    A. call for a doctor to help the woman
    B. give the woman first aid to make her conscious
    C. move the woman to a safe place
    D. stay with the woman in case she becomes conscious

18. Firefighters often make their way through a burning room by crawling along the floor because
    A. they are less likely to lose their balance
    B. it is easier for them to avoid flying sparks
    C. fires does not often spread along the floor
    D. there is less smoke at floor level

19. In order to enforce the fire safety laws, firefighters must inspect buildings and stores.
    It is *NOT* a good idea for firefighters to let owners of buildings and stores know when they are coming because
    A. firefighters will waste valuable time if the owner breaks the appointment
    B. owners might try to hide fire hazards from the firefighters
    C. firefighters can make the inspection faster without an appointment
    D. owners would be angry if the firefighters were unable to keep the appointment

20. Three fires occurred in an unused school building during one month. The firefighters believed that arsonists had started these fires. The fire department decided to take photographs of the crowds watching any more fires in this school building.
    This was a *good* idea MAINLY because
    A. it would help the fire department's public relations program
    B. it would be useful in getting the city to tear down the building
    C. taking pictures forces the crowd to stand back out of danger
    D. people who set fires sometimes appear in the crowd watching the fire

21. Firefighters probably would be in GREATEST personal danger from a fire in a
    A. florist shop             B. food store
    C. paint store              D. bank

22. Firefighters answering an alarm find a badly beaten and unconscious man lying next to the alarm box.  
    Of the following, the LEAST important thing the firefighters should do is  22. ...
    A. call the police       B. administer first aid
    C. call for an ambulance   D. question nearby residents

23. At several fires in one neighborhood, people threw bricks and bottles at firefighters who were fighting fires.  23. ...
    To try to solve this problem, it would be BEST to
    A. talk to neighborhood leaders to reduce these attacks
    B. refuse to answer alarms in the neighborhood
    C. turn the hoses on the people if it happens again
    D. allow firefighters to carry guns or other weapons

24. Between fires, firefighters clean and check their equipment and vehicles.  24. ...
    They *probably* do this because they want to
    A. look busy when the public visits
    B. have more free time to watch T.V. or play cards
    C. make the neighborhood proud of the appearance of the equipment and vehicles
    D. keep the equipment and vehicles in good working order

25. Storekeepers are *most likely* to be willing to follow fire safety rules if they  25. ...
    A. understand the reasons for them   B. have plenty of time
    C. are ordered to follow them
    D. have just opened up a new store

# TEST 2

DIRECTIONS: This test presents problem situations in which firefighters have to deal with other people. Read the problem, study the answer choices, and pick the one that you think would BEST solve the problem. *THEN, PRINT THE LETTER OF THE CORRECT ANSWER IN THE SPACE AT THE RIGHT.*

1. When a firefighter arrives at a fire, an angry woman screams at the firefighter for not coming sooner. She says it has been nearly half an hour since she called and all her things will be burned up before the firefighter gets the fire out. The firefighter knows it has been only 6 minutes since the alarm came in.  1. ...
   *What* should the firefighter do?
   A. Ask her exactly what time she called and show her it was only 6 minutes ago
   B. Explain to her how firefighters respond to a fire and go on fighting the fire
   C. Tell her that time seems longer when people are worried and she is wrong
   D. Say nothing and get to work on the fire

2. When inspecting a store, a firefighter sees some trash piled on a stair landing. This is a dangerous fire condition which violates the law. The owner says that the last inspector said it was okay because the people can use the elevator instead of the stairs.  2. ...

*What* should the firefighter do *FIRST*?
- A. Ignore the violation since firefighters should back each other up in dealing with the public
- B. Insist that the owner remove the trash since it is a violation of the law
- C. Ask the owner for the name of the previous inspector
- D. Try to find out why the owner wants to store trash on the stair landing

3. While on fire inspection duty, a firefighter enters a restaurant during a very busy lunch time. The owner, who usually goes along on the inspection, says he is short-handed and asks the firefighter to come back when he will be able to show the firefighter around.
*What* should the firefighter do?
- A. Agree to come back later but inform the owner that the inspection will be more strict on the next visit
- B. Go ahead and inspect without the owner since it would be a good time to catch violations
- C. Tell the owner that he will be reported to the authorities
- D. Wait around and inspect when the crowd has gone

4. Firefighters have almost put a fire out in an apartment building. A couple who live on the top floor ask a firefighter if they can go back to their apartment to bring out some clothing.
*What* should the firefighter do?
- A. Let the couple go back to their apartment since the fire is now almost put out
- B. Offer to go back and get the clothes for them
- C. Tell them that only one or the other, not both, can go back inside
- D. Tell them that they will be allowed back into the building when it is completely safe

5. A man rushes into the firehouse telling the firefighters on duty that some children are throwing large rocks off a nearby overpass onto cars passing underneath.
*What* should the firefighters do?
- A. Go to the overpass with the man and stop the children
- B. Report it to their superior officer
- C. Drive the man to the nearest police station
- D. Tell him this is not a firefighter's problem

6. During a dangerous fire, a citizen complains to a firefighter that another firefighter swore at her for being in the way.
*What* should the firefighter do?
- A. Apologize to the citizen and explain in detail why the firefighter acted that way
- B. Nothing, since the citizen is clearly wrong
- C. Tell the woman to report the incident to the supervisor after the fire
- D. Tell the firefighter to apologize or the citizen might make trouble

7. Twenty firefighters in a firehouse want to get a color T.V. to replace their old set which is broken. The other two firefighters who want the set say they can't afford to pay their shares now.

The BEST solution is for the twenty firefighters to
- A. suggest that the two take part-time jobs to pay their shares
- B. forget about buying a set
- C. suggest that the two borrow the money to pay their shares
- D. buy the set without the contribution from the two and allow them more time to pay

8. While inspecting a small store during business hours, a firefighter finds an exit door padlocked. According to fire safety laws, exit doors must not be locked while the store is open for business. The owner says burglars had once come in through that door, and she has put the padlock key on a nail beside the door and shown it to all her employees.
   What should the firefighter do?
   - A. Explain the fire safety law requirements and order the owner to remove the padlock
   - B. Get all the employees to show the firefighter they can open the locked door
   - C. Do nothing because the key is easy to see hanging from the nail
   - D. Tell the owner to give a key to each employee

9. A fire truck is present at a fireworks display to put out any fires which may be started by the fireworks. Just when the fireworks begin, some children start climbing up on the truck.
   What should the firefighters do?
   - A. Show the children around on the truck and explain how it works
   - B. Let only one or two of the children on the truck at a time so that the firefighters can watch them
   - C. Tell the children to get off the truck because they will be in the way if a fire starts
   - D. Move the truck away from the fireworks so the children will not be hurt

10. During a fire a superior officer orders a firefighter to use a certain type of hose. The firefighter feels very strongly that a different type of hose should be used.
    In this situation the firefighter should
    - A. use the different hose if the officer is not watching
    - B. ask the officer the reasons for the order
    - C. do what the officer says and ask for an explanation of the order after the fire is out
    - D. tell the officer that the different hose is better and explain why

11. On a firefighter's first day on the job, a neighborhood resident visits the firehouse and complains to the firefighter that too much of the taxpayers' money is being spent on expensive firefighting equipment.
    The firefighter should say:
    - A. "I'm new on this job so let me get my superior officer to discuss this with you."
    - B. "Since this is the biggest city, it needs the most expensive equipment."

C. "Sir, you are entitled to your opinion even if you are wrong."
D. "Why don't you write a letter of complaint and send it to the Mayor?"

12. A man who is drunk staggers into the firehouse and asks a firefighter for help in getting his car started. It is parked less than a block away.
 *What* should the firefighter do?
 A. Go with him and see what is wrong with the car
 B. Ask him how much he has had to drink
 C. Tell him he shouldn't drive and suggest he take a cab
 D. Offer to take him home

13. A Scout troop visits a firehouse to see the equipment. The firefighters show them around the firehouse.
 Letting Scouts visit the firehouse is
 A. *good*, because firefighters should be kept busy at all times
 B. *bad*, because firefighters should rest when not fighting fires
 C. *good*, because it gives the firefighters a chance to teach the Scouts about fire safety
 D. *bad*, because the Scouts can cause damage to the equipment in the firehouse

14. During an inspection, a building manager becomes angry and tells a firefighter that the fire department does a rotten job and inspections are a waste of time.
 The firefighter should
 A. tell the building manager to clean up his own place first before complaining about the fire department
 B. suggest that they trade jobs for a few hours
 C. try to find out why he feels this way
 D. inform the building manager that the real problem is his bad attitude

15. While putting firefighting equipment back on the fire truck after an apartment fire, a firefighter is falsely accused by a woman of stealing ten dollars she had kept hidden in a sugar bowl in her apartment.
 The firefighter should
 A. ask her why firefighters would risk their lives for ten dollars
 B. give her ten dollars to get her out of the way
 C. tell her she had no business keeping money in a sugar bowl
 D. deny it and tell her she may report it to a superior officer

16. After firefighters had put out a fire in a store, the owner yelled to a firefighter that another firefighter had chopped a hole in the roof and had caused more damage than the fire.
 *What* should the firefighter do *FIRST*?
 A. Tell the owner insurance pays for the damage
 B. Tell the owner to talk to the firefighter who chopped the hole
 C. Explain that it was necessary to make a hole or the firefighter wouldn't have done it

D. Suggest to the owner that he put his complaint in writing to the Fire Commissioner

17. After giving a talk on fire prevention to a group of school children, a firefighter finds that the children have more questions than can be answered in the time allowed.
The firefighter should
    A. answer as many questions as possible and try to arrange another visit
    B. let only the teacher ask questions
    C. stay with the children and answer all their questions
    D. refuse to answer any questions

18. Some neighborhood children have been coming to the firehouse several times a day. They mean to be friendly, but they are keeping the firefighters from doing their work.
The firefighters should
    A. tell them not to come back to the firehouse anymore
    B. call their parents and ask them to keep the children away
    C. suggest that they start visiting the neighborhood police station
    D. ask them to leave because the firefighters have a lot of work to do

19. After a fire has been put out, a firefighter sees a newly appointed firefighter pulling down loose plaster from the ceiling, without wearing a helmet.
The firefighter should
    A. report the new firefighter to the officer in charge
    B. say nothing about what happened
    C. tell the new firefighter to put the helmet on because falling plaster can be dangerous
    D. use force, if necessary, to make the new firefighter wear the helmet

20. While on duty, firefighters usually prepare their meals in the firehouse. Most of the firefighters in a certain firehouse like to take turns cooking meals. However, one of them offers to clean up the dishes rather than having to cook.
The other firefighters should
    A. tell the firefighter that cooking can be fun
    B. agree to the firefighter's offer
    C. let the firefighter make sandwiches instead of meals for dinner
    D. excuse the firefighter from cooking and doing the dishes

## KEYS (CORRECT ANSWERS)

| TEST 1 | | | TEST 2 | |
|---|---|---|---|---|
| 1. A | 11. D | 21. C | 1. D | 11. A |
| 2. D | 12. B | 22. D | 2. B | 12. C |
| 3. C | 13. C | 23. A | 3. B | 13. C |
| 4. B | 14. D | 24. D | 4. D | 14. C |
| 5. B | 15. B | 25. A | 5. B | 15. D |
| 6. A | 16. A | | 6. C | 16. C |
| 7. D | 17. C | | 7. D | 17. A |
| 8. A | 18. D | | 8. A | 18. D |
| 9. C | 19. B | | 9. C | 19. C |
| 10. B | 20. D | | 10. C | 20. B |

# READING COMPREHENSION
## UNDERSTANDING AND INTERPRETING WRITTEN MATERIAL

# EXAMINATION SECTION
## TEST 1

DIRECTIONS: Each question or incomplete statement is followed by several suggested answers or completions. Select the one that BEST answers the question or completes the statement. *PRINT THE LETTER OF THE CORRECT ANSWER IN THE SPACE AT THE RIGHT.*

Questions 1-4.

DIRECTIONS: Questions 1 through 4 are to be answered SOLELY on the basis of the following paragraph.

    The canister-type gas mask consists of a tight-fitting face piece connected to a canister containing chemicals which filter toxic gases and smoke from otherwise breathable air. These masks are of value when used with due regard to the fact that two or three percent of gas in air is about the highest concentration that the chemicals in the canister will absorb and that these masks do not provide the oxygen which is necessary for the support of life. In general, if flame is visible, there is sufficient oxygen for firefighters although toxic gases may be present. Where there is heavy smoke and no flame, an oxygen deficiency may exist. Fatalities have occurred where filter-type canister masks have been used in attempting rescue from manholes, wells, basements, or other locations deficient in oxygen.

1. If the mask described above is used in an atmosphere containing oxygen, nitrogen, and carbon monoxide, we would expect the mask to remove from the air breathed

    A. the nitrogen only
    B. the carbon monoxide only
    C. the nitrogen and the carbon monoxide
    D. none of these gases

1.____

2. According to the above paragraph, when a fireman is wearing one of these masks at a fire where flame is visible, he can GENERALLY feel that as far as breathing is concerned, he is

    A. *safe*, since the mask will provide him with sufficient oxygen to live
    B. *unsafe*, unless the gas concentration is below 2 or 3 percent
    C. *safe*, provided the gas concentration is above 2 or 3 percent
    D. *unsafe*, since the mask will not provide him with sufficient oxygen to live

2.____

3. According to the above paragraph, fatalities have occurred to persons using this type gas mask in manholes, wells, and basements because

    A. the supply of oxygen provided by the mask ran out
    B. the air in those places did not contain enough oxygen to support life
    C. heavy smoke interfered with the operation of the mask
    D. the chemicals in the canister did not function properly

3.____

4. The following shorthand formula may be used to show, in general, the operation of the gas mask described in the above paragraph:
(Chemicals in canister) →(Air + gases) = Breathable Air.
The arrow in the formula, when expressed in words, means MOST NEARLY

   A. replace
   B. are changed into
   C. act upon
   D. give off

Questions 5-7.

DIRECTIONS: Questions 5 through 7 are to be answered SOLELY on the basis of the following paragraph.

The only openings permitted in fire partitions, except openings for ventilating ducts, shall be those required for doors. There shall be but one such door opening unless the provision of additional openings would not exceed in total width of all doorways 25 percent of the length of the wall. The minimum distance between openings shall be three feet. The maximum area for such a door opening shall be 80 square feet, except that such openings for the passage of motor trucks may be a maximum of 140 square feet.

5. According to the above paragraph, openings in fire partitions are permitted ONLY for

   A. doors
   B. doors and windows
   C. doors and ventilation ducts
   D. doors, windows, and ventilation ducts

6. In a fire partition 22 feet long and 10 feet high, the MAXIMUM number of doors 3 feet wide and 7 feet high is

   A. 1    B. 2    C. 3    D. 4

7.

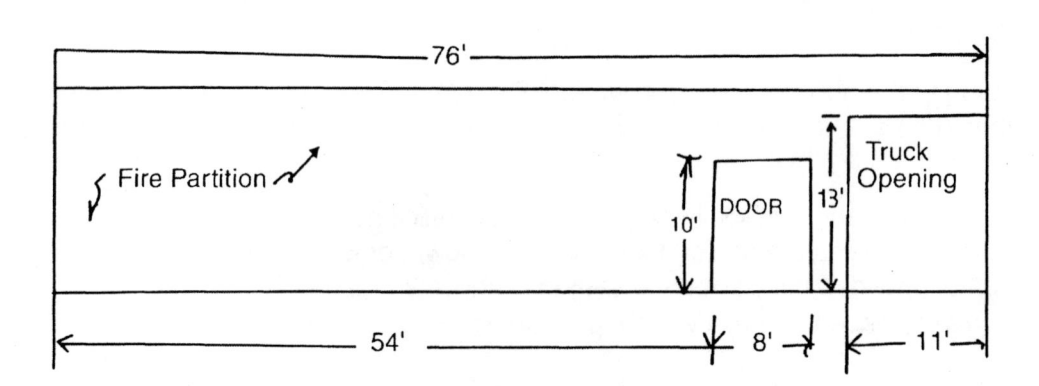

The one of the following statements about the layout shown above that is MOST accurate is that the

A. total width of the openings is too large
B. truck opening is too large
C. truck and door openings are too close together
D. layout is acceptable

Questions 8-11.

DIRECTIONS: Questions 8 through 11 are to be answered SOLELY on the basis of the following paragraph.

Division commanders shall arrange and maintain a plan for the use of hose wagons to transport members in emergencies. Upon receipt of a call for members, the deputy chief of the division from whom the men are called shall have the designated hose wagon placed out of service and prepared for the transportation of members. Hose wagons shall be placed at central assembly points, and members detailed instructed to report promptly to such locations equipped for fire duty. Hose wagons designated shall remain at regular assignments when not engaged in the transportation of members.

8. Preparation of the hose wagon for this special assignment of transporting of members would MOST likely involve  8.____

   A. checking the gas and oil, air in tires, and mechanical operation of the apparatus
   B. removal of hose lines to make room for the members being transported
   C. gathering of equipment which will be needed by the members being transported
   D. instructing the driver on the best route to be used

9. Hose wagons used for emergency transportation of members are placed out of service because they are  9.____

   A. not available to respond to alarms in their own district
   B. more subject to mechanical breakdown while on emergency duty
   C. engaged in operations which are not the primary responsibility of their division
   D. considered reserve equipment

10. Of the following, the BEST example of the type of emergency referred to in the above paragraph is a(n)  10.____

    A. fireman injured at a fire and requiring transportation
    B. subway strike which prevents firemen from reporting for duty
    C. unusually large number of false alarms occurring at one time
    D. need for additional manpower at a fire

11. A *central assembly point*, as used in the above paragraph, would MOST likely be a place  11.____

    A. close to the place of the emergency
    B. in the geographical center of the division
    C. easily reached by the members assigned
    D. readily accessible to the intersection of major highways

Questions 12-14.

DIRECTIONS: Questions 12 through 14 are to be answered SOLELY on the basis of the following paragraph.

A plastic does not consist of a single substance, but is a blended combination of several. In addition to the resin, it may contain various fillers, plasticizers, lubricants, and coloring material. Depending upon the type and quantity of substances added to the binder, the properties, including combustibility, may be altered considerably. The flammability of plastics depends upon the composition and, as with other materials, upon their physical size and condition. Thin sections, sharp edges, or powdered plastics will ignite and burn more readily than the same amount of identical material in heavy sections with smooth surfaces.

12. The one of the following conclusions that is BEST supported by the above paragraph is that the flammability of plastics

    A. generally is high
    B. generally is moderate
    C. generally is low
    D. varies considerably

13. According to the above paragraph, *plastics* can BEST be described as

    A. a trade name
    B. the name of a specific product
    C. the name of a group of products which have some similar and some dissimilar properties
    D. the name of any substance which can be shaped or molded during the production process

14. According to the above paragraph, all plastics contain a

    A. resin
    B. resin and a filler
    C. resin, filler, and plasticizer
    D. resin, filler, plasticizer, lubricant, and coloring material

Questions 15-18.

DIRECTIONS: Questions 15 through 18 are to be answered SOLELY on the basis of the following paragraph.

To guard against overheating of electrical conductors in buildings, an overcurrent protective device is provided for each circuit. This device is designed to open the circuit and cut off the flow of current whenever the current exceeds a predetermined limit. The fuse, which is the most common form of overcurrent protection, consists of a fusible metal element which when heated by the current to a certain temperature melts and opens the circuit.

15. According to the above paragraph, a circuit which is NOT carrying an electric current is a(n)

    A. open circuit
    B. closed circuit
    C. circuit protected by a fuse
    D. circuit protected by an overcurrent protective device other than a fuse

16. As used in the above paragraph, the one of the following which is the BEST example of a   16.____
    *conductor* is a(n)

    A. metal table which comes in contact with a source of electricity
    B. storage battery generating electricity
    C. electrical wire carrying an electrical current
    D. dynamo converting mechanical energy into electrical energy

17. A fuse is NOT   17.____

    A. an overcurrent protective device
    B. the most common form of overcurrent protection
    C. dangerous because it allows such a strong flow of electricity that the wires carrying it may become heated enough to set fire to materials in contact with them
    D. a safety valve

18. According to the above paragraph, the MAXIMUM number of circuits that can be handled by a fuse box containing 6 fuses   18.____

    A. is 3
    B. is 6
    C. is 12
    D. cannot be determined from the information given in the above Paragraph

Questions 19-21.

DIRECTIONS: Questions 19 through 21 are to be answered SOLELY on the basis of the following paragraph.

Unlined linen hose is essentially a fabric tube made of closely woven linen yarn. Due to the natural characteristics of linen, very shortly after water is introduced, the threads swell after being wet, closing the minute spaces between them making the tube practically water tight. This type of hose tends to deteriorate rapidly if not thoroughly dried after use or if installed where it will be exposed to dampness or the weather. It is not ordinarily built to withstand frequent service or for use where the fabric will be subjected to chafing from rough or sharp surfaces.

19. Seepage of water through an unlined linen hose is observed when the water is first turned on.   19.____
    From the above paragraph, we may conclude that the seepage

    A. indicates that the hose is defective
    B. does not indicate that the hose is defective provided that the seepage is proportionate to the water pressure
    C. does not indicate that the hose is defective provided that the seepage is greatly reduced when the hose becomes thoroughly wet
    D. does not indicate that the hose is defective provided that the seepage takes place only at the surface of the hose

20. Unlined linen hose is MOST suitable for use

    A. as a garden hose
    B. on fire department apparatus
    C. as emergency fire equipment in buildings
    D. in fire department training schools

21. The use of unlined linen hose would be LEAST appropriate in a(n)

    A. outdoor lumber yard
    B. non-fireproof office building
    C. department store
    D. cosmetic manufacturing plant

Questions 22-25.

DIRECTIONS: Questions 22 through 25 are to be answered SOLELY on the basis of the following paragraph.

    The velocity of moving water droplets decreases because of aerodynamic drag forces and gravitational effects. In the case of droplets of the sizes more favorable for fire extinguishment, these aerodynamic drag forces, opposing the motion of the droplets, are proportional to the square of the diameters of the droplets and to the square of their velocity. If the initial velocity of the droplets leaving the spray nozzles is resolved into a horizontal and vertical component, the aerodynamic drag affects the horizontal component, and both the aerodynamic drag and gravitation affect the vertical component. In still air, the horizontal velocity of a moving droplet approaches zero. The vertical velocity of the droplet approaches the terminal velocity of a free falling body, which is attained when the aerodynamic drag forces are in equilibrium with the weight of the droplet. The terminal velocity represents the lower limit of the relative velocity of water drops in air. From the standpoint of fire fighting, the absolute velocity of the moving drops is also important, since the horizontal component of the absolute velocity must be sufficient for the droplets to reach the heated area surrounding the fire, and to penetrate the updraft to the seat of the fire.

22. The one of the following forces which would contribute MOST to *aerodynamic drag forces*, as that term is used in the above paragraph, is

    A. friction   B. gravity   C. inertia   D. momentum

23. Assume that water droplets in one stream have four times the diameter and the same initial velocity as droplets in a second stream.
    From the above paragraph, we may conclude that the aerodynamic drag forces on the first stream, compared to the second, initially are _____ as much.

    A. twice              B. four times
    C. eight times        D. sixteen times

24. The horizontal velocity of a moving droplet approaches zero when the

    A. horizontal velocity approaches the terminal velocity of a free falling body
    B. square of the diameter of the droplet is proportional to the square of the velocity of the droplet
    C. vertical velocity is in equilibrium with the aerodynamic drag forces
    D. maximum horizontal reach of the stream is obtained

25. The relative velocity of water droplets is equal to the absolute velocity when      25._____
    A. aerodynamic drag forces are in equilibrium with the weight of the droplets
    B. the square of the diameter of the droplets is proportional to the square of the velocity
    C. the air through which the droplets pass is still
    D. the aerodynamic drag forces equal the gravitational effects on the droplets

## KEY (CORRECT ANSWERS)

| | | | | |
|---|---|---|---|---|
| 1. | B | | 11. | C |
| 2. | B | | 12. | D |
| 3. | B | | 13. | C |
| 4. | C | | 14. | A |
| 5. | C | | 15. | A |
| 6. | A | | 16. | A |
| 7. | B | | 17. | C |
| 8. | B | | 18. | B |
| 9. | A | | 19. | C |
| 10. | D | | 20. | C |

21. A
22. A
23. D
24. D
25. C

# TEST 2

Questions 1-4.

DIRECTIONS: Questions 1 through 4 are to be answered SOLELY on the basis of the following paragraph.

During fire operations, all members shall be constantly alert to possibility of the crime of arson. In the event conditions indicate this possibility, the officer in command shall promptly notify the Fire Marshal. Unauthorized persons shall be prohibited from entering premises and actions of those authorized carefully noted. Members shall refrain from discussion of the fire and prevent disturbance of essential evidence. If necessary, the officer in command shall detail one or more members at location with information for the Fire Marshal upon his arrival.

1. From the above paragraph, it may be inferred that the reason for prohibiting unauthorized persons from entering the fire premises when arson is suspected is to prevent such persons from

    A. endangering themselves in the fire
    B. interfering with the firemen fighting the fire
    C. disturbing any evidence of arson
    D. committing acts of arson

2. The one of the following titles which BEST describes the subject matter of the above paragraph is

    A. TECHNIQUES OF ARSON DETECTION
    B. THE ROLE OF THE FIRE MARSHAL IN ARSON CASES
    C. FIRE SCENE PROCEDURES IN CASES OF SUSPECTED ARSON
    D. EVIDENCE IN ARSON INVESTIGATIONS

3. The one of the following statements that is MOST correct and complete is that the responsibility for detecting signs of arson at a fire belongs to the

    A. Fire Marshal
    B. Fire Marshal and officer in command
    C. Fire Marshal, officer in command, and any members detailed at location with information for the Fire Marshal
    D. members present at the scene of the fire regardless of their rank or position

4. From the above paragraph, it may be inferred that the Fire Marshal USUALLY arrives at the scene of a fire

    A. before the fire companies
    B. simultaneously with the fire companies
    C. immediately after the fire companies
    D. some time after the fire companies

Questions 5-8.

DIRECTIONS: Questions 5 through 8 are to be answered SOLELY on the basis of the following paragraph.

## FIRES

The four types of fires are called Class A, Class B, Class C, and Class D. Examples of Class A fires are paper, cloth, or wood fires. The types of extinguishers used on Class A fires are foam, soda acid, or water. Class B fires are those in burning liquids. They require a smothering action for extinguishment. Carbon dioxide, dry chemical, vaporizing liquid, or foam are the types of extinguishers that are used on burning liquids. Electrical fires, such as in motors and switches, are Class C fires. A non-conducting extinguishing agent must be used for this kind of fire. Therefore, carbon dioxide, dry chemical, or vaporizing liquid extinguishers are used. Fires in motor vehicles are Class D fires; and carbon dioxide, dry chemical, or vaporizing liquid extinguishers should be used on them.

5. According to the information in the above paragraph, a fire in a can full of gasoline would be a Class _____ fire.

   A. D      B. C      C. B      D. A

6. In the above paragraph, the extinguishers recommended are entirely the same for Class _____ and Class _____ fires.

   A. B; D      B. C; D      C. B; C      D. A; B

7. According to the information in the above paragraph, a water extinguisher would MOST likely be suitable for use on which one of the following fires? A(n)

   A. fire in a truck engine
   B. fire in an electrical switch
   C. oil fire
   D. lumber fire

8. According to the information in the above paragraph, dry chemical

   A. should NOT be used on a burning liquid fire
   B. is a conducting extinguishing agent
   C. should NOT be used on a fire in a car
   D. smothers fires to put them out

Questions 9-10.

DIRECTIONS: Questions 9 and 10 are to be answered SOLELY on the basis of the following passage.

One of the greatest hazards to an industrial plant is fire. Consequently, a rigid system should be set up for periodic inspection of all types of fire protective equipment. Such inspections should include water tanks, sprinkler systems, standpipes, hose, fire plugs, extinguishers, and all other equipment used for fire protection. The schedule of inspections should be closely followed and an *accurate* record kept of each piece of equipment inspected and tested.

Along with this scheduled inspection, a careful survey should be made of new equipment needed. Recommendations should be made for replacement of defective and obsolete equipment, as well as the purchase of any additional equipment. As new processes and products are added to the manufacturing system, new fire hazards may be introduced that require individual treatment and possible special extinguishing devices. Plant inspection personnel should be sure to follow through.

Surveys should also include all means of egress from the building. Exits, stairs, fire towers, fire escapes, halls, fire alarm systems, emergency lighting systems, and places seldom used should be thoroughly inspected to determine their adequacy and readiness for emergency use.

9. Of the following titles, the one that BEST fits the above passage is

   A. NEW, USED, AND OLD FIRE PROTECTION EQUIPMENT
   B. MAINTENANCE OF FIRE PROTECTION EQUIPMENT
   C. INSPECTION OF FIRE PROTECTION EQUIPMENT
   D. OVERHAUL OF WORN OUT FIRE FIGHTING EQUIPMENT

10. As used in the above passage, the word *accurate* means

    A. exact     B. approximate     C. close     D. vague

Questions 11-15.

DIRECTIONS: Questions 11 through 15 are to be answered SOLELY on the basis of the following passage.

The sizes of living rooms shall meet the following requirements:

   a. In each apartment, there shall be at least one living room containing at least 120 square feet of clear floor area, and every other living room except a kitchen shall contain at least 70 square feet of clear floor area.
   b. Every living room which contains less than 80 square feet of clear floor area or which is located in the cellar or basement shall be at least 9 feet high and every other living room 8 feet high.

Apartments containing three or more rooms may have dining bays, which shall not exceed 55 square feet in floor surface area and shall not be deemed separate rooms or subject to the requirements for separate rooms. Every such dining bay shall be provided with at least one window containing an area at least one-eighth of the floor surface area of such dining bay.

11. The MINIMUM volume of a living room, other than a kitchen, which meets the minimum requirements of the above paragraph is one that measures _____ cubic feet.

    A. 70     B. 80     C. 630     D. 640

12. A builder proposes to construct an apartment house containing an apartment consisting of a kitchen which measures 10 feet by 6 feet, a room 12 feet by 12 feet, and one 11 feet by 7 feet.
    This apartment

    A. does not comply with the requirements of the above paragraph
    B. complies with the requirements of the above paragraph provided that it is not located in the cellar or basement

C. complies with the requirements of the above paragraph provided that the height of the smaller rooms is at least 9 feet
D. may or may not comply with the requirements of the above paragraph, depending upon the clear floor area of the kitchen

13. The one of the following definitions of the term *living room* which is MOST in accord with its meaning in the above paragraph is

   A. a sitting room or parlor
   B. the largest room in an apartment
   C. a room used for living purposes
   D. any room in an apartment containing 120 square feet of clear floor Area

14. Assume that one room in a four-room apartment measures 20 feet by 10 feet and contains a dining bay 8 feet by 6 feet. According to the above passage, the dining bay MUST be provided with a window measuring AT LEAST _____ square feet.

   A. 6   B. 7   C. 25   D. 55

15. Kitchens, according to the above passage, are

   A. not considered *living rooms*
   B. considered *living rooms* and must, therefore, meet the height and area requirements of the paragraph
   C. considered *living rooms* but they need not meet either the height or area requirements of the paragraph
   D. considered *living rooms* but they need meet only the height requirements, not the area requirements, of the paragraph

Questions 16-20.

DIRECTIONS: Questions 16 through 20 are to be answered SOLELY on the basis of the following paragraph.

Cotton fabrics treated with the XYZ Process have features which make them far superior to any previously known flame-retardant-treated cotton fabrics. XYZ are glow resistant; when exposed to flames or intense heat form tough, pliable, and protective chars; are inert physiologically to persons handling or exposed to the fabric; are only slightly heavier than untreated fabrics; and are susceptible to further wet and dry finishing treatments. In addition, the treated fabrics exhibit little or no adverse change in feel, texture, and appearance, and are shrink-, rot-, and mildew-resistant. The treatment reduces strength only slightly. Finished fabrics have *easy care* properties in that they are wrinkle-resistant and dry rapidly.

16. It is MOST accurate to state that the author, in the above paragraph, presents

   A. facts but reaches no conclusion concerning the value of the process
   B. his conclusion concerning the value of the process and facts to support his conclusion
   C. his conclusion concerning the value of the process unsupported by facts
   D. neither facts nor conclusions, but merely describes the process

17. The one of the following articles for which the XYZ Process would be MOST suitable is   17.___

    A. nylon stockings  B. woolen shirt
    C. silk tie  D. cotton bedsheet

18. The one of the following aspects of the XYZ Process which is NOT discussed in the above paragraph is its effects on   18.___

    A. costs  B. washability
    C. wearability  D. the human body

19. The MAIN reason for treating a fabric with the XYZ Process is to   19.___

    A. prepare the fabric for other wet and dry finishing treatments
    B. render it shrink-, rot-, and mildew-resistant
    C. increase its weight and strength
    D. reduce the chance that it will catch fire

20. The one of the following which would be considered a MINOR drawback of the XYZ Process is that it   20.___

    A. forms chars when exposed to flame
    B. makes fabrics mildew-resistant
    C. adds to the weight of fabrics
    D. is compatible with other finishing treatments

Questions 21-25.

DIRECTIONS: Questions 21 through 25 are to be answered SOLELY on the basis of the following paragraph.

In order to help prevent the spread of fire, it is necessary to understand the means by which heat is transmitted. Heat is transmitted through solids by a method called *conduction*. Materials vary greatly in their ability to transmit heat. Metals are good conductors of heat. On the other hand, wood, glass, pottery, asbestos, and many like substances are very poor conductors of heat and are termed insulators. It should be remembered, however, that there are no perfect insulators of heat. All will conduct heat to some extent; and if the heat continues long enough, it will be transmitted through the solid. The hazard of heat transmission is illustrated by the fact that a fire on one side of a metal wall could start a fire on the other side if combustibles were close to the wall.

21. Of the following, the BEST material to use for the handle of a metal pan to guard against heat is   21.___

    A. copper  B. iron  C. wood  D. steel

22. According to the above paragraph, *conduction* applies to the traveling of heat through a   22.___

    A. solid  B. liquid
    C. slow-moving fluid  D. gas

23. According to the information in the above paragraph, when storing combustible materials in a room with metal walls, it is BEST to

    A. keep the combustibles close together
    B. keep the combustibles away from the metal walls
    C. put the non-metals nearest the metal walls
    D. separate metal materials from non-metal materials

23._____

24. Based on the information in the above paragraph, which one of the following objects is the BEST conductor of heat?

    A. Pottery                                       B. An oak desk
    C. A glass jar                              D. A silver spoon

24._____

25. Of the following, the title which BEST describes what the above paragraph is about is

    A. USES OF CONDUCTORS AND INSULATORS
    B. THE REASONS WHY FIRE SPREADS
    C. HEAT TRANSMISSION AND FIRES
    D. THE HAZARDS OF POOR CONDUCTION

25._____

---

## KEY (CORRECT ANSWERS)

1. C
2. C
3. D
4. D
5. C

6. B
7. D
8. D
9. C
10. A

11. C
12. C
13. C
14. A
15. D

16. B
17. D
18. A
19. D
20. C

21. C
22. A
23. B
24. D
25. C

---

# EXAMINATION SECTION
## TEST 1

DIRECTIONS: Each question or incomplete statement is followed by several suggested answers or completions. Select the one that BEST answers the question or completes the statement. *PRINT THE LETTER OF THE CORRECT ANSWER IN THE SPACE AT THE RIGHT.*

1. Assume that you are called on to render first aid to a man injured in an accident. You find he is bleeding profusely, is unconscious, and has a broken arm. There is a strong odor of alcohol about him.
   The FIRST thing for which you should treat him is the
   A. bleeding
   B. unconsciousness
   C. broken arm
   D. alcoholism

   1.___

2. In applying first aid for removal of a foreign body in the eye, an IMPORTANT precaution to be observed is:
   Do not
   A. attempt to wash out the foreign body
   B. bring the upper eyelid down over the lower
   C. rub the eye
   D. touch or attempt to remove a speck on the lower lid

   2.___

3. The one of the following symptoms which is LEAST likely to indicate that a person involved in an accident requires first aid for shock is that
   A. he has fainted twice
   B. his face is red and flushed
   C. his skin is wet with sweat
   D. his pulse is rapid

   3.___

4. When giving first aid to a person suffering from shock as a result of an auto accident, it is MOST important to
   A. massage him in order to aid blood circulation
   B. have him sip whiskey
   C. prop him up in a sitting position
   D. cover the person and keep him warm

   4.___

5. Assume that you are about to apply artificial respiration to a person.
   The LEAST useful of the following items is a(n)
   A. blanket
   B. inhalator
   C. hot water bottle
   D. radiant heater

   5.___

6. Assume that you are called on to render first aid to a man injured in an accident. You find he is bleeding profusely in spurts, has a rash indicating food poisoning, has a broken leg, and is not breathing.
   The FIRST thing for which you should treat him is
   A. profuse bleeding
   B. not breathing
   C. the broken leg
   D. food poisoning

   6.___

7. Assume that you are called to render first aid to a person who is unconscious. Your first glance indicates that the victim's face is cherry red.
You would IMMEDIATELY start treatment for
   A. heat exhaustion
   B. sunstroke
   C. gas asphyxiation
   D. red unconsciousness

8. Of the following statements concerning the treatment of wounds with severe bleeding, the LEAST accurate is:
   A. The chief duty of the first aider is to stop the bleeding at once
   B. Application of digital pressure in most severe venous bleeding may well be recommended
   C. In all serious bleeding, the first aider should think first of pressure
   D. Stimulants should be given so that the patient will not go into shock

9. Of the following statements concerning the use of tourniquets, the LEAST accurate is:
   A. Tourniquets are most frequently used in cases of severe venous bleeding
   B. It is preferable to use a pad over the artery with a tourniquet
   C. A tourniquet is correctly applied in only two places
   D. A tourniquet should be loosened every fifteen or twenty minutes

10. Suppose that you are called to administer first aid to an unconscious person.
Of the following, the BEST reason for not attempting to administer a liquid stimulant to this person is that
   A. he may have poor circulation of blood
   B. he may choke on the liquid
   C. stimulants affect the heart
   D. stimulants should be administered at the direction of a physician

11. Assume that it is necessary for you to apply a tourniquet in order to stop serious bleeding.
The one of the following MOST properly used for this purpose is
   A. thin cord
   B. thick rope
   C. a necktie
   D. wire

12. Suppose than an elderly man has met with an accident and is lying on the floor awaiting the arrival of a doctor.
Of the following, the BEST action to take in order to prevent shock is to
   A. raise him to a sitting position
   B. apply a wet cloth to his head
   C. apply artificial respiration
   D. cover him with a coat

13. While you are on duty, a fellow officer suddenly turns pale and his breathing becomes rapid and shallow. He is apparently suffering from heat exhaustion.
Of the following, the LEAST desirable action for you to take under the circumstances is to
   A. apply cold cloths to his head
   B. place him in a reclining position
   C. give him a stimulant
   D. have him sip salt water

14. Assume that a fellow officer is in contact with an electrically charged wire.
Of the following, the BEST reason for not grasping the victim's clothing with your bare hands in order to pull him off the wire is that
   A. his clothing may be damp with perspiration
   B. his clothing may be 100% wool
   C. you may be standing on a dry surface
   D. you may be wearing rubber-soled shoes

15. The recommended first aid procedure for a person who has fainted is to lay him down with his head lower than his body.
Such a position is used because it
   A. quickly relieves exhaustion
   B. is the most comfortable position
   C. speeds the return of blood to his head
   D. retards rapid breathing

16. If an ambulance is required for an injured passenger, all subway employees including railroad clerks are instructed to call the transit police department and have them call the ambulance.
An IMPORTANT reason for such a procedure is to
   A. enable the clerk to concentrate on his regular duties
   B. provide faster service
   C. fix responsibility
   D. avoid possible duplication of calls

17. According to the latest recommended first aid practice, a cut finger should be cleaned with
   A. soap and water        B. phenol
   C. mercurochrome         D. iodine

18. If a clerk has to telephone for an ambulance for an injured person, the MOST important information he must transmit is
   A. where the ambulance is needed
   B. the name of the injured person
   C. how the accident occurred
   D. what part of the body has been injured

19. When an ambulance arrives to take away an unconscious person, it would probably be MOST difficult for an officer to obtain the name of the
    A. station
    B. ambulance attendant
    C. hospital
    D. injured person

20. The first aid procedure of not moving a person unless absolutely necessary is MOST important in the case of a person who has
    A. fainted
    B. collapsed from heat
    C. fractured his leg
    D. broken a finger

21. Shock, a condition often brought on by a serious injury to any part of the body, is dangerous MAINLY because
    A. body temperature rises too high
    B. blood pressure becomes very high
    C. the injured person remains unconscious for a long time
    D. there is a reduction in the flow of blood to the vital organs

22. If a little *battery fluid* accidentally gets into a person's eye, the FIRST thing to do is to
    A. call a doctor or ambulance
    B. find out what safety rule was broken
    C. put several drops of clean olive oil in the eye
    D. wash the eye with large quantities of plain water

23. If an unconscious person is found on the sidewalk, the BEST of the following to do right away is to
    A. cover him to keep him warm
    B. give him sips of hot tea or coffee
    C. move him into the nearest building
    D. shake him gently to arouse him

24. To keep germs from entering a wound, it is BEST to
    A. apply a sterilized dressing to the wound
    B. put an antiseptic on the wound
    C. squeeze the wound gently to make it bleed
    D. wash the wound with soap and hot water

25. If several persons are injured in an accident, the one who should be treated FIRST is the person who
    A. has a compound fracture
    B. has severe burns
    C. is bleeding seriously
    D. is in the greatest pain

# KEY (CORRECT ANSWERS)

| | | | | |
|---|---|---|---|---|
| 1. A | 6. A | 11. C | 16. D | 21. D |
| 2. C | 7. C | 12. D | 17. A | 22. D |
| 3. B | 8. D | 13. A | 18. A | 23. A |
| 4. D | 9. A | 14. A | 19. D | 24. A |
| 5. B | 10. B | 15. C | 20. C | 25. C |

# TEST 2

DIRECTIONS: Each question or incomplete statement is followed by several suggested answers or completions. Select the one that BEST answers the question or completes the statement. *PRINT THE LETTER OF THE CORRECT ANSWER IN THE SPACE AT THE RIGHT.*

1. An injured person who is unconscious should *not* be given a liquid to drink MAINLY because
   A. cold liquid may be harmful
   B. he may choke on it
   C. he may not like the liquid
   D. his unconsciousness may be due to too much liquid

   1.____

2. The MOST important reason for putting a bandage on a cut is to
   A. help prevent germs from getting into the cut
   B. hide the ugly scar
   C. keep the blood pressure down
   D. keep the skin warm

   2.____

3. In first aid for an injured person, the MAIN purpose of a tourniquet is to
   A. prevent infection      B. restore circulation
   C. support a broken bone  D. stop severe bleeding

   3.____

4. Artificial respiration is given in first aid MAINLY to
   A. force air into the lungs
   B. force blood circulation by even pressure
   C. keep the injured person awake
   D. prevent shock by keeping the victim's body in motion

   4.____

5. The aromatic spirits of ammonia in a first aid kit should be used to
   A. clean a dirty wound
   B. deaden pain
   C. revive a person who has fainted
   D. warm a person who is chilled

   5.____

6. Suppose that you come upon an old man with blood on his face, seated on the sidewalk leaning against the tire of a parked car.
   Of the following, the BEST action for you to take FIRST is to
   A. ask the man for identification
   B. call a policeman to move him from his dangerous position
   C. examine him to see what first aid help you can give
   D. look up and down the block to find a witness to the accident

   6.____

7. A person trips on a station stairway, striking his head so severely that his breathing is stopped.
   First aid treatment should consist of the IMMEDIATE application of
   A. a bandage
   B. a compress
   C. cold water
   D. artificial respiration

8. When a passenger becomes seriously ill, it is advisable to call an ambulance PRIMARILY to
   A. save expense for the city
   B. provide adequate treatment
   C. save money for the passenger
   D. remove him from city property

9. The procedure of not moving a person unless absolutely necessary is MOST essential in the case of a person who has
   A. fainted
   B. collapsed from heat exhaustion
   C. fractured his leg
   D. a severe nose bleed

10. A railroad clerk sees a passenger, apparently ill, fall to the floor some distance from his booth during a quiet period.
    The railroad clerk should
    A. immediately close the booth and go to the passenger
    B. not leave the booth since a hold-up may be planned
    C. remain in the booth and call the nearest hospital
    D. send the next passenger to the person's assistance

11. If an artery has been cut, you can tell by the
    A. quick clotting of the blood
    B. RH factor of the blood
    C. slow, steady flow of blood
    D. spurting of the blood

12. The BEST material to be used directly over a wound or burn is
    A. absorbent cotton
    B. adhesive tape
    C. sterile gauze
    D. tourniquet

13. Aromatic spirits of ammonia is used as a(n)
    A. antidote for arsenic poisoning
    B. stimulant
    C. sedative drug
    D. sterilizing solution

14. A compound fracture is one in which
    A. broken bones protrude through the skin
    B. bones are broken and shattered
    C. a large bone and its adjoining smaller bones are broken
    D. two or more bones are broken

15. If you accidentally get a liquid chemical into your eye, the FIRST thing you should do is
    A. try to rub the chemical out of your eye
    B. rinse your eye with cold water
    C. bandage your eye
    D. put eye drops in your eye

16. If the label on a bottle of cleaning fluid has the word *flammable* on it, it means that the fluid
    A. is strong enough to remove grease stains
    B. must be mixed with water before use
    C. can easily be set on fire
    D. is used to kill germs

17. When a fire occurs in or near electrical equipment, the MOST suitable method of extinguishing it is to
    A. drench it with water
    B. use rags to beat it out
    C. use a fire extinguisher of the proper type
    D. smother it with grease

18. The BEST way to treat a person who has fainted is to
    A. place him gently on his back
    B. give him a cold glass of water to drink
    C. give him artificial respiration
    D. revive him immediately by placing him in a sitting position

19. The BEST thing to do immediately for a person who has suffered a severe blow to his head in a fall is to
    A. have him lie down and remain quiet until medical attention is obtained
    B. quickly transport him to a bed
    C. have him sit down and give him a glass of water
    D. get him up and walk him around

20. Of the following, the one which is LEAST likely to be a symptom of shock is that the victim
    A. feels cold
    B. feels weak
    C. has a rapid but weak pulse
    D. looks flushed

21. In attempting to revive a person who has stopped breathing after receiving an electric shock, it is MOST important to
    A. start artificial respiration immediately
    B. wrap the victim in a blanket
    C. massage the ankles and wrists
    D. force the victim to swallow a stimulant

22. Artificial respiration after a severe shock is ALWAYS necessary when the shock results in
    A. unconsciousness      B. a burn
    C. stoppage of breathing   D. bleeding

23. If a maintainer makes contact with a 600-volt conductor and remains in contact, your FIRST action should be to
    A. search for the disconnecting switch
    B. ground the conductor with a bare wire
    C. pull him loose by his clothing
    D. cut the conductor

24. Assume that you have burned your hand accidentally while on the job.
    The POOREST first aid remedy for the burn would be
    A. tannic acid      B. iodine
    C. vaseline         D. baking soda

25. Small cuts or injuries should be
    A. taken care of immediately to avoid infection
    B. ignored because they are seldom important
    C. ignored unless they are painful
    D. taken care of at the end of the day

# KEY (CORRECT ANSWERS)

1. B
2. A
3. D
4. A
5. C

6. C
7. D
8. B
9. C
10. A

11. D
12. C
13. B
14. A
15. B

16. C
17. C
18. A
19. A
20. D

21. A
22. C
23. C
24. B
25. A

# FIRST AID

# Table of Contents

|  | Page |
|---|---|
| BASIC PRINCIPLES AND PRACTICES | 1 |
|   Caution | 1 |
|   General Rules | 1 |
|   Emergency Actions | 1 |
|     1. For Bleeding | 1 |
|     2. For Burns | 2 |
|     3. For Broken | 2 |
|     4. For Shock | 2 |
|     5. For Suffocation | 3 |
|       Artificial Respiration | 3 |
|       Mouth-to-mouth (mouth-to-nose) method | 3 |
|       Mouth-to-mouth technique for infants and small children | 4 |
|       Other manual methods of artificial respiration | 5 |
|     6. To move injured persons | 5 |
| CURRENT CHANGES IN FIRST-AID METHODS | 6 |
|   Cuts | 6 |
|   Bleeding from artery | 6 |
|   Choking | 6 |
|   Burns | 7 |
|   Diving accident | 7 |
|   Nosebleed | 8 |
|   Poison | 8 |
|   Accident | 9 |
| FIRST AID SUMMARY CHART | 10 |

# FIRST AID

## Basic Principles and Practices

CAUTION
 These are emergency actions only. Always call a doctor if possible. If you cannot get a doctor or trained first-aider and the injured person is in danger of losing his life, take one of the six emergency actions described in this section.

BUT, FIRST, OBSERVE THESE GENERAL RULES:
 Keep the injured person lying down, with his head level with the rest of his body unless he has a head injury. In that case raise his head slightly. Cover him and keep him warm.
 Don't move the injured person to determine whether emergency action is necessary. If he is NOT in danger of bleeding to death, or is NOT suffocating or has NOT been severely burned, or is NOT in shock, IT IS BETTER FOR THE UNTRAINED PERSON TO LEAVE HIM ALONE.
 Do NOT give an unconscious or semiconscious person anything to drink.
 Do NOT let an injured person see his wounds.
 Reassure him and keep him comfortable.

EMERGENCY ACTIONS
 I. FOR BLEEDING
  TAKE THIS EMERGENCY ACTION
   Apply pressure directly over the wound. Use a first aid dressing, clean cloth, or even the bare hand. When bleeding has been controlled, add extra layers of cloth and bandage firmly. Do NOT remove the dressing. If the wound is in an arm or leg, elevate it with pillows or substitutes. Do NOT use a tourniquet except as a last resort.

II. FOR BURNS
   TAKE THIS EMERGENCY ACTION
   Remove clothing covering the burn unless it sticks. Cover the burned area with a clean dry dressing or several layers of cloth folded into a pad. Apply a bandage over the pad, tightly enough to keep out the air. Don't remove the pad. DON'T USE GREASE, OIL OR ANY OINTMENT EXCEPT ON A DOCTOR'S ORDER. On chemical burns, such as caused by acid or lye, wash the burn thoroughly with water before covering with a dry dressing.

III. FOR BROKEN BONES
   TAKE THIS EMERGENCY ACTION
   Unless it is absolutely necessary to move a person with a broken bone, don't do anything except apply an ice bag to the injured area to relieve pain. If you must move him, splint the broken bone first so the broken bone ends cannot move. Use a board, thick bundle of newspapers, even a pillow. Tie the splint firmly in place above and below the break, but not tightly enough to cut off circulation. Use layers of cloth or newspapers to pad a hard splint.
   Broken bones in the hand, arm, or shoulder should be supported by a sling after splinting. Use a triangular bandage or a substitute such as a scarf, towel, or torn width of sheet and tie the ends around the casualty's neck. Or place his forearm across his chest and pin his sleeve to his coat. In this way the lower sleeve will take the weight of the injured arm.
   If you suspect a broken neck or back do not move the casualty except to remove him from further danger that may take his life. If you must remove the casualty, slide him gently onto a litter or a wide, rigid board. Then leave him alone until trained help arrives.
   If a bone has punctured the skin, cover the wound with a first aid dressing or clean cloth and control bleeding by hand pressure.

IV. FOR SHOCK
   TAKE THIS EMERGENCY ACTION
   Shock may result from severe burns, broken bones, or other wounds, or from acute emotional disturbance. Usually the person going into shock becomes pale. His skin may be cold and moist. His pulse may be rapid. He may become wet with sweat. He may become unconscious.

Keep the casualty lying down. His head should be level with or lower than his body unless he has a head injury. In the latter case his head should be raised slightly. Wrap the casualty warm but do not permit him to become overheated. Try to avoid letting him see his injury. If he is able to swallow, give hime plenty of water to drink, with salt and baking soda added. Mix one teaspoonful of salt and one-half teaspoonful of baking soda to one quart of water. This will help to prevent severe shock.

Do NOT give anything by mouth to a person who is vomiting, is unconscious, or semiconscious, or has an abdominal wound.

V. FOR SUFFOCATION

TAKE THIS EMERGENCY ACTION

Suffocation can result from pressure on the neck or chest, contact with a live electric wire, drowning or breathing-in foreign substances such as liquids, smoke, or gas. The usual signs of suffocation are coughing and sputtering or other difficulty in breathing. As breathing becomes difficult or stops, the face may turn purple and lips and fingernails become blue. Unconsciousness will follow quickly unless you act at once.

First, remove the person from the cause of suffocation. If he is in contact with a live wire, don't touch him. Shut off the current if you can. If not, stand on a piece of dry wood or on paper and remove the wire from the person with a long dry stick or other nonmetallic object.

If the person is in a room filled with gas, smoke, or water, get him out quickly. Remove any objects from his mouth or throat that may obstruct breathing. Then apply artificial respiration immediately, as follows:

ARTIFICIAL RESPIRATION

Mouth-to-Mouth (Mouth-to-Nose) Method

Tilt the head back so the chin is pointing upward, and pull or push the jaw into a jutting out position. (These maneuvers should relieve obstruction of the airway by moving the base of the tongue away from the back of the throat.)

Open your mouth wide and place it tightly over the casualty's nostrils shut or close the nostrils with your cheek. Or close the casualty's mouth and place your mouth over the nose. Blow into his mouth or nose. (Air may be blown through the casualty's teeth, even though they may be clenched.) The first blowing efforts should determine whether or not obstruction exists.

Remove your mouth, turn your head to the side, and listen for the return rush of air that indicates air-exchange. Repeat the blowing effort. For an adult, blow vigorously at the rate of 12 breaths per minute. For a child, take relatively shallow breaths appropriate for the child's size at the rate of about 20 per minute.

If you are not getting air-exchange, recheck the head and jaw position. If you still do not get air-exchange, quickly turn the casualty on his side and administer several sharp blows between the shoulder blades in the hope of dislodging foreign matter. Again sweep your fingers through the casualty's mouth to remove any foreign matter.

Those who do not wish to come in contact with the person may hold a cloth over the casualty's mouth or nose and breathe through it. The cloth does not greatly affect the exchange of air.

Mouth-To-Mouth Technique For Infants And Small Children

If foreign matter is visible in the mouth, wipe it out quickly with your fingers or a cloth wrapped around your fingers.

Place the child on his back and use the fingers of both hands to lift the lower jaw from beneath and behind, so that it juts out.

Place your mouth over the child's mouth and nose making a relatively leakproof seal, and breathe into the child, using shallow puffs of air. The breathing rate should be about 20 per minute.

If you meet resistance in your blowing efforts, recheck the position of the jaw. If the air passages are still blocked, the child should be suspended momentarily by the ankles or inverted over one arm and given two or three sharp pats between the shoulder blades, in the hope of dislodging obstructing matter.

Other Manual Methods Of Artificial Respiration

Persons who cannot, or will not, use the mouth-to-mouth (mouth-to-nose) method of artificial respiration should use another manual method. The nature of the injury in any given case may prevent the use of one method, while favoring another. Other methods suggested for use by the American National Red Cross are THE CHEST PRESSURE-ARM LIFT METHOD (Silvester) and THE BACK PRESSURE-ARM LIFT METHOD (Holger-Nielsen).

When performing any method of artificial respiration, remember to time your efforts to coincide with the casualty's first attempt to breathe for himself.

Be sure that the air passages are clear of all obstructions, that the casualty is positioned in a manner that will keep the air passages clear, and that air is forced into the lungs as soon as possible.

If vomiting occurs, quickly turn the casualty on his side, wipe out his mouth, and reposition him.

When the casualty is revived, keep him as quiet as possible until he is breathing regularly. Loosen his clothing, cover him to keep him warm, and then treat for shock.

Whatever method of artificial respiration you use, it should be continued until the casualty begins to breathe for himself, or until there is no doubt that the person is dead.

VI. TO MOVE INJURED PERSONS
TAKE THIS EMERGENCY ACTION

Do NOT move an injured person except to prevent further injury or possible death. If you must move him, keep him lying down flat. Move him on a wide board, such as an ironing board or door, and tie him to it so he won't roll off.

If you have nothing to carry him on, get two other persons to help you carry. You must kneel together on the same side of the casualty and slide your hands under him gently. Then lift carefully, keeping his body level. Walk in step to prevent jarring, and carry him only far enough to remove from danger.

## CURRENT CHANGES IN FIRST-AID METHODS

When an accident occurs and before medical help arrives, the victim often can be helped by someone who has knowledge of first aid. However, a person who does not know the recent developments in treatment may find that he is endangering the physical well being of the victim by using an improper method. Many of the methods once used are now obsolete. For example:

CUTS

    OLD METHOD
        Apply an antiseptic such as iodine, to a cut to kill germs.

    CURRENT METHOD
        Wash the cut with gauze dipped in soap and water. Antiseptics can destroy living tissue around the wound and retard healing. Soap and water, however does not destroy tissue, and it provides a flushing action that washes away dirt and some bacteria.

BLEEDING FROM ARTERY

    OLD METHOD
        Apply a tourniquet to stop bleeding from a cut artery.

    CURRENT METHOD
        The best way to control any bleeding is to apply sterile compresses directly over the wound, and bandage them tightly in place. The pressure of the bandage will stem the flow of blood. Medical attention is indicated for any cut artery. The old method of using a tourniquet, say medical authorities, can be dangerous because it cuts off all circulation to the limb, which can lead to a risk of gangrene and even amputation. Also, if muscles begin to die from lack of oxygen, poisonous substances may form and get into the victim's circulation, causing "tourniquet shock."

CHOKING

    CURRENT METHOD
        Perform the Heimlich method by hugging the victim with his back against your body, placing your arms around his body. Make a fist with one hand, hold your fist with the other hand and place it under victim's diaphragm and forcefully push air up forcing food up windpipe and out of mouth. If necessary, make several separate forceful movements until successful.

OLD METHOD
   If a person is choking, slap him on the back repeatedly in order to dislodge the obstruction.
   Do nothing for a while in order to give the person's voice box (where food usually lodges) enough time to relax. At this stage the person ordinarily coughs up the object. If nothing happens and the person stops breathing, lean him forward, then slap him on the back to dislodge the obstruction. A young child may be held upside down to help dislodge any obstruction. If the obstruction can be reached with the fingers, it should be removed. Slapping a person immediately may cause the object to be sucked, by a sudden rush of air, into his windpipe. If the object has slipped into the windpipe, a slap may make him cough, forcing the object up against the narrower opening of the vocal cords. This can cause a blockage and asphyxiation.

BURNS

   OLD METHOD
   When someone is burned, apply butter or other household grease to the area.

   CURRENT METHOD
   Never apply grease. The sterility of household greases cannot be guaranteed and therefore there is a risk of introducing infection. In serious burns, any grease or ointment must be scraped off before treatment at a hospital, and the patient experiences more pain. If the burn is minor (one that does not require medical attention and when the skin is not broken), sterile commercial products can be used. Another method is to submerge the burned area in cold water (under 70 degrees) and keep adding ice to maintain the temperature. Parts that cannot be submerged should be treated with a cloth dipped in cold water. Treatment should continue until the burned parts can be kept out of the cold water without recurrence of pain. However, there is still some controversy about the use of this treatment when the burn is extensive. In a serious burn, the Red Cross recommends the application of a dry sterile dressing, bandaged securely in place to protect the burn from contamination and to prevent exposure to air.

DIVING ACCIDENT

   OLD METHOD
   If a person diving into the water appears to have struck his head, pull him out of the water as quickly as possible.

CURRENT METHOD

Many cases of paralysis have resulted from rough handling of a person dragged out of the water. Instead, the person should be supported in the water and kept afloat until the ambulance arrives. Quite often in this type of accident, the person's neck is fractured, and moving his head roughly is likely to cause irreparable injury to the spinal cord. If, however, it is necessary to remove a person from the water, he should be placed on something rigid so that his head will be at the same level as his body.

NOSEBLEED

OLD METHOD

Use an ice pack to stop a nosebleed.

CURRENT METHOD

Tilt the person's head all the way back so that his nose becomes the highest point of his body, and pinch his nostrils. It is important to keep the head tilted to lessen pressure. However, if the bleeding is severe, roll a piece of gauze and use it to plug his nostril, making sure that a long piece hangs out to facilitate removal. Gentle pressure can be exerted on the outside of the nostril. In severe bleeding, it is necessary to have medical attention.

POISON

OLD METHOD

Use a mixture of burned toast, tea and milk to counteract accidental swallowing of poisons.

CURRENT METHOD

Poison-control authorities say that the homemade antidote of burned toast, tea and milk is useless because the charcoal from the toast is not the kind that absorbs poisons. Call a physician immediately. Begin mouth-to-mouth resuscitation if the victim has difficulty breathing. Actually, the nature of the poison will determine the first-aid measure to use. Give water or milk. Do NOT induce vomiting if a petroleum product, such as gasoline, kerosene or turpentine has been ingested. With poisons such as an overdose of aspirin, induce vomiting by either placing a finger at the back of the victim's throat, or by giving salt water (two teaspoons to a glass) or syrup of ipecac (one ounce for adults and half an ounce for children).

ACCIDENT

OLD METHOD
Rush a person to the hospital as quickly as possible after an accident.

CURRENT METHOD
Proper carrying of an injured person is necessary in order to avoid the possibility of permanent damage. To move a person too quickly may cause spinal injury, hemorrhage or shock. Unless the person must be moved out of danger, it is BEST to apply first aid on the spot and wait until the ambulance arrives. The American Red Cross says: "The principle of first aid is to get the victim to medical attention in the best possible manner."

## FIRST AID SUMMARY CHART

| FOR THESE PURPOSES | USE THESE | OR THESE | SUGGESTED QUANTITY |
|---|---|---|---|
| For open wounds, scratches, and cuts. Not for burns. | 1. Antiseptic Solution: Benzalkonium Chloride Solution, U.S.P., 1 to 1,000 parts of water. | Quaternary ammonium compounds in water. Sold under trade names as Zephiran, Phemerol, Ceepryn, and Bactine. | 3-to 6-oz. bottle. |
| For faintness, adult dose 1/2 teaspoon in cup of water; children 5 to 10 drops in 1/2 glass of water. As smelling salts, remove stopper, hold bottle under nose. | 2. Aromatic Spirits of ammonia. | | 1-to 2-oz. bottle. |
| For shock -- dissolve 1 teaspoonful salt and 1/2 teaspoonful baking soda in 1 quart water. Have patient ink as much as he ..ll. Don't give to unconscious person or semiconscious person. If using substitutes dissolve six 10-gr. sodium chloride tablets and six 5-gr. sodium bicarbonate (or sodium citrate) tablets in 1 qt. water. | 3. Table salt. | Sodium chloride tablets, 10 gr., 50 tablets in bottle. | 1 box. |
| | 4. Baking soda. | Sodium bicarbonate or sodium citrate tablets, 5 gr., 50 tablets in bottle. | 8-to 10 oz. box. |
| For a sling; as a cover; for a dressing. | 5. Triangular bandage, folded, 37 by 37 by 52 in., with 2 safety pins. | Muslin or other strong material. Cut to exact dimensions. Fold and wrap each bandage and 2 safety pins separately in paper. | 4 bandages. |

## FIRST AID SUMMARY CHART (Cont'd)

| FOR THESE PURPOSES | USE THESE | OR THESE | SUGGESTED QUANTITY |
|---|---|---|---|
| For open wounds or for dry dressings for burns. These are packaged sterile. | 6. Two medium first aid dressings, folded, sterile with gauze enclosed cotton pads, 8 in. by 7 1/2 in. Packaged with muslin bandage and 4 safety pins. | a) Two emergency dressings 8 in. by 7 1/2 in., in glassine bags, sterilized. One roller bandage, 2 in. by 10 yds. b) Four large sanitary napkins wrapped separately and sterilized. One roller bandage, 2 in. by 10 yards. | As indicated. |
| For open wounds or for dry dressings for burns. These are packaged sterile. | 7. Two small first aid dressings, folded, sterile with gauze enclosed cotton pads and gauze bandage, 4 in. by 7 in. | Twelve sterile gauze pads in individual packages, 3 in. by 3 in. One roller bandage, 1 in. by 10 yards. | As indicated. |
| For eyes irritated by dust, smoke, or fumes. Use 2 drops in each eye. Apply cold compresses every 20 minutes if possible. | 8. Eye drops. | Bland eye sold by druggists under various trade names. | 1/2-to 1-oz. bottle with dropper. |
| For splinting broken fingers or other small bones and for stirring solutions. | 9. Twelve tongue blades, wooden. | Shingles, pieces of orange crate, or other light wood cut to approximately 1 1/2 in. by 6 in. | As indicated. |

## FIRST AID SUMMARY CHART (Cont'd)

| FOR THESE PURPOSES | USE THESE | OR THESE | SUGGESTED QUANTITY |
|---|---|---|---|
| For purifying water when it cannot be boiled. (Radioactive contamination cannot be neutralized or removed by boiling or by disinfectants.) | 10. Water purification tablets Iodine (trade names--Globaline, Bursoline, Potable Aqua) Chlorine (trade name--Halazone). | Tincture of iodine or iodine solution (3 drops per quart of water). Household bleach (approx. 5% available chlorine) 3 drops per quart of water. | Tablets-- Bottle of 50 or 100. Liquid-- One Small bottle. |
| For bandages or dressings: Old soft towels and sheets are best. Cut in sizes necessary to cover wounds. Towels are burn dressings. Place over burns and fasten with triangular bandage or strips of sheet. Towels and sheets should be laundered, ironed and packaged in heavy paper. Relaunder every 3 months. | 11. Large bath towels. | | 2. |
| | 12. Small bath towels. | | 2. |
| | 13. Bed Sheet. | | 1. |
| For administering stimulants and liquids. | 14. Paper drinking cups. | | 25 to 50. |
| Electric lights may go out. Wrap batteries separately in moisture-proof covering. Don't keep in flashlight. | 15. Flashlight. | | 1. |
| | 16. Flashlight batteries. | | 3. |
| For holding bandages in place. | 17. Safety pins, 1 1/2 in. long. | | 12 to 15. |
| For cutting bandages and dressings, or for removing clothing from injured body surface. | 18. Razor blades, single edge. | Sharp knife or scissors. | 3. |
| For cleansing skin. | 19. Toilet soap | Any mild soap. | 1 bar. |
| For measuring or stirring solutions. | 20. Measuring spoons. | Inexpensive plastic or metal. | 1 set. |
| For splinting broken arms or legs. | 21. Twelve splints, plastic or wooden, 1/8 to 1 1/4 in. thick, 3 1/2 in. wide by 12 to 15 in. long. | A 40-page newspaper folded to dimensions, pieces of orange crate sidings, or shingles cut to size. | As indicated. |

# Basic Emergency Procedures

## Contents

|    |                                      | Page |
|----|--------------------------------------|------|
| I. | ABDOMINAL AND CHEST THRUSTS          | 1    |
| II.| CARDIOPULMONARY RESUSCITATION (CPR)  | 2    |
| III.| EMERGENCY CART                      | 4    |
| IV.| ROTATING TOURNIQUETS                 | 5    |

# BASIC EMERGENCY PROCEDURES

## 1. ABDOMINAL AND CHEST THRUSTS
## (FOR AIRWAY OBSTRUCTION)

PURPOSE

To clear an airway obstruction and ensure adequate ventilation

PROCEDURE

- Identify condition.
  - If unconscious, manage as cardiopulmonary arrest.
  - If victim is conscious and appears unable to speak or cough, ask "Can you speak?"
  - If patient can speak, remain with victim and encourage to continue spontaneous coughing and breathing efforts.
  - If patient cannot speak, proceed immediately to next step.

Abdominal Thrust

- Rescuer standing, victim standing or sitting
  - Stand behind victim and wrap your arms around victim's waist.
  - Grasp one of your fists with your other hand and place fist against victim's abdomen slightly above navel and below rib cage. See figure 1.
  - Press your fist into victim's abdomen with quick upward thrust 4 times.
  - Repeat several times as necessary.

- Rescuer kneeling, victim lying face up
  - Place victim flat on back.
  - Kneel astride victim.
  - Grasp one of your fists with your other hand and place fist directly in the middle of abdomen as shown in figure 2.
  - Press your fist into victim's abdomen with quick upward thrust 4 times.
  - Repeat several times as necessary.

SPECIAL CONSIDERATIONS

See CPR procedure.

Victim may use distress signal of choking by clutching his neck.
Do not interfere with victim's attempt to expel foreign body.

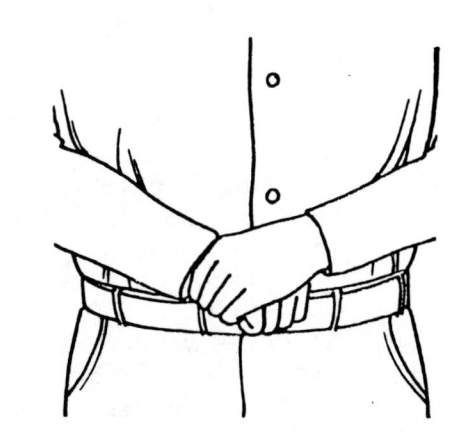

Figure 1. Correct Hand Placement, Victim Standing.

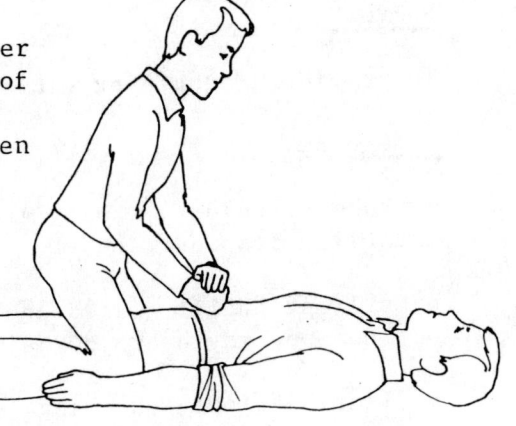

Figure 2. Correct Hand Placement, Victim Lying Down.

ABDOMINAL AND CHEST THRUSTS (cont)

PROCEDURE

- Victim alone
  - Victims should attempt to perform abdominal thrusts on themselves by pressing their own fist upward into abdomen.
  - Victim should lean forward and press abdomen quickly over any firm object.
  - Repeat several times as necessary.

Chest Thrust

- Rescuer standing, victim standing or sitting
  - Stand behind victim and wrap your arms around victim's waist.
  - Grasp one of your fists with your other hand and place at level just above xiphoid process as illustrated in figure 3.
  - Press your fist into victim's chest with a sharp backward thrust.
  - Repeat several times as necessary.

- Rescuer kneeling, victim lying face up
  - Place victim flat on back.
  - Kneel astride victim.
  - Grasp one of your fists with other hand and place at level just above xiphoid process.
  - Press your fist into victim's chest with a sharp inward thrust.
  - Repeat several times as necessary.

SPECIAL CONSIDERATIONS

Use in advanced pregnancy or marked obesity.

Figure 3. Correct Hand Placement, Chest Thrust.

## II. CARDIOPULMONARY RESUSCITATION (CPR)

PURPOSE

To provide adequate oxygen and blood to the body's vital organs

PROCEDURE

- Shake shoulder, shout "Are you O.K.?" to establish responsiveness.

- Call out "Help!" (No one may be in sight, but someone may hear you call.)

- Place patient on back on hard surface supporting extremities, head, and neck to prevent further injury.

# CARDIOPULMONARY RESUSCITATION (cont)

## PROCEDURE

- Kneel at victim's side.

- Open victim's airway by tilting head and lifting neck. (Many times this alone will establish patent airway.) See figure 4.

- Place ear over victim's mouth.
  - Look for chest to rise and fall.
  - Listen for air escaping during exhalation.
  - Feel for flow of air on your cheek.

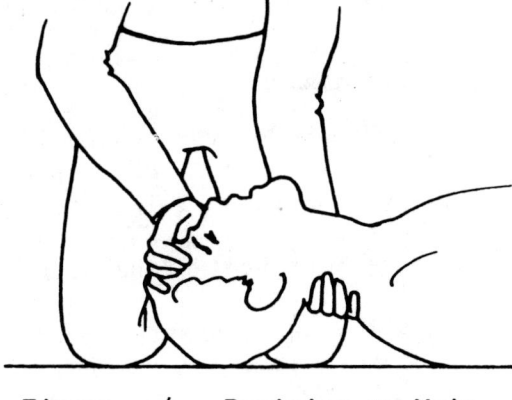

Figure 4. Position to Maintain Airway.

- Assume mouth-to-mouth position as shown in figure 5.

- Prevent air escape from nostrils.

- Quickly ventilate 4 times ensuring that chest rises each time.
  - Do not allow lungs to deflate between breaths.

- Palpate for carotid pulse keeping 1 hand on forehead to maintain head tilt.
  - If pulse cannot be felt, proceed with external heart compressions.

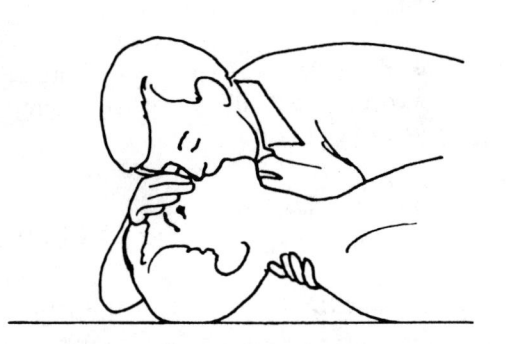

Figure 5. Mouth-to-Mouth Position.

- Locate compression landmark 2 fingers above xiphoid process. See figure 6.

- Position your hands for compression as illustrated in figure 7. Place heel of 1 hand 2 fingers above xiphoid process and heel of other on top of first.

- Interlock fingers; KEEP THEM OFF VICTIM'S CHEST!

- Keep your elbows straight as shown in figure 8 on the following page.

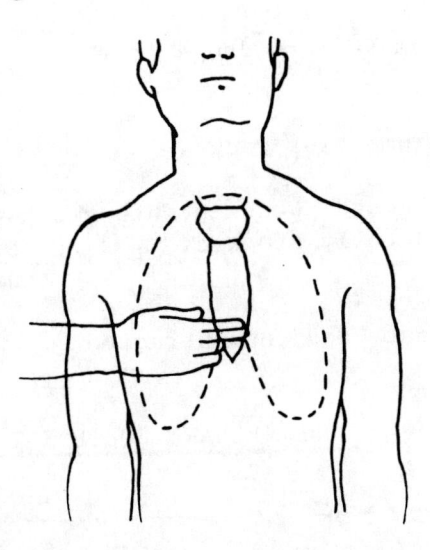

Figure 6. Compression Landmark.

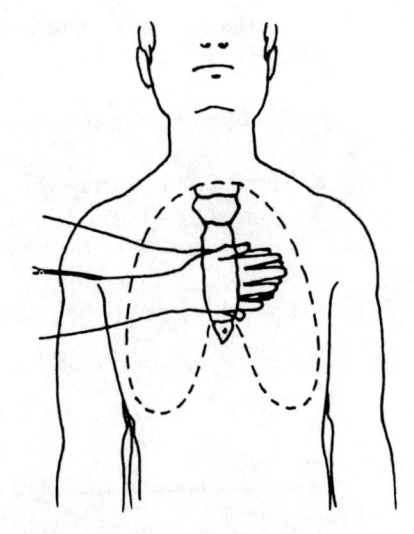

Figure 7. Hand Placement for Compression.

## CARDIOPULMONARY RESUSCITATION (cont)

### PROCEDURE

- Compress vertically 15 compressions to 2 ventilations or 80 compressions a minute.
- Compress 1 1/2 to 2 inches on normal sized adult.
- Keep heel of hand on chest.

- Release pressure to allow blood to flow into heart.

- Check for return of pulse and spontaneous breathing every fourth through sixth cycle (15/2).

- For two rescuer CPR, administer 5 compressions and 1 ventilation with no pause for ventilation.

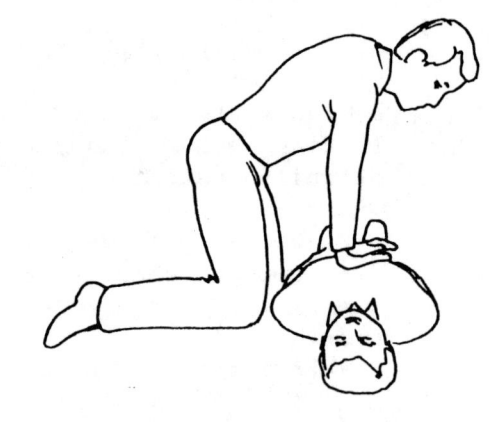

Figure 8. Rescuer's Position for Compression.

# III. EMERGENCY CART

### PURPOSE

To have equipment and drugs readily available to manage emergency situations

### PROCEDURE

- Check emergency cart for completeness, expiration dates, and equipment operation at least daily and after each use.

- Replace missing equipment or drugs immediately.

- Remove any excess equipment or drugs.

- Sign Daily Inventory Record when inventory is completed and cart is fully stocked.

- Keep cart in prominent and unobstructed area.

### SPECIAL CONSIDERATIONS

Follow local policy.

Record usually attached to cart. Person completing inventory must sign it.

### SUPPLIES AND EQUIPMENT

List locally used drugs and equipment. Use as many pages as required and and make the list a permanent part of your manual.

# IV. ROTATING TOURNIQUETS

PURPOSE

To systematically restrict venous return to the heart to reduce acute pulmonary edema

| PROCEDURE | SPECIAL CONSIDERATIONS |
|---|---|
| • Verify doctor's orders. | |
| • Assemble equipment and take to bedside. | A rotating tourniquet machine may be used which automatically rotates the pressure in the tourniquets. Attach a copy of operating instructions to machine. |
| • Explain procedure to patient. | |
| • Place patient in high Fowler's position unless contraindicated. | Promotes natural collection of fluid in bases of lungs. |
| • Take arterial pulse and BP in each extremity and record on flowsheet. | Only venous circulation is obstructed. |
| • If using rubber tourniquets, place towel or ABD pad around each extremity at level where tourniquets will be applied. | Avoids skin irritation. |
| • Apply tourniquets up high on 3 extremities (near axilla and groin) as shown in figure 1-9 on the following page. | Do not use on any extremity through which patient is receiving IV fluids. |
| • BP cuffs used as tourniquets should be inflated to a level just below systolic blood pressure readings. | Cuff should not restrict arterial flow. |
| • Recheck and record arterial pulses in each extremity to be sure they have not been obliterated. | Extremities may become discolored. |
| • Drape patient to expose extremities. | |
| • At time interval ordered by physician, remove one tourniquet and apply it to free (previously nonrestricted) extremity. | Rotate free extremity in a clockwise pattern. Direction of rotation must be the same throughout procedure (figure 9). |
| • Maintain flowsheet as each tourniquet is released and rotated. | |

## ROTATING TOURNIQUETS (cont)

### PROCEDURE

- Discontinue procedure by releasing tourniquets one at a time in same rotation pattern and interval as had been established.

- Remove, clean, and store equipment.

- Record pertinent observations and patient's response on Nursing Notes.

### SPECIAL CONSIDERATIONS

Avoid forcing large volume of blood to the heart. Allow time to adjust to increased venous return.

### SUPPLIES AND EQUIPMENT

Antibacterial cleaner   Hand towel or ABD pad (4)   Tourniquet (3) or BP cuff (4) or Rotating tourniquet machine

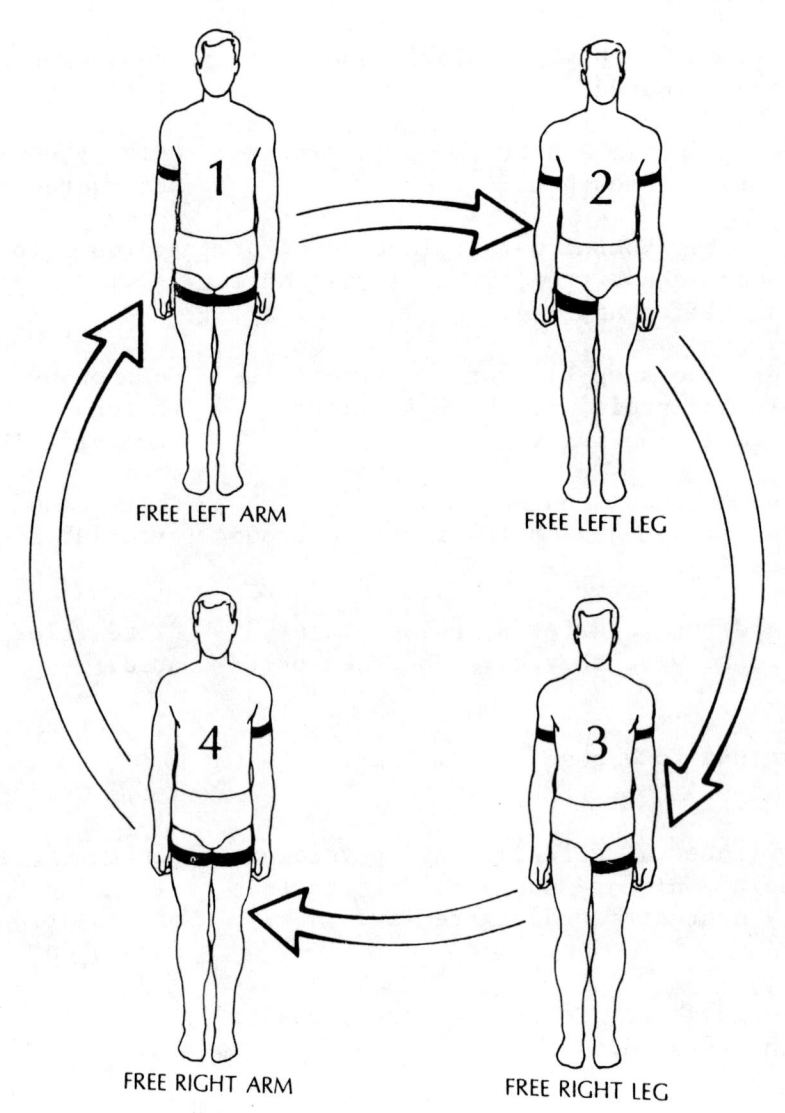

Figure 9. Tourniquet Placement and Rotation.

# ANSWER SHEET

TEST NO. _____ PART _____ TITLE OF POSITION _____
(AS GIVEN IN EXAMINATION ANNOUNCEMENT - INCLUDE OPTION, IF ANY)

PLACE OF EXAMINATION _____ _____ DATE _____
(CITY OR TOWN) (STATE)

RATING

USE THE SPECIAL PENCIL. MAKE GLOSSY BLACK MARKS.

|     | A B C D E |     | A B C D E |     | A B C D E |     | A B C D E |     | A B C D E |
|-----|-----------|-----|-----------|-----|-----------|-----|-----------|-----|-----------|
| 1   | ⋮ ⋮ ⋮ ⋮ ⋮ | 26  | ⋮ ⋮ ⋮ ⋮ ⋮ | 51  | ⋮ ⋮ ⋮ ⋮ ⋮ | 76  | ⋮ ⋮ ⋮ ⋮ ⋮ | 101 | ⋮ ⋮ ⋮ ⋮ ⋮ |
| 2   | ⋮ ⋮ ⋮ ⋮ ⋮ | 27  | ⋮ ⋮ ⋮ ⋮ ⋮ | 52  | ⋮ ⋮ ⋮ ⋮ ⋮ | 77  | ⋮ ⋮ ⋮ ⋮ ⋮ | 102 | ⋮ ⋮ ⋮ ⋮ ⋮ |
| 3   | ⋮ ⋮ ⋮ ⋮ ⋮ | 28  | ⋮ ⋮ ⋮ ⋮ ⋮ | 53  | ⋮ ⋮ ⋮ ⋮ ⋮ | 78  | ⋮ ⋮ ⋮ ⋮ ⋮ | 103 | ⋮ ⋮ ⋮ ⋮ ⋮ |
| 4   | ⋮ ⋮ ⋮ ⋮ ⋮ | 29  | ⋮ ⋮ ⋮ ⋮ ⋮ | 54  | ⋮ ⋮ ⋮ ⋮ ⋮ | 79  | ⋮ ⋮ ⋮ ⋮ ⋮ | 104 | ⋮ ⋮ ⋮ ⋮ ⋮ |
| 5   | ⋮ ⋮ ⋮ ⋮ ⋮ | 30  | ⋮ ⋮ ⋮ ⋮ ⋮ | 55  | ⋮ ⋮ ⋮ ⋮ ⋮ | 80  | ⋮ ⋮ ⋮ ⋮ ⋮ | 105 | ⋮ ⋮ ⋮ ⋮ ⋮ |
| 6   | ⋮ ⋮ ⋮ ⋮ ⋮ | 31  | ⋮ ⋮ ⋮ ⋮ ⋮ | 56  | ⋮ ⋮ ⋮ ⋮ ⋮ | 81  | ⋮ ⋮ ⋮ ⋮ ⋮ | 106 | ⋮ ⋮ ⋮ ⋮ ⋮ |
| 7   | ⋮ ⋮ ⋮ ⋮ ⋮ | 32  | ⋮ ⋮ ⋮ ⋮ ⋮ | 57  | ⋮ ⋮ ⋮ ⋮ ⋮ | 82  | ⋮ ⋮ ⋮ ⋮ ⋮ | 107 | ⋮ ⋮ ⋮ ⋮ ⋮ |
| 8   | ⋮ ⋮ ⋮ ⋮ ⋮ | 33  | ⋮ ⋮ ⋮ ⋮ ⋮ | 58  | ⋮ ⋮ ⋮ ⋮ ⋮ | 83  | ⋮ ⋮ ⋮ ⋮ ⋮ | 108 | ⋮ ⋮ ⋮ ⋮ ⋮ |
| 9   | ⋮ ⋮ ⋮ ⋮ ⋮ | 34  | ⋮ ⋮ ⋮ ⋮ ⋮ | 59  | ⋮ ⋮ ⋮ ⋮ ⋮ | 84  | ⋮ ⋮ ⋮ ⋮ ⋮ | 109 | ⋮ ⋮ ⋮ ⋮ ⋮ |
| 10  | ⋮ ⋮ ⋮ ⋮ ⋮ | 35  | ⋮ ⋮ ⋮ ⋮ ⋮ | 60  | ⋮ ⋮ ⋮ ⋮ ⋮ | 85  | ⋮ ⋮ ⋮ ⋮ ⋮ | 110 | ⋮ ⋮ ⋮ ⋮ ⋮ |

Make only ONE mark for each answer. Additional and stray marks may be counted as mistakes. In making corrections, erase errors COMPLETELY.

|     | A B C D E |     | A B C D E |     | A B C D E |     | A B C D E |     | A B C D E |
|-----|-----------|-----|-----------|-----|-----------|-----|-----------|-----|-----------|
| 11  | ⋮ ⋮ ⋮ ⋮ ⋮ | 36  | ⋮ ⋮ ⋮ ⋮ ⋮ | 61  | ⋮ ⋮ ⋮ ⋮ ⋮ | 86  | ⋮ ⋮ ⋮ ⋮ ⋮ | 111 | ⋮ ⋮ ⋮ ⋮ ⋮ |
| 12  | ⋮ ⋮ ⋮ ⋮ ⋮ | 37  | ⋮ ⋮ ⋮ ⋮ ⋮ | 62  | ⋮ ⋮ ⋮ ⋮ ⋮ | 87  | ⋮ ⋮ ⋮ ⋮ ⋮ | 112 | ⋮ ⋮ ⋮ ⋮ ⋮ |
| 13  | ⋮ ⋮ ⋮ ⋮ ⋮ | 38  | ⋮ ⋮ ⋮ ⋮ ⋮ | 63  | ⋮ ⋮ ⋮ ⋮ ⋮ | 88  | ⋮ ⋮ ⋮ ⋮ ⋮ | 113 | ⋮ ⋮ ⋮ ⋮ ⋮ |
| 14  | ⋮ ⋮ ⋮ ⋮ ⋮ | 39  | ⋮ ⋮ ⋮ ⋮ ⋮ | 64  | ⋮ ⋮ ⋮ ⋮ ⋮ | 89  | ⋮ ⋮ ⋮ ⋮ ⋮ | 114 | ⋮ ⋮ ⋮ ⋮ ⋮ |
| 15  | ⋮ ⋮ ⋮ ⋮ ⋮ | 40  | ⋮ ⋮ ⋮ ⋮ ⋮ | 65  | ⋮ ⋮ ⋮ ⋮ ⋮ | 90  | ⋮ ⋮ ⋮ ⋮ ⋮ | 115 | ⋮ ⋮ ⋮ ⋮ ⋮ |
| 16  | ⋮ ⋮ ⋮ ⋮ ⋮ | 41  | ⋮ ⋮ ⋮ ⋮ ⋮ | 66  | ⋮ ⋮ ⋮ ⋮ ⋮ | 91  | ⋮ ⋮ ⋮ ⋮ ⋮ | 116 | ⋮ ⋮ ⋮ ⋮ ⋮ |
| 17  | ⋮ ⋮ ⋮ ⋮ ⋮ | 42  | ⋮ ⋮ ⋮ ⋮ ⋮ | 67  | ⋮ ⋮ ⋮ ⋮ ⋮ | 92  | ⋮ ⋮ ⋮ ⋮ ⋮ | 117 | ⋮ ⋮ ⋮ ⋮ ⋮ |
| 18  | ⋮ ⋮ ⋮ ⋮ ⋮ | 43  | ⋮ ⋮ ⋮ ⋮ ⋮ | 68  | ⋮ ⋮ ⋮ ⋮ ⋮ | 93  | ⋮ ⋮ ⋮ ⋮ ⋮ | 118 | ⋮ ⋮ ⋮ ⋮ ⋮ |
| 19  | ⋮ ⋮ ⋮ ⋮ ⋮ | 44  | ⋮ ⋮ ⋮ ⋮ ⋮ | 69  | ⋮ ⋮ ⋮ ⋮ ⋮ | 94  | ⋮ ⋮ ⋮ ⋮ ⋮ | 119 | ⋮ ⋮ ⋮ ⋮ ⋮ |
| 20  | ⋮ ⋮ ⋮ ⋮ ⋮ | 45  | ⋮ ⋮ ⋮ ⋮ ⋮ | 70  | ⋮ ⋮ ⋮ ⋮ ⋮ | 95  | ⋮ ⋮ ⋮ ⋮ ⋮ | 120 | ⋮ ⋮ ⋮ ⋮ ⋮ |
| 21  | ⋮ ⋮ ⋮ ⋮ ⋮ | 46  | ⋮ ⋮ ⋮ ⋮ ⋮ | 71  | ⋮ ⋮ ⋮ ⋮ ⋮ | 96  | ⋮ ⋮ ⋮ ⋮ ⋮ | 121 | ⋮ ⋮ ⋮ ⋮ ⋮ |
| 22  | ⋮ ⋮ ⋮ ⋮ ⋮ | 47  | ⋮ ⋮ ⋮ ⋮ ⋮ | 72  | ⋮ ⋮ ⋮ ⋮ ⋮ | 97  | ⋮ ⋮ ⋮ ⋮ ⋮ | 122 | ⋮ ⋮ ⋮ ⋮ ⋮ |
| 23  | ⋮ ⋮ ⋮ ⋮ ⋮ | 48  | ⋮ ⋮ ⋮ ⋮ ⋮ | 73  | ⋮ ⋮ ⋮ ⋮ ⋮ | 98  | ⋮ ⋮ ⋮ ⋮ ⋮ | 123 | ⋮ ⋮ ⋮ ⋮ ⋮ |
| 24  | ⋮ ⋮ ⋮ ⋮ ⋮ | 49  | ⋮ ⋮ ⋮ ⋮ ⋮ | 74  | ⋮ ⋮ ⋮ ⋮ ⋮ | 99  | ⋮ ⋮ ⋮ ⋮ ⋮ | 124 | ⋮ ⋮ ⋮ ⋮ ⋮ |
| 25  | ⋮ ⋮ ⋮ ⋮ ⋮ | 50  | ⋮ ⋮ ⋮ ⋮ ⋮ | 75  | ⋮ ⋮ ⋮ ⋮ ⋮ | 100 | ⋮ ⋮ ⋮ ⋮ ⋮ | 125 | ⋮ ⋮ ⋮ ⋮ ⋮ |

# ANSWER SHEET

TEST NO. _____ PART _____ TITLE OF POSITION _____
(AS GIVEN IN EXAMINATION ANNOUNCEMENT - INCLUDE OPTION, IF ANY)

PLACE OF EXAMINATION _____ DATE _____
(CITY OR TOWN)                    (STATE)

RATING

USE THE SPECIAL PENCIL.  MAKE GLOSSY BLACK MARKS.

|     | A B C D E |     | A B C D E |     | A B C D E |     | A B C D E |      | A B C D E |
|-----|-----------|-----|-----------|-----|-----------|-----|-----------|------|-----------|
| 1   | :: :: :: :: :: | 26 | :: :: :: :: :: | 51 | :: :: :: :: :: | 76 | :: :: :: :: :: | 101 | :: :: :: :: :: |
| 2   | :: :: :: :: :: | 27 | :: :: :: :: :: | 52 | :: :: :: :: :: | 77 | :: :: :: :: :: | 102 | :: :: :: :: :: |
| 3   | :: :: :: :: :: | 28 | :: :: :: :: :: | 53 | :: :: :: :: :: | 78 | :: :: :: :: :: | 103 | :: :: :: :: :: |
| 4   | :: :: :: :: :: | 29 | :: :: :: :: :: | 54 | :: :: :: :: :: | 79 | :: :: :: :: :: | 104 | :: :: :: :: :: |
| 5   | :: :: :: :: :: | 30 | :: :: :: :: :: | 55 | :: :: :: :: :: | 80 | :: :: :: :: :: | 105 | :: :: :: :: :: |
| 6   | :: :: :: :: :: | 31 | :: :: :: :: :: | 56 | :: :: :: :: :: | 81 | :: :: :: :: :: | 106 | :: :: :: :: :: |
| 7   | :: :: :: :: :: | 32 | :: :: :: :: :: | 57 | :: :: :: :: :: | 82 | :: :: :: :: :: | 107 | :: :: :: :: :: |
| 8   | :: :: :: :: :: | 33 | :: :: :: :: :: | 58 | :: :: :: :: :: | 83 | :: :: :: :: :: | 108 | :: :: :: :: :: |
| 9   | :: :: :: :: :: | 34 | :: :: :: :: :: | 59 | :: :: :: :: :: | 84 | :: :: :: :: :: | 109 | :: :: :: :: :: |
| 10  | :: :: :: :: :: | 35 | :: :: :: :: :: | 60 | :: :: :: :: :: | 85 | :: :: :: :: :: | 110 | :: :: :: :: :: |

Make only ONE mark for each answer.  Additional and stray marks may be counted as mistakes.  In making corrections, erase errors COMPLETELY.

|     | A B C D E |     | A B C D E |     | A B C D E |     | A B C D E |      | A B C D E |
|-----|-----------|-----|-----------|-----|-----------|-----|-----------|------|-----------|
| 11  | :: :: :: :: :: | 36 | :: :: :: :: :: | 61 | :: :: :: :: :: | 86 | :: :: :: :: :: | 111 | :: :: :: :: :: |
| 12  | :: :: :: :: :: | 37 | :: :: :: :: :: | 62 | :: :: :: :: :: | 87 | :: :: :: :: :: | 112 | :: :: :: :: :: |
| 13  | :: :: :: :: :: | 38 | :: :: :: :: :: | 63 | :: :: :: :: :: | 88 | :: :: :: :: :: | 113 | :: :: :: :: :: |
| 14  | :: :: :: :: :: | 39 | :: :: :: :: :: | 64 | :: :: :: :: :: | 89 | :: :: :: :: :: | 114 | :: :: :: :: :: |
| 15  | :: :: :: :: :: | 40 | :: :: :: :: :: | 65 | :: :: :: :: :: | 90 | :: :: :: :: :: | 115 | :: :: :: :: :: |
| 16  | :: :: :: :: :: | 41 | :: :: :: :: :: | 66 | :: :: :: :: :: | 91 | :: :: :: :: :: | 116 | :: :: :: :: :: |
| 17  | :: :: :: :: :: | 42 | :: :: :: :: :: | 67 | :: :: :: :: :: | 92 | :: :: :: :: :: | 117 | :: :: :: :: :: |
| 18  | :: :: :: :: :: | 43 | :: :: :: :: :: | 68 | :: :: :: :: :: | 93 | :: :: :: :: :: | 118 | :: :: :: :: :: |
| 19  | :: :: :: :: :: | 44 | :: :: :: :: :: | 69 | :: :: :: :: :: | 94 | :: :: :: :: :: | 119 | :: :: :: :: :: |
| 20  | :: :: :: :: :: | 45 | :: :: :: :: :: | 70 | :: :: :: :: :: | 95 | :: :: :: :: :: | 120 | :: :: :: :: :: |
| 21  | :: :: :: :: :: | 46 | :: :: :: :: :: | 71 | :: :: :: :: :: | 96 | :: :: :: :: :: | 121 | :: :: :: :: :: |
| 22  | :: :: :: :: :: | 47 | :: :: :: :: :: | 72 | :: :: :: :: :: | 97 | :: :: :: :: :: | 122 | :: :: :: :: :: |
| 23  | :: :: :: :: :: | 48 | :: :: :: :: :: | 73 | :: :: :: :: :: | 98 | :: :: :: :: :: | 123 | :: :: :: :: :: |
| 24  | :: :: :: :: :: | 49 | :: :: :: :: :: | 74 | :: :: :: :: :: | 99 | :: :: :: :: :: | 124 | :: :: :: :: :: |
| 25  | :: :: :: :: :: | 50 | :: :: :: :: :: | 75 | :: :: :: :: :: | 100 | :: :: :: :: :: | 125 | :: :: :: :: :: |